Primary Elections
AND
American Politics

Primary Elections AND American Politics

The Unintended Consequences of Progressive Era Reform

Chapman Rackaway and Joseph Romance

SUNY PRESS

Published by State University of New York Press, Albany

© 2022 State University of New York

All rights reserved

Printed in the United States of America

No part of this book may be used or reproduced in any manner whatsoever without written permission. No part of this book may be stored in a retrieval system or transmitted in any form or by any means including electronic, electrostatic, magnetic tape, mechanical, photocopying, recording, or otherwise without the prior permission in writing of the publisher.

For information, contact State University of New York Press, Albany, NY
www.sunypress.edu

Library of Congress Cataloging-in-Publication Data

Names: Rackaway, Chapman, author. | Romance, Joseph, 1966– author.
Title: Primary elections and American politics : the unintended consequences of Progressive era reform / Chapman Rackaway, Joseph Romance.
Description: Albany : State University of New York Press, 2022. | Includes bibliographical references and index.
Identifiers: LCCN 2022006889 | ISBN 9781438490571 (hardcover : alk. paper) | ISBN 9781438490595 (ebook)
Subjects: LCSH: Primaries—United States—History. | Political parties—United States—History. | Progressivism (United States politics)—History. | Representative government and representation—United States—History.
Classification: LCC JK2071 .R34 2022 | DDC 324.273/154—dc23/eng/20220707
LC record available at https://lccn.loc.gov/2022006889

10 9 8 7 6 5 4 3 2 1

Contents

Chapter 1	Making Parties into Machines	1
Chapter 2	Parties Ascendant	15
Chapter 3	What the Progressives Were For	35
Chapter 4	Why the Machines Were Targeted	55
Chapter 5	The Early Primary Era	79
Chapter 6	The Pivotal 1968 Democratic National Convention	103
Chapter 7	What Direct Primaries Have Done	125
Chapter 8	The Problem with Primaries	149
Chapter 9	Conclusion	175
Notes		191
Bibliography		227
Index		251

Chapter 1

Making Parties into Machines

If I could not go to heaven but with a party, I would not go there at all.[1]

—Thomas Jefferson

The Tale of Eric Cantor

One of the informal prerequisites for a potential member of party leadership in the US Congress today is representing a safe district. Modern-day legislative leaders spend much of their time not only on the internal management of their chamber but traveling the country fundraising and supporting fellow partisans seeking election to the US Congress. Only three times in US history has a sitting Speaker of the House been defeated in reelection. Party members and other leaders want to know that their party's leadership will be stable, so safe-district candidates are inherently more appealing than swing-district candidates. The Majority Leader, often the Speaker's closest ally, needs a similar level of electoral safety to do their job effectively. Thus, Eric Cantor's defeat in 2014 sent political shockwaves and provided an example of the unique challenges presented by the American system of direct primary elections.

Most elections to the US Congress are quite stable. District composition and boundaries, partisanship, and incumbency provide significant protections for those already in office. Once in, candidates are difficult to remove from office through the ballot box. The defeat of an incumbent is rare in any circumstances, but particularly in a primary election. Cantor, a Republican who had represented a strongly Republican district in central

Virginia since 2001, appeared to have only token primary opposition from Randolph-Macon College economics professor David Brat. However, Brat defeated Cantor in a shocking primary upset.

Cantor ascended to the role of House Majority Leader in 2011, when Republicans wrested majority control of the chamber from Democrats. In his safe district, Cantor would be able to spend less time taking care of his district and expend more effort campaigning for fellow Republicans. Brat, a member of the surging Tea Party fiscal conservative movement, decided to mount a primary challenge to Cantor for the 2014 cycle.

Like most primary challengers against incumbents, Brat's campaign was a tiny operation, especially when compared with the might a multi-term incumbent and party leader like Cantor had available. Cantor spent $5 million on the campaign; Brat, less than $200,000.[2] Brat accepted no donations from political action committees.[3] Leveraging media stars of the Tea Party movement like radio host Mark Levin, Brat's campaign portrayed Cantor as focused on crony relationships with major corporations to the detriment of small businesses in the district. Brat also embraced a populist message that would hallmark Donald Trump's presidential campaign two years later, emphasizing a hard line on illegal immigration and opposition to government bailouts.

In almost any campaign season Brat should have had no chance at victory. Spending little money, having a small professional staff, and facing off against an entrenched incumbent are all warning signs of an unsuccessful candidacy. But Brat played on feelings of disconnect between constituents and Cantor, defeated the Majority Leader, and went on to easily beat the Democratic nominee in the general election.

Another aspect of Brat's unlikely victory was its occurrence not during a general election contest, but in a primary. Incumbent legislators lose their reelection bids in general elections less than 10 percent of the time, but the loss percentage in primaries is even a fraction of that, at around one-hundredth of one percent. If primaries are that uncompetitive, what exact purpose do they serve in a functioning democracy? Unlike the parties themselves, the vast majority of polities conduct their elections without primary elections. The direct primary is a peculiarly American invention that few other nations have adopted, and with more than a century of electoral history behind them, primaries give us a test bed to understand parties and their role in a democracy better. In this book, we seek to provide more of that understanding of primaries.

Primaries are important because of their significant power over one of the basic functions of a political party: the nomination of candidates to represent that party in a general election. All parties nominate candidates, and most allow the parties to do so without input or interference from the voting public. Parties choose the candidates they believe best represent their ideologies and vision, and let the public choose which of those party nominees best serves the office. A David Brat would not be able to wrest his party's nomination from an entrenched party leader like Eric Cantor without the presence of direct primary elections.

Cantor's defeat at Brat's hands is emblematic of the substantive shift in politics brought about since the advent of the direct primary election in the early 1900s. Unlike almost every other country in the world, the US puts the power of partisan candidate nominations in the hands of voters rather than party leadership. As such, primaries shape elections by altering the relationship between voters and their party. In particular, by stripping party leadership of their ability to control the party's message through its candidates, the direct primary has weakened the parties' ability to link a disconnected and disinterested public with the political process. Many of the ills of modern-day politics can be traced back to the advent and evolution of the direct primary. And these ills are not just because a party leader can be defeated. They are wider than that and go the heart of what it means to have a well-functioning representative democracy.

What is at stake here is an understanding of how parties function in such a democracy. They are not simply a neutral calculating institution that passively records votes to determine a nominee. At least they have not done so historically. Parties have, as Steven Levitsky and Daniel Ziblatt remind us in *How Democracies Die*, functioned as gatekeepers who "screen out those who pose a threat to democracy or are otherwise unfit to hold office."[4] The rise of primaries and the embrace of direct democracy has weakened that essential function. These ills have been present for some time; however, they have become even more apparent in recent years.

Of course, one of the appeals of primaries is to create a greater sense of democracy and to foster a sense of equality between people. Parties should be, to the champions of primaries, the tool of fully equal citizens. On the surface, we all have an equal vote and apparently equal influence over the outcome. The seemingly oligarchic nature of parties means that, to their critics, they undermine democratic ideas and mock the notion that we are all equal citizens. However, this is far too simplistic—everyone realizes that we are not truly equal in influence concerning the outcome of primaries. Furthermore, as James Lindley Wilson argues in *Democratic Equality*, the ideal of equality "requires a richer conception of deliberative fairness."[5] To make democracy work and to ensure true equality it takes more than imposing rigid procedural structures, such as primaries, to create an illusion of equality. While it is certainly correct, for those committed to democracy, to view inequality with suspicion, the best response to inequality requires nuance, and forms of inequality can, in the long run, enhance democratic decision-making on the part of citizens. As Wilson aptly writes, "Political equality requires the maintenance of equal rule over time, rather than merely sharing in rule at individual moments, such as election day."[6] It is our contention that a more prominent role for parties in the nomination process is only unfair in a superficial reading of politics. Rightly imagined, stronger political parties will provide an enhanced process that is more fair overtime.

To put our cards on the table, we believe not only that parties are essential to democracy—that is a common belief of many political scientists going back decades—but that rightly functioning parties are central to democracy. Rightly functioning parties are not completely democratic in nature and include a strong role for an educated elite not beholden to every impulse of the voter.

What Is Democracy?

To better grasp what we are calling for, it is necessary to review what we mean by "democracy." A reasonable place to start is the word *democracy* itself, which can be traced to its Greek roots—*demos* meaning "people" and *kratia* meaning "rule." Thus, it simply means the people rule. But who are the people and how do they rule? Aristotle argued, "the virtue of a citizen is held to be that capacity to rule and be ruled finely."[7] That issue, complicated enough in a Greek city-state, becomes even more vexing in a large, diversely populated nation. Somehow the views of the ruler and the views of the average citizen must be aligned. For the ancient democrats, that meant drawing lots to fill that many offices—thus anyone had an equal chance at office (and, thus, not just the "unfairly" popular would hold office). On many issues the citizens themselves decided on policy. This was the essence of democracy to the ancient Greeks and what is commonly termed *direct democracy* today. However, this was, through the ages, criticized for a host of reasons, not least of which was that the average citizen might not have the intelligence or dispassion to administer a government. This challenge about how to make democracy work was the issue the United States took up from its very beginning.

Of course, *democracy* has been defined in a number of ways.[8] As noted, the ancient Greeks defined it in ways that are much more participatory than we think of it today. We might suggest three ways of looking at democracy.

On one end there is a democracy that we could call deliberative. James Lindley Wilson writes that "political deliberation involves the formation, through individual reflection and interpersonal interaction, of judgments about what the regime ought to do."[9] This deliberative ideal was most clearly captured by the ancient Greeks, who met collectively to discuss policy and make decisions by consensus.[10] People were highly attuned to politics, and decision-making was as close as possible to being collective. Man was, to use Aristotle's terms, a political animal. Citizens partook in debate and discussion about what a society should do. This kind of democracy requires a small community. And for it to be truly effective it is probably a requirement that people know and trust each other—they are friends in some sense, or at most distant, neighbors. In the United States, something similar is captured in the New England town hall meetings. Present-day caucuses during the nomination process can also, at times, reach toward the deliberative ideal. People must make arguments about what we should do, what is important, and what policies to adopt. Of course, establishing and developing such a system is going to take a lot of time. It is the kingdom of the political animal, a kind of democracy for the highly politically engaged.

At the other end of the spectrum is representative democracy. As the word *representative* implies in this system, people choose their leaders. Of course, elections can make these leaders accountable. But there is no way to force people to think and talk about politics. They can do that; however, no one is required to do so as a prerequisite to political participation. Indeed, in this ideal, sometimes advocates really desire that people reflect on what they believe in and what they want done. Then, silently and without pressure, they go to the voting place and cast their ballots. In fact, as we do today, candidates and their surrogates are not supposed to conduct any politicking close to the polling station, and one's vote is secret. This kind of democracy has its defenders because of its practicality and the way it is well adapted to a large polity. However, it might actually create barriers between the government and citizenry. As Robert Dahl observed,

> these institutions of representative democracy removed government so far from the direct reach of the demos that one could reasonably wonder, as some critics have, whether the new system was entitled to call itself by the venerable name of democracy.[11]

To many of its defenders, such as James Madison, this removal of government from "the direct reach of the demos" was precisely its most appealing aspect. Yet, as the direct democratic impulse grew stronger in the nineteenth and twentieth centuries, this became a problem to overcome.

The United States was becoming a bold experiment in finding ways to give people more of a voice in government. Christopher Achen and Larry Bartels, in *Democracy for Realists*, argue that there is a "folk theory" of democracy that values ordinary people's preferences as paramount:

> In the convention view, democracy begins with the voters. Ordinary people have preferences about that their government should do. They choose leaders who will do those things, or they enact their preferences directly in referendums. . . . Democracy makes the people the rulers, and legitimacy derives from consent. In Abraham Lincoln's stirring words from the Gettysburg Address, democratic government is "of the people, by the people, and for the people." That way of thinking about democracy has passed into everyday wisdom, not just in the United States but in a great many other countries around the globe. It constitutes a kind of "folk theory" of democracy.[12]

Could the nation find a middle ground between Madisonian vision of a partyless representative democracy and the very problematic ancient ideal of deliberative and highly participatory democracy? Progressives came to believe that middle way was in what we might call *direct democracy*. This upset the sense of balance created by the founders and, later, modified and augmented by the creators of the major political parties. In Achen and Bartels's telling, "The direct primary represented an unprecedented attempt to impose the folk theory of democracy on the nominating process."[13] Citizens would have more avenues to influence politics—more than Madison could have imagined. At the same time, they would not meet and set policy as Athenian citizens might. Citizens in isolation, unable to truly collectively deliberate as the ancient ideal of democracy demanded, were instead given power to select candidates for office in the rather naive belief that collective folk wisdom would simply spring forth. Thus, the Progressives did not just support primaries, but also urged the adoption of initiative, referendum, and recall. Theodore Roosevelt supported all these reforms and expanded them with a desire to make it easier to amend the Constitution itself.[14] There has been, for well over 100 years, an impulse to expand democracy into areas in which it did not hither thereto exist.

The political theorist Robert Talisse is one of many who worry about "overdoing democracy"—the title of his recent book. Talisse is concerned with the way "politics is being overdone" and how it is detrimental to democracy.[15] His concern is not about the internal workings of parties, and he may very well disagree with the ideas presented here. But his thesis is valuable to the argument of this book. The expansion of democracy, its very tyrannizing quality, has become a problem and accentuates some of the worst tendencies of our politics. We don't suggest that technological innovations, or the media, the rise of money in politics, or changing economic conditions are unimportant in explaining how our politics have reached the state they are in. However, we do believe that the politically polarized world we live in today, in part, reflects structural changes in our political parties that long predate many of the causes often suggested. And the most important structural transformation is the way the political parties went about selecting candidates for office. The impulse for democracy led to the rise of the direct primaries, and that led, in the long run, to weaker political parties and the unhealthy political world we live in today.

The Direct Primary in America

The direct primary is a nearly unique American political invention and practice.[16] Most states have featured sub-presidential direct primaries for a century, and direct, binding presidential primaries have been in effect since the 1970s. Primaries are controversial, not only because of their near-exclusivity in the United States' political milieu but also because of the effects they have on political party organizations, electoral systems, governing, and even the electorates themselves. This controversy stems from a fundamental political science question concerning the role of citizens in the political process. While democratic theory called for citizen participation in the electoral process, where and when this occurs is open to debate. The direct democratic impulse drove the adoption of the primaries, and we can think of primaries as efforts to advance direct democratic practices into the US's historically republican system. In short, how much direct democracy is a good thing?

Primary elections are ubiquitous in American politics today. In a political environment dominated by two major political parties, some believe that primaries give voters an expanded set of choices, often ideological, among the often many primary candidates, where a general-only election would limit them to two effective nominees. Others see the primary election as increasing polarization in the electorate, higher campaign costs, and polarization in government.[17]

The direct primary was a product of the Progressive Era, and its origins at that time tell us much about their effect on American politics. The strongly anti-partisan Progressives wanted to curtail party politicking and governing as much as possible, mostly due to the excesses of urban machines. To achieve this, the Progressives wanted to boost direct democratic impulses among the electorate. The historical record shows the direct primary achieves neither of these goals. Yet, though the primaries did not achieve these goals, they were a product of Progressive thinking, even when Progressives as a group held mixed views about them.

While it is true that the creation of the first primaries predated the Progressives and not all Progressives favored the primaries, many Progressives were quite enthusiastic about them. Progressive ideas about direct democracy easily found expression in the primary. Furthermore, Progressives and their political descendants were the ones who either pushed for the adoption of primaries or, in the 1970s, created the conditions in which primaries flourished.

The Progressive Movement, shaping political currents that had existed for a long time in American history, helped foster a certain notion of direct democracy that was appealing to many. It was hard to argue against respecting the will of the people, and primaries seem to do just that. While some Progressives, such Herbert Croly, saw problems with the direct primary, it is hard to stop a mechanism that appears to be democratic. It was also the case that even people who were not Progressive were influenced by these ideals. Thus, non-Progressives could reflect and embrace these reforms for any number of reasons. Embracing the language of democracy is bound to unleash further demands for giving more people more voice in the system.[18] This made direct primaries, if not exactly inevitable, probable.

The push for more direct democracy is where we find the great challenge presented by primary elections. Progressives may have conflated frustration with the existing machine parties with a desire for less republican democracy and thus advocated for more direct reforms. In that way, the primaries were the wrong solution to the problem. The main effect that direct primaries have had is a weakening of the parties as a linkage institution between the public and their government.

In this book, we will develop a theory of the direct primary as a flawed initiative for direct democracy, and trace the challenges presented by the direct primary through the lens of representative versus direct democracy.

The Accidental Nature of Parties

Any exploration of the role of political parties in American politics must account for the tension between their integral position in representative democracy and the intense distaste for their very existence. That stress between two forces—the impetus toward a direct democracy that seeks to limit the role of parties and the vitality of parties as central linkage institutions—marks the history of American political parties and informs the development of the direct primary election.

Primaries are an important part of the political process because of how they affect the key linkage institution between a public and its politics: the parties themselves. The effect of primaries on the general public is indirect, because their most significant impact is on the parties. Understanding primaries thus means understanding parties, which itself is a large task.

Parties are ubiquitous in politics, but their genesis was accidental. Despite the great care that the Constitution put into governmental design, parties were not part of it. Particularly in the US, parties are both essential to political participation and extraconstitutional, which puts them in a precarious position, fraught with contradictions: parties are robust, yet constantly under threat; emic to politics, yet popular sentiment often tends toward their abolition; powerful, yet susceptible to outside forces.

Thus, primaries are an important area of study because of the impact they have had on this key political institution. Parties are widespread in their effect because of their connection with every element of politics. Parties connect, perhaps better than any other institution, the citizenry to both the elective and governmental processes. Certainly, parties are the most effective linkage institution in politics.

Parties are nebulous because of their lack of constitutional definition and their scope. There is no baseline against which to measure party activity in the Constitution as there is, say, executive power. Parties are generally free to do what they want. But parties also have shifting centers of power because of their *sui generis* creation. There are no rules in the Constitution restraining political parties. As we will see, over time that led to parties accumulating an incredible amount of power, which led to a regulatory backlash. The same parties that had built themselves into all-powerful local machines would become gutted by external rules, most especially the direct primary.

The American political party is unique in the world in being in such a position. Most other nations have some form of partisan acknowledgment built into their constitutions, though those descriptions can be seen as other nations founded after the United States learning from our mistakes. The parties' roles in American government and politics are informal, extraconstitutional, and fluid.

Parties, if they existed at all, were supposed to be ephemeral but instead have paradoxically persisted for two centuries and more. We can thus see parties as robust institutions due to their longevity but also weak ones due to their susceptibility to etic influences. This unique situation makes parties excellent areas for study but difficult organizations about which to draw stable conclusions. Parties are a free-floating anomaly within the American political milieu.

That does not mean that parties are purely nebulous entities, however. Parties are important elements in any polity, hence why so many other countries have accounted for them in their basic governing documents. Post–World War II Europe featured many of its nations specifically granting status to political parties in their constitutions: Italy, France, and Germany all noted parties as having a recognized and official role in elections and governance. Political parties are ubiquitous in democracies for a number of reasons, but the most significant one is that they provide a connection between the electorate and their elected officials that is unsurpassed by any other entity.

While a debate has continued since Ancient Greece over whether or not people are naturally inclined toward political activity, one consistent truth has been that when the public have had robust political party connections, they have also had strong participatory relationships with their governments. An incontrovertible truth is that parties create a vital linkage between the public and government. Laws and exogenous shocks that weaken political parties also tend to weaken public participation. As linkage institutions connecting people to government, parties are unrivaled. So those activities and occurrences that, intentionally or not, strain the linkage relationship that parties foster are worthy of understanding. Weakened political parties subsequently weaken citizen political engagement.

There are many ways to look at political parties: some as rational creations of office-seekers,[19] some as natural outgrowths of social movements,[20] and others as electioneering entities.[21] All of these views are valid and reflective of the multifaceted nature of parties. Mostly within this work we will focus on the party as a linkage institution between the public and its government. Linkage institutions connect people to their government, providing education and mobilization pathways that citizens would otherwise not utilize.

In this book we argue that no exogenous shock has been more damaging to the political parties than the introduction of the direct nominating primary election. The direct primary was originally created as a method to rein in the excesses of urban party machines, but its choice as the mechanism to accomplish this was based on a flawed view of it as a necessary shift toward direct democracy. To explore the flaws in the direct primary, we must be cognizant of three interlinked concepts: 1) political parties as linkage institutions; 2) participatory democracy, where the public is engaged but uses a series of intermediary institutions to facilitate that engagement; and 3) direct democracy, where elected representatives are minimized and the general public has more immediate input into policymaking.

The primary's architects, loosely described as the Progressive Movement of the late 1800s and early 1900s, conflated participatory and direct democracy. However, a century of evidence has shown that direct democracy and participatory democracy are two different things entirely, and the public has not at all embraced the more direct democratic impulses embodied in the nominating primary. As an experiment in direct democracy, as a reform to an admittedly corrupt party system, and as an effort to empower the public, the creation and development of the direct nominating primary has been an overall failure. In this book we will explore how, in intent and design, the direct nominating primary is a flawed political process that has done more damage to parties as linkage institutions than it has bolstered citizen engagement.

Parties and Democracy

Democracy and political parties are so connected that it is easy to think one does not exist without the other. Through most of the history of democratic governance, parties have existed as a vital entity in each citizen-governed system. But parties often operate outside of direct sanction by the state's fundamental law, which can make them more independent and variable. Parties have existed in democracies because of a basic but necessary service they provide: connecting the public with their politics. Without parties, democracies rarely survive.

Political parties occupy a unique space in American politics partly because they were never intended to be a part of the system. The writers of the United States Constitution constructed the document with very specific intent, careful design of governmental institutions, and thoughtful allocations of powers to those institutions to keep them in balance. For example, as the Congress was directly elected by the public, that branch was designed to initiate public policy. The House would write and pass any taxing or spending legislation to keep itself accountable to the electorate. The writers of the Constitution thus were very intentional in every institution, every power, each clause included to achieve a specific purpose. The Constitution is also notable for those things it left out, with the same intentional and methodical approach. Nowhere in the US Constitution are political parties directly mentioned, which in itself signals the preferences of its writers.[22]

Most specifically, the United States was designed to prevent the emergence of parties at the national level. The framers created the federal Constitution of 1789 with the intent of using the large geographic space of the thirteen states as an impediment to the natural formation of organized interests or parties.[23] Madison's reformulation of republican theory, which previously demanded republics be small and compact in nature, meant that "a greater variety . . . [of] interests would exist in the United States. This would necessitate a system of representation that would result in a government of nationally minded elites who would largely see beyond the many parochial interests of the states (though they would be cognizant of those state interests)." There would be no national parties and the interests, though quite real, would be numerous, often cross-cutting in their influences, and usually state focused. Alliances of such interests would be temporary and unstable—not unstable in such a way as to threaten the new nation; rather, it would be a salutary fluidity that would leave national elites free to forge a consensus on most policies that concerned the nation as a whole.

The Federalist promoters of the Constitution believed that there was no difference between organized interests, what we would commonly call "interest groups" today, and political parties. Both parties and interests, according to the Constitution's writers, were minority splinter groups that put their particular preferences over that of the public good. Madison and his fellows thought that parties would undermine the public consensus so carefully designed to be extracted by the federal government. As Madison famously warned,

> So strong is the propensity to fall into mutual animosities that where no substantial occasion presents itself, the most frivolous and fanciful distinctions have been sufficient to kindle their unfriendly passions, and excite their most violent conflicts.[24]

Thus, parties had all the vices associated with the crassness that critics of interest groups see in them.

Mostly, parties threatened a tyranny of the minority, and therefore the Constitution intended to keep them from becoming federally organized. Parties had already organized at the state level, reinforcing the idea that they were a net negative contributor to American politics. The Federalists' hope was that permanent national parties would not exist, and a more fluid world of constantly shifting and reforming alliances between interest groups would prevail. This more flexible political world would have the consequence of less rigidly constraining politicians by the very real pressure of local factional demands as they sought to achieve the greater good. The framers were not naive and did not expect saints in politics. But they did seek to create a world that filtered public demands through the considered judgment of an educated and more farsighted elite.

Certainly, the idea of long-lasting national parties was something the Constitution's authors never envisioned. For some time after parties formed, many earlier leaders hoped that such national organizations would be, at most, temporary creations. Jefferson certainly thought so, seeing the Republican Party as a one-time creation that would eventually die a natural death, not to be replaced.[25]

Parties had already formed in the colonies prior to the War of Independence, though, so the Constitution's writers also knew that they were inevitable.[26] Even if parties only existed at the local or state level, Madison admitted that the only way to prevent the emergence of parties anywhere was to restrict the liberties of free speech, assembly, and petitioning the government for a redress of grievances. To eliminate parties, freedom itself would have to be abolished, an exchange the writers of the Constitution were unwilling to make. *Federalist* no. 10 posited that the large geographic footprint of the United States would create a logistical barrier to national-level party organization emergence. There was no specific prohibition on parties written into the Constitution, itself an admission that national party organization development was possible and indeed probable.

With many other elements of government, a structure or strategy exists in the Constitution.[27] For instance, as much as the presidency has evolved over more than 200 years, it remains tethered in a variety of ways to the rules laid out in Article II. Nevertheless, the Constitution's drafters did not intend for political parties to emerge at the federal level, so there is no roadmap for their operation.[28] The lack of guidance from government may help explain why American parties developed and progressed in haphazard ways, with a history of making up their own rules as they went along. Parties also were much stronger at the local and state levels than at the national level, though that may have been because of the self-same geographic limitations Madison referenced in *Federalist* no. 10.[29] Even as national-level parties emerged, they quickly followed the model of local party organizations. Local party organizations would fade during the Era of Good Feelings, however, and not return until they followed suit of their national-level counterparts.[30]

Post-Independence Americans were partisans because of their local organization. The federal government's operations were minimal and distant, but local government was omnipresent in the citizenry's lives, and their political party was their lifeline to what was happening in the most active and relevant levels of government: the local community and state.

For those early citizens, the story of Thaddeus McCotter and Kerry Bentivolio would have seemed like democracy run amok. McCotter was a multiple-term incumbent in the US House of Representatives from Michigan. Bentivolio entered the 2012 primary against McCotter as a long-shot candidate, but relied on a primary-era requirement with which the incumbent had surprisingly failed to comply: submitting enough qualified petition signatures to be eligible to run for reelection. McCotter was thus off the ballot, which never would have happened in a system where party organizations conduct their own nomination processes. As an untested candidate who had never sought elective office before, Bentivolio was a rarity: an accidental party nominee. Because of the strength of his Republican Party affiliation in the district, Bentivolio secured the nomination in McCotter's absence and won the seat.

Voters did not embrace Bentivolio, however, and a primary challenge to him two years later resulted in the "accidental" 2012 nominee being replaced after a single term. Bentivolio's candidacy, and the confusion it caused among voters, is a byproduct of the era of the direct primary. When candidates can self-select without any vetting by or connection to a party, they make political information and partisan political linkage much weaker.

Chapter 2

Parties Ascendant

Creating a Political Party without a Model

American political parties used examples from prior party-like organizations in their creation and development. Parties were non-existent during the first attempts at self-government in Greece, while the Roman Empire had patricians and plebeians emerge as proto-parties representing specific segments of the population.[1] After Rome fell, parties vanished for a millennium, as any semblance of representative government disappeared. Organized parties were unwelcome in a world dominated by kings and aristocrats. Such a world is one of cabals and cliques, not parties. Political parties in the modern sense are a product of seventeenth-century England.

After the English Parliament's creation, the legislature became a place where the public, in an admittedly limited way at first, was to have input on government. Even so, parties were not an immediate byproduct of Parliament's founding. Only after issues emerged that divided crown loyalists from other citizens did parties arise in Parliament.

In 1678, a rumor spread through England that Roman Catholics were plotting to kill the Protestant King Charles II and give the throne to Charles's Catholic brother, James, Duke of York. While no concrete evidence was ever unearthed of an actual plot, the rumor was enough to spread throughout the public and stoke fears. Overreacting, Parliament passed a ban on Catholics holding public office, even stripping the Duke of York's birthright to inherit the throne. King Charles II responded by dissolving the entire Parliament.[2]

Throughout England outrage seethed over Parliament's dissolution. Those who wanted a new Parliament created took the name Petitioners.

Loyalists to the king called themselves Abhorrers from their disdain for any limitation on the king's power. Quickly the groups solidified and took new names. Petitioners were called Whigs, a Scottish name for religious opposition. The king's supporters became known as Tories, a name first given to Irish Catholics who suffered under Protestant rule.[3]

The Whigs and Tories of the 1600s bore an important resemblance to their modern counterparts that marks them as the first modern parties: their view of government's scope and role. Tories wanted rule by a strong king, accountable not to man but to God alone. Whigs wanted the public to have more rights and a government responsive to the public. Over time as Parliament expanded its power relative to the king, Whigs and Tories developed into organized parties similar to the kind we see today. The central issue of the creation of Whigs and Tories was the role of accountability for elected leaders, a concept that carries through the history of parties and was central to the circumstances that brought primary elections into being.[4]

These British precedents were central to the American political experience prior to the revolution. In the colonies, disputes emerged between groups that would develop into parties, just as the Whigs and Tories did. American parties did not begin with the debate over constitutional ratification (though those ratifications debates had significant partisan implications—they took place on an already established partisan field). Three camps, or social movements, emerged in the lead-up to the War of Independence: supporters of the English crown, rebels who wanted independence, and the ambivalent. Each group took on names: Loyalists, Patriots, and Neutralists. The Loyalists, similar to the Tories before them, maintained ties to England and wanted to stay colonies of the British Empire.[5] Patriots pressed for a breakaway from England entirely, and the Neutralists refused to take a side.[6] As armed conflict forced the issue, the Neutralists dissipated and migrated into either the Loyalist or Patriot camps.

Here we note that parties of that era were creatures of the legislatures in which they operated only. The parties did not run elections under their banners, and no party organization worth the name existed. Loyalty to the parties among the electorate was minimal at best. Parties would develop and institutionalize later. These parties were legislative factions and thus ephemeral. As issues changed, the parties would disappear, only to be replaced by others.

After the War of Independence, the passions of the public that had stoked the rebellion did not dissipate. This is not surprising. Revolutions are often vague in the exact kind of politics they want, uniting people only by a more concrete agreement about what is wrong. The Loyalist and Patriot division became less salient and definitive to the public, but the same divisions between philosophy and social class manifested in different views of the role of government. There was always a group that was more comfortable with centralized power and another group suspicious of anything that smacked of monarchy and jealously protective of their local rights.

A strong relationship existed between philosophies of government power and social class in the new United States.[7] In the cities, educated elites saw a floundering post-Independence economy and a weak national government unable to accommodate even basic needs such as paying the war debt. These elites saw a stronger federal government as necessary to ensure protection of citizens' natural rights, and after Shays' Rebellion inspired a critical eye on the Articles of Confederation's governmental design, they took on the name Federalists to incorporate their vision for an invigorated national government.[8]

Outside of the cities, rural citizens saw powerful government as a sign that the English model of governing was not necessary and, indeed, was a threat to everyday civil liberties for which they had fought during the War of Independence. Farmers had seen, especially in states like Massachusetts, powerful and expansive governments taxing family farms into foreclosure and worried that a strong government would invalidate their new hard-earned freedoms. As the Federalists organized, particularly in cities, these rural preferences coalesced into a counterpart movement, the Anti-Federalists. The need to translate policy preferences into a coherent government program made party organizations inevitable.[9]

Parties often form out of social movements, as the first true US parties certainly did. The Federalists and Anti-Federalists may have begun as pamphleteering entities trading arguments over the proposed Constitution, but they quickly developed fully into stable political parties in their own right, even carrying forward into government once the Federalists won ratification of the Constitution with the compromise of adding the Bill of Rights to allay Anti-Federalist fears.

Contra Parties: A Brief and Futile Attempt

Federalists and Anti-Federalists organized at the federal level immediately, forming political party-like structures in Congress while the local level parties exploded. Even *Federalist* no. 10 author James Madison abandoned the anti-party spirit of the Constitution immediately with one very important dissident: President George Washington.

Fearful of the nascent parties spreading and stabilizing their influence on government, Washington intentionally tried to keep their advance at bay. Washington designed his cabinet as a place to stem off partisanship by placing high-profile national leaders from each party in key positions in it.[10] Surmising that despite their distinct ideological differences a personal friendship and mutual respect between Anti-Federalist Thomas Jefferson and Federalist Alexander Hamilton would allow for compromise on policy as well as a lessening of tensions, Washington placed both in his cabinet. Significant compromises did occur, such as the deal that had the federal government accept debt from the War of Independence in exchange for placing the national capital near the South.[11] However, dissent within the administration festered and finding common purpose became progressively more difficult as partisan tensions overrode the cooperative venue Washington provided. In fact, Jefferson and Hamilton were instrumental in forming the first two parties: Jefferson's Republicans and Hamilton's Federalists.[12]

Even as George Washington tried to provide a bulwark against the formation of parties within his own administration, though, parties were developing. Factions had emerged during the fight for constitutional ratification, and despite Washington's efforts to maintain a balanced and nonpartisan administration, differences of opinion and tactic led to parties emerging, prompting him to warn against their presence and advancement in his farewell speech.[13]

Washington's retirement inevitably opened the floodgates for partisan development. Washington is the only president in American history to serve without a party label. However, as strenuously as Washington fought to keep party advancement at bay, he was functionally a Federalist.[14] Washington never joined the party or publicly declared allegiance to the group, but ideologically he favored a strong federal government, and most of the policies he promoted were consistent with the Federalist platform. He would have disdained the idea of being a party member in any meaningful sense, however, and only Washington would be able to maintain such an Olympian detachment from partisan wrangling that was occurring all around him. Partisanship is inevitable, even when government design suppresses it. Simply put, the idea of making democracy work without political parties is an unattainable goal. As E. E. Schattschneider famously asserted, "political parties created democracy, and democracy is unthinkable save in terms of parties."[15] Direct democratic impulses of the nonpartisan ideal fail to function in geographically large and highly populated constituencies such as the US.

Parties, or some semblance of them, thus preceded Independence, and Washington's effort to quash parties was a doomed enterprise. Political parties are ingrained into the very fabric of representative government, because the public needs a liaison to bring them into political engagement. Parties provide that opportunity for the public to activate their own latent interest in politics and give them a method by which they can direct their energies.[16]

Nonetheless, the anti-party concerns of many remained even as parties were forming and became an inevitability. Washington's worries, the same expressed by Madison in *Federalist* no. 10, were legitimate ones. Minority factions (to use Madison's terminology) who conflate their interests with those of the common good could undermine a nation built on majoritarian consensus.[17] Parties in that sense were no different from organized interests, so much so that Madison combined the two types of organization under the same banner, calling them all factions. Some in the public shared Washington's fears about parties, but they were not as vocal as their organized opponents, who had embraced partisanship in the new republic. Madison's admonition was quickly ignored, forgotten, or rejected outright.

While parties fit Madison's definition of factions, they also serve a grander and more essential role in politics than Madison foresaw. Parties are linkage institutions. The general American public are not intrinsically self-motivated to participate in mass politics. An intermediary body is needed to bring the public to politics, to provide enthusiasm and reason to participate.[18] Parties also provide an easier way to foster democratic accountability in a world where the public at large is not engaged in politics on a day-to-day basis. Despite their very real flaws, parties are the most effective and efficient mechanism to link the public with political participation. Thus, although it took a few decades, the democratic impulses that existed within political system and culture necessitated the creation of parties to make politics sensible to a voting public. Yet, that democratic impulse also contained within it a strong revulsion against the very idea of parties. In short, America needs parties and, simultaneously, many citizens hate them.

To understand parties is to reconcile the very real tension between the vital linkage they provide and the threat to democratic rule that they present. Parties live at the intersection of the necessary and dangerous, and the knife-edge closeness of the two roles reflects the volatile history of parties throughout the American experiment. Primary elections emerged from a misinterpretation of the parties as a linkage institution as well as a misunderstanding of how rank-and-file citizens participate in politics.

Parties at the Beginning

Early parties bore little resemblance to those of today, as the early parties were mostly coalitions of like-minded elected officials. The Federalists and Anti-Federalists evolved at the elite level, to use contemporary language, long before they existed in the minds or shaped the identity of the average citizen.[19] The federal partisan caucuses did develop a very important precedent that would become vitally important to understand the advent of primary elections: presidential nomination.[20] Over a widespread geographic nation, it would be very difficult for all states to develop enough consensus over candidates to win a majority of the Electoral College's votes. One can envision the Electoral College as a de facto nomination mechanism rather than a final arbiter of the election's winner. However, parties emerged and filled a gap that would turn the Electoral College into a decisive body, cuing voters by placing the names of candidates into nomination for president.

Neither the Romans nor the English Parliament had used their parties (or party-like entities) to nominate a candidate for office before, so the American parties created an innovation through formally recommending candidates for office. The practice would become commonplace, spreading from the federal level down to the local. The process of winnowing candidates from a large pool of office-seekers to an easily manageable short list was a powerful change. Not only did party nomination ensure that majority winners would be commonplace in the Electoral College, it created an expectation that the party organization was the best entity to make the initial selection of candidate qualifications to stand for election.[21]

Initially, the party in the electorate and organization, to use V. O. Key's (1955) famous model, barely existed.[22] The party in government, the caucus, handled nominations and organized legislative action. Where state or local party organizations did exist, they were ad hoc self-appointed community organizers: gathering locals to hear speeches at a stump or securing food and drink to distribute to traveling voters on hay carts.[23]

The Anti-Federalists rechristened themselves as Republicans, and did not only organize in their federal offices. The same can be said about their rivals, the Federalists. Local party organizations immediately began emerging in strongholds of Federalist and Republican support. The local organizers had no guidelines or model to follow, since parties had exclusively been legislative bodies before. Local party organizations were thus free to make up their own rules, policies, and philosophies for themselves. The local party could even be independent and differ in important ways from its federal affiliate.

Formal party organizations themselves were an accidental creation, developed by Andrew Jackson to ensure his renomination for president over the machinations of his party's congressional caucus.[24] Parties over time have reacted to changes in their environment, in ways that have both corrected for mistakes of the past and created solutions to problems they faced. The most significant of these adaptations was the development of the urban political party machine.

The First Party Organizations

From the beginning days of the republic, political parties were elite institutions. The first parties were composed of office-seekers and office-holders as well as affiliated pamphleteers. Parties caucused in office and promoted their agendas, but they were not mass entities at their core: they were mechanisms for winning office and overcoming institutional barriers.[25]

Since parties are such a vital linkage institution, even elite-centered parties will not remain elite-only for a prolonged time. Parties would expand beyond their initial caucus structures as America's nascent democracy took root. As the early party organizations began to reach out—in New York and Boston to localities around the republic—a subtle shift toward parties as mass outreach entities also emerged. Rationally minded elected officials knew they needed votes, and the party became an effective mechanism to deliver those votes in large numbers.[26] Simply put, parties developed at the elite level as they governed the nation and, over time, these same elites saw the need to mobilize voters and the value of creating lasting loyalty among a mass public. For a variety of reasons, another unique American political party facet is the two-party nature of government. American parties emerged as a duopoly for a variety of reasons, including the sociocultural agreement on the US as an emerging capitalist enterprise that restricted most policy debates to those over variations that embraced capitalism; the binary nature of the constitutional ratification argument that spawned the first two parties; and, most importantly, the first-past-the-post, single-member-district structure of American elections, which has been historically consistent with eventually producing a two-party system.²⁷ The two-party nature of the republic would contribute to the development of the party machines that would spawn the reforms bringing primary elections into the system.

Even with the federal caucus and local party organizations in operation, parties were still only beginning and thus inconsistent in their structure, processes, and success. Some of the delay in local party emergence can be understood by the elite nature of the early party system. Since only landowners could vote and only for the House of Representatives, the scope of local party organizations was somewhat limited. The local entity had little to do with presidential or even senatorial politics. A significant gap existed between the parties, which had a federal emphasis, and their local organizations, who focused on a completely different politics.²⁸

Local and state politics dominated the early days of the republic. The Constitution put significant limitations on federal power and the first era of the republic was a state- and local-centric politics. Citizens of the new United States did not consistently look to the federal level for policy and leadership; they looked to local-level government, where they had more direct understanding and input. The higher level of engagement at the local level meant fewer felt the need to attach themselves to intermediary institutions. Parties lagged at the local level for this reason, but also because the elite nature of federal politics did not yet attract voters as effectively.

The Populist Turn

Local politics slowly adapted to partisanship, and so some significant changes would empower those organizations to take the lead among all partisan groups. As the public adapted to having input in public decisions, they began to yearn for even more. Voting for state, local, and US House races was not enough for people who wanted more direct input into the presidential election process. As media moved to regional and national distribution, a common vernacular about national politics emerged.²⁹

Along with that shared language, a transformative figure would enter into American politics, both for better and for worse. Andrew Jackson had served as a member of the US House and Senate from Tennessee, was later renowned as the hero of 1815's Battle of New Orleans, and in the early 1820s used his newfound fame to inject himself into the national political conversation. Jackson was a firebrand while in office, a dissident during a time of elite one-party rule.[30] Indeed, he was the first president not associated with the old political elite of either Massachusetts or Virginia.

Jackson was denied the presidency after his first campaign in 1824. No Electoral College majority emerged, and in the House, the final decision favored one of the elites, John Quincy Adams. Jackson perceived the loss as a personal attack on him—he was always prickly about his honor and especially anything that could be seen as a slight—particularly because in advisory elections across the country Jackson had won the popular vote.[31] The powerful charge of a "corrupt" deal being struck between Adams and one of the other candidates in the election—Henry Clay—also came into play. It tells us something of the emerging sense of democracy among many that a perfectly valid constitutional way of selecting the president in a close election was illegitimate in the minds of many. Jackson would win in 1828, and once in the presidency deployed two significant changes that affected parties and would help speed the deployment of primaries: expanded suffrage and patronage.[32]

The rest of Jackson's philosophy was equally transformative, for good and ill, including manifest destiny and a strong adherence to state sovereignty over federal policy initiatives. None of those state-supporting acts was more significant than Jackson's opposition to, and eventual dissolution of, the Bank of the United States. Nevertheless, Jackson's desire to tear down the elite structures of partisan rule would bring about a massive transformation in how the public viewed parties and how they conducted their business.[33]

To understand the impetus for reform it is imperative to understand the Jacksonian model of political parties, starting in 1832. Jackson transformed the party system, railing against the party elites who had denied him the presidency in 1824. Jackson's unfavorable view of party elites would remain embedded in the public and emerge with force during the Progressive Era. When Jackson won the 1828 election, not coincidentally at the same time many states began to hold public votes on presidential candidates, he was determined to not let the elites who had denied him the White House before deprive him of it in 1832. Jackson, favored by voters across the country, took his populist message into his policy and structural recommendations. He used the same mass appeal that catapulted him to the presidency to reshape the parties into his own image and conform to his vision of popular democracy. Jackson's vision, and his continued presence in the White House, was under threat from the congressional party nominating body he came to call "King Caucus."[34]

Jackson's hostility toward the congressional caucus was understandable. He had performed well among the public in 1824's election, but when no majority in the Electoral College emerged and the final decision went to the House of Representatives, the old-guard elite-model members of his own National Republican Party turned against him in favor of fellow elite John Quincy Adams.[35] What the founders envisioned as a common occurrence—the House selecting the president—was by the 1820s seen as suspect. The deal-making, alleged if never proven, that put Adams in the White House struck at the emerging sense of democracy that Jackson embodied.

In a way, Jackson's radical vision of democracy was a precursor to the Progressives. A significant proportion of the population wanted access to the ballot, which had previously been denied them. The burgeoning electorate provided a model that Progressives would later rely on in their reforms, because this newly enfranchised population was hungry to participate. Eliminating the barriers to their participation caused a surge in voter turnout and engagement, setting a standard for future efforts to enhance democracy. Jackson's democracy was somewhat more direct than the version that preceded it, but there were many forces at work to connect them to their politics. Jackson's Democratic Party served as the vital linkage between this new electoral bloc and the polling place. Jacksonian democracy was thus a strongly participatory one in the context of the times and in principle. Even if the convention system that grew out of the Jacksonian era was viewed with great hostility by later Progressive and twentieth-century reformers, we must nonetheless recognize that kinship between the Progressives and Jackson in their interest in directly linking voters to candidates. And while the public wanted a vote, they did not want more direct votes on legislation. The newly empowered electorate wanted to vote for representatives and maintain the more indirect elements of the emerging more participatory democracy.

Jackson saw his enemies, even within his own parties, as having the potential to thwart his renomination in 1832 and functionally remove him from the presidency. To ensure his ability to contest reelection, Jackson leveraged his public popularity to create the first national political convention. By integrating the party organization as a nominating mechanism (as opposed to the party in government), Jackson innovated what would quickly become the standard method by which parties choose candidates at all levels. Unchecked nomination power was not seen as the threat it would later become, however, so Jackson's idea gained widespread acceptance among party organizations.[36]

The first Democratic National Convention combined the populist fervor of Jackson's age with the power to select candidates for office by leadership within the party's membership hierarchy, bypassing its elected segment. The combination of Jackson's populist beliefs and empowered local organizations would drastically alter the nature of parties, turning them primarily into local entities. Citizens flocked to their local party organizations, as they provided not only a simplified vote decision but often employment and social support. Those local entities would quickly grow in power, begin to abuse that power, help lead to the downfall of machines, and the advent of the direct primary.

One other important practice emerged under Jackson's eight years in office: an aggressive use of the spoils system. Spoils emerged from a simple democratic principle: that anyone who remained in an office for too long became eventually and inescapably corrupt. Jackson's ire worsened against the reticence of those government employees already in positions upon his inauguration who were not true believers in Jackson's philosophy. Those existing bureaucrats represented barriers to the implementation of Jacksonian democracy, and he sought a way to remove and replace them with adherents to his own view of governing. Jackson wanted to infuse the same kind of thinking into the federal bureaucracy, leading him to advocate rotation in office. He was a "man of the people" and firmly believed that there were too many aristocratic career politicians in the bureaucracy and upper-class Congress that were out of touch with the American public. He adopted the policy of removing the old office-holders and replacing them with those recommended by fellow partisans who had won election to office. This went against the practice that preceded his presidency, where partisan loyalty was considered, but was never the primary criterion for selecting office-holders. When Jefferson came to the presidency, as the first president from a differing party, he had not generally engaged in the wholesale removal of Federalists from their offices. Although he effected some removals, he waffled about their necessity and never came to the kind of understanding of patronage that would later characterize Jackson.[37] Later still, President John Quincy Adams left most of Monroe's civil servants in place and even offered to let a presidential opponent, William Crawford, stay at the treasury.[38] The implementation of the system of rotating experienced but different people in office, coupled with Jackson's demand for strict loyalty, evolved into the spoils system.[39]

Jackson had made parties into military-structured and disciplined organizations. The Jacksonian party took its orders from the president instead of following loose coalitions of elected office-holders. Jackson's party had clearly delineated responsibilities, and executed orders without question. Jackson's philosophy of employment even took a turn of phrase from the military: "to the victor go the spoils." The military-like processes developed made party organizations operate nearly automatically, like a machine.

State and Local Party Development

The state- and local-level parties, having been distinct and disconnected from their national counterparts, would begin to align more with the federal party under Jackson's rule as well. Jackson's model of party organization had a lot to offer to the lower-level parties: instead of deferring to the natural aristocracy of the national elite, the local party adjunct could follow Jackson's model and mobilize voters with the promise of having many jobs to dole out to supporters after electoral victory. Voters followed their livelihoods and supported their party in government at the ballot box. The spoils promise was a powerful one and it drew local parties along.[40]

Spoils helped local governments and party organizations solve the main problem they had faced since their beginning: how to mobilize voters. Identifying potential voters and enticing them to the polls was incredibly difficult, since the promise of good public policy was the most concrete expectation one could have for casting a ballot. With the spoils system, voters could be enticed with a tangible benefit for their vote: stable work with stable pay.[41] The linkage between parties and voters was thus complete. It is highly likely that without parties the electorate would not have expanded, and if it did that participation would not have been as high as it was.

Following the Jackson model, local party organizations exploded. Armed with their new mobilization tool, parties became a ready linkage between the public and their government. The US's population was growing, and with it demand for more governmental services. Not only could party organizations use their elected power to dole out jobs, the number of jobs to hand out was growing. Across the country, hastily developed party organizations were becoming highly influential power players in their communities.[42] In this regard, Jackson found help in his second vice president, Martin Van Buren, one of the first to provide the intellectual foundation of the absolute good of organized parties, as opposed to simply seeing them as unavoidable.[43]

During Jackson's rise, American parties were developing into mass coalitional bodies. Not only was politics becoming progressively more popular, the rise of a war hero to national political prominence accelerated the movement toward mass appeal for the parties. Andrew Jackson captivated the nation's attention, solidifying support among the public for the newly christened Democratic Party through popular conventions, state-level candidate recruitment, and support for partisan newspapers. As Jackson spread the Democratic message, party organizations followed at the local level.[44] Voter turnout began to increase as the party organization advanced and matured.

Part of the appeal of local party organizations was the access they provided to jobs. Citizens wanted trash collected and snow removed from sidewalks. The country was growing in population quickly and basic infrastructure needs exploded. This groundwork needed to be built and then maintained. As roads, water lines, and other public works were created, offices to supervise and maintain them had to be populated with staff. Government jobs were growing in number, and whoever won the most recent local election could distribute them all. Since local elected officials controlled the day-to-day employment of government workers, they distributed them to supportive volunteers during their campaigns. Regular citizens, especially those with unsteady employment prospects, saw opportunities to get steady work by involving themselves in party politics, thus earning the spoils of campaign war by being first in line for the government jobs that were available to party loyalists after winning a contest. Local officials saw Jackson's unabashed use of the patronage system at the federal level as a model from which they could borrow, and did. Local governments began growing and providing employment to active members of the party.[45] Although it is seen as quite corrupt today, at the time it was defended on democratic grounds. Elections should have consequences, and the entrenched bureaucracy could be seen as thwarting the will of the people. Jacksonians advocated for the spoils system using the rationale of rotation in office—letting more people have a chance at government. In President Jackson's first message to Congress, he argued that "in a country where offices are created solely for the benefit of the people no man has any more intrinsic right to office than another."[46] Of course, Jackson did make one requirement for office-seekers—that they be loyal to him and his ideas.

Simultaneously, demographic changes occurred that would provide great demand for those spoils jobs. Beginning in the late 1840s, European immigrants began following the dream of success and prosperity to the United States.[47] Primarily hailing from Catholic areas such as Ireland and the scattered principalities of what would later become Italy, waves of immigrants flooded into the US over two decades, most with no family connections or prearranged work. Coming with faith and little else, these new Americans sought open job opportunities.

Clever party officials sensed an opportunity. Job-seeking new arrivals had sought out what work was available, with mixed success. Unsuccessful job seekers turned to the one common resource they knew: the Roman Catholic Church. When the diocese in their new communities ran out of resources, they turned to their parishioners who were Democratic Party officials as they tried to make work for their new members. The Roman Catholic Church and the Democratic Party aligned strongly with each other in most places, especially in the urban northeast where so many of the new immigrants congregated.[48]

Rapid growth of the urban areas also necessitated growth in government services, which meant more need for more employees. The recursive need helped the party in control of the city's government to provide ever more employment opportunities for more participants in the growing party organization.

Rise of the Machines

The political party was about to become much more central to people's lives than ever intended or envisioned by the Constitution's authors. The party organizations found a base of new members, employees, and voters. Once the party organizations hired these new Americans, even to menial jobs, they gained adherents for life. A brief mention to the new employees that, if the opposing party won the upcoming election, their new job would be in jeopardy was enough to ensure that they voted for their party whenever possible. While the party was in power, it also gave them access to a large fundraising base, which they used not only to employ citizens but also to provide a rudimentary social welfare provision. In *Plunkitt of Tammany Hall*, ward heeler George Washington Plunkitt describes having ready cash available to distribute to party members who were in between jobs or had suffered some disability, to help them make ends meet. Party events made sure all participants were well fed and sated with drink. With participation and employment, the new American immigrants quickly attained money and social status.[49]

In return, hordes of new voters locked their ballots for their new party. In urban areas such as New York, the new party arrangements turned races that favored the majority party (usually the Democratic Party) into a dominant party, a machine that would go of itself. Because of the automatic and preordained return to power that the new arrangement provided, the party organizations became machine-like. The pejorative term "machine" stuck, and the organizations became known as "party machines."[50]

Machines were a natural outgrowth of the unintended consequences of Jacksonian democracy. The combination of using the spoils model of government employment with popular democracy and partisan nomination of candidates created a closed system. The party leaders, once in power, could install party members in jobs and assess their salaries to fund the next campaign. The party in power had enough loyal voters in their employment base alone to ensure victory in subsequent elections. Internal dissenters need not apply, nor should the out-party. Party leaders would not renominate internal reformers to office, ensuring that loyalty to the party was the true litmus test of one's electability. As caucuses faded under the convention nomination model, without the support of one's party organization one would not be eligible to run for office.

The machine eliminated nearly all measures of accountability for those in public office. Instead of voting their ideology, or their pocketbooks, people voted for their employer. The stakes were so high for those who owed their employment to the party that they were willing to sacrifice even basic democratic elements such as accountability. Party loyalists looked the other way as organized crime elements infiltrated the parties. The machines were subverting the very popular democracy from which they spawned.[51]

Machines Overpower Democracy

Growing organizations required strong leadership, and the machines had such leaders. William "Marcy" Tweed in New York may have become the most notorious of the party machine bosses, but he was far from alone in holding massive power over his machine and thus his community. James Curley in Boston, Tom Pendergast in Kansas City, Louisiana's Huey Long, and Richard Daley in Chicago were other highly notable and powerful machine bosses.[52]

The growing power over large masses of people that the bosses and their machines wielded was necessary in large organizations, but the demands that placed upon the machines would never be able to be fully satisfied. The machines quickly began assessing the pay of their partisan-appointed employees, and when that was not enough entrepreneurial leaders began looking for other revenue streams, leading some to connect with organized crime operatives.[53]

The machines became emboldened with their power, since the large cadre of supporters who owed their jobs to the party ensured that elections would not be competitive. Party government became machine-like in the automatic nature of the party's return to office, usually crushing all in its path, and with it the growing number of corrupt officials that were blurring the lines between partisanship and organized crime.[54]

Machines would grant not only jobs but also government building contracts to supporters. Business owners sought lucrative government contracts. When the machine bosses gave out contracts, with new buildings for example, they would expect repayment in the form of kickbacks. Businesses built the cost of kickbacks into their bids, essentially earning their normal take and providing an extra percentage for the machine bosses. The public was unaware of this high-level theft, known as graft. In some cases, what many saw as corrupt was, nevertheless, legal. Hence, Plunkitt's famous line that he was engaged in "honest graft"—his belief that what he was doing furthered both the public interest and his personal interest at the same time.[55]

Political machines also often accepted payments from criminal enterprises in exchange for the police looking the other way when they engaged in illegal acts. In New York City, for example, protection money paid by gambling and prostitution rackets offered the Tweed Ring a stable income stream throughout his leadership. The gangsters paid the Tweed Ring back by stuffing ballot boxes with votes for Tweed's party on Election Day.

Much later, Richard Daley's Chicago machine operated in much the same way. Daley controlled roughly 35,000 patronage jobs, giving him the ability to reward many party loyalists and decimate the formerly competitive Republican Party in the city. Daley consistently circumvented civil service laws by hiring loyal Democrats to temporary jobs, which were not regulated the same as protected non-patronage positions. As full-time protected government workers left, the party machine filled their positions temporarily pending civil service exams that were never given, thus ensuring party discipline over the massive Chicago public works apparatus that built the city's expressways and even O'Hare International Airport.[56] Temporary jobs, ones that sometimes lasted 20 to 30 years, had the dual benefit of rewarding party loyalists while at the same time reminding the occupant of his need to produce for the machine or he could easily be replaced. The lack of civil service protection provided job opportunities for some and yet kept them ever nervous and attentive to the machines' needs.

Where the party machines failed democracy was in the core concept of accountability. Elections provide voters the opportunity to remove people from office, providing turnover and the chance for dissent from the majority party in government to become policy. Elections are the core mechanism through which voters hold their elected officials accountable. By functionally bypassing the electoral accountability element of elections, machine rule ensured a type of oligarchy in the growing urban centers of the mid-1800s.[57] The parties may have maximized their linkage role, but they failed on grounds of accountability.

Dissent became impossible in the cities where complete machine rule took hold. Bosses and their allies ignored or quashed members of the minority party and factions within the majority party who were not involved in the machine apparatus. At the local level, the clear lines between a given political party and the government itself were blurred or erased. "Boss" William Tweed was the government of New York City during his reign, as was Tom Pendergast in Kansas City, and in almost any major urban area machine bosses ruled with iron fists and little thought to anything other than the maintenance of their own power.[58]

The machine era took away competition and accountability, and with them representation. The linkage institution had become an impediment. Citizens had little choice, if they wanted to have a voice in their government or even to receive the basic services government provided, but to select the machine party. One of the most pernicious aspects of the machine was how its inevitable victories drew otherwise good government types into the machine's grasp. Accessing the center of power required compliance and assimilation. Yet, in so doing, reform-minded people sometimes became machine worker and leaders. Boss E. H. Crump of Memphis created a powerful machine in his city; however, he was also a great believer in efficiency and providing quality municipal services. Daley actually campaigned initially as a reformer, although he was loyal to the Democratic Party from the beginning.[59] State-level reforms could have contained machine rule in the cities, but the corruption embraced by the machines began to spread to cities' state governments and eventually to the US Senate. At the time, state legislatures appointed their representatives in the US Senate, thereby ensuring cooperation at the federal level as well.

Citizens had no accountability to hold over their elected officials and party leaders in two ways: the public had no input at all on the candidates put forward by the party leadership for nomination, and the public had already chosen their party of preference before the general election occurred. Once party leaders had selected their nominees, the election winners would have been publicly known, as any uncertainty over outcomes was obviated by the machines' advantages.

Change Comes to the Machine

While enough supporters existed to maintain the machine, their excesses were ever harder to ignore. Newspapers, especially those supporting minority parties in machine-run communities, exposed the failings and corruption inherent in the machines. Out-party members and in-party dissenters became so frustrated they would choose to find alternate means of pleading their cases. The machine became the public image of a crooked, even broken, political process. As the strength of the machines allowed them to withstand the early attacks on their rule, opposition to them began to coalesce under the growing frustration of reform-minded inability to change the machines. By the mid-1880s the problem reached crisis proportions. Reform was necessary and inevitable.

The federal use of spoils continued, and the issue was so divisive it threatened to split the dominant Republican Party over its presidential nomination. The 1880 Republican national convention took thirty-six ballots. Fourteen serious contenders were eventually winnowed down to two. In the end, spoils supporters, known as Stalwarts, promoted New York Port Authority director Chester Arthur. Reformers, who had adopted the moniker Mugwumps, eventually chose a dark horse from Ohio, James A. Garfield, as their standard-bearer. Once the field had narrowed to the two, a compromise ticket emerged of Garfield as the nominee and Arthur as his vice president.[60] The Garfield-Arthur ticket won the general election, but the controversy over spoils followed them into their administration. Halfway through the first year of his presidency, Garfield was assassinated by a frustrated office-seeker whose only words after shooting him were "I am a Stalwart, and Arthur is President now."[61]

Arthur quickly soured on the spoils system that had resulted in a president's death and became an advocate for reform. By 1883, Arthur signed merit protections for federal bureaucrats into law, thus eliminating the federal model for spoils used at the local level.[62] Local-level machines did not intend to dismantle their spoils-based electioneering methods, and they persisted. However, the public had become aware of reform and the drumbeat of support for changes to the machines would only grow louder. The days of machine rule were numbered, though it would persist in some places—such as Chicago—until the 1960s. The reformers were ascendant, transforming one city after another, and the primary election would be one of the most significant components of reform to emerge.

Machine rule was destined to fail, but its eventual downfall was accelerated by the rise of the reform movement that would remake American politics: the Progressives. As we discussed in this chapter, the Progressives were a committed and diverse group, one that found common purpose in defeating the excesses of the machine politics era.

Progressives were not of any single political or demographic group. Western expansionists and bootstrapping libertarians joined urban intellectuals. Progressives drew support from the middle class, and supporters included many lawyers, teachers, physicians, ministers, and business people. Frustrated Republicans and suffragettes saw similar goals and coalesced. While the groups would find disagreement on many things, they saw the old machine ways as corrupt, wicked, and ripe for reform. The reform they chose would alter the very nature of American parties.

Chapter 3

What the Progressives Were For

We seek to restore the government of the Republic to the hands of "the plain people," with which class it originated.[1]

—People's Party Platform, 1892

Abolish the caucus and the convention. Go back to the first principles of democracy; go back to the people. Substitute for both the caucus and the convention a primary election.[2]

—Robert La Follette

The Progressives believed in fixing things. They saw a world that was not working well and that, with the application of reason and a devotion to the high ideals of classical democracy, could be improved. In many ways, we live in the world they produced, a century after their efforts. Furthermore, many of the reforms they made were praiseworthy and helpful to eradicate the scourge of urban political machines. However, those beneficial results came with unintended consequences. Especially concerning political parties and their view of the electoral process, it is our contention the Progressives made dire mistakes, ones that we also live with to the current day. Their devotion to direct democracy in the creation of the primary system was misguided.

The Progressives were moralists. While they looked forward as their name suggests, and believed in technology and knowledge to better the world, they also looked back to the democratic ideals—a belief in the public good, an engaged citizenry—that animated the American founding.

Progressives espoused Protestant values and were middle to upper middle class in socioeconomic status. An abiding religious belief held throughout Progressive thought. The mixture of Newtonian scientific thinking and Protestant optimism led to a corresponding belief in the goodness of mankind, a philosophy that humanity could for the first time see the divine design of the university and bring itself into harmony with it.[3] That combination manifested many of their strengths, as well as their blind spots.

The Progressives were, in the end, believers in a specific kind of democracy, and they sought to adapt that conception of democracy to a fast-changing world. As Wilson Carey McWilliams observed, "Progressives were engaged in a quest for democracy on a grand scale, informed by the belief that the human spirit or conscience, guided by social science, could eventually create a vast and brotherly republic of public-spirited citizens."[4] These ideals were in some ways very consistent with the Constitution's own design, especially in the idea of a universal commitment to the common good. However, in their haste to embrace new ways of thinking they frequently slighted or overlooked the vital roles of linkage institutions played by the traditional American political parties. Their fervor for reform made the Progressives see only corruption in parties and not the very central roles they play in engaging voters and making representative democracy function. The Progressive belief in democracy was limited by their prejudice in favor of the engaged middle class and by an unrealistic belief that all people happily and robustly participated in politics without external assistance or encouragement. The Progressives forgot—or did not realize—that the day-to-day life of the working class presented very real difficulties to individual voters in being highly informed and engaged citizens. However, to fully appreciate their ideas—for good or ill—we need to understand the world in which they lived. The American political milieu was changing and the manifestations of political failings in the late nineteenth and early twentieth centuries were metastasizing within the machines. Reform was necessary.

The World the Progressives Faced

Americans tend to believe, at least about the nation if not the entire world, that economic prosperity, freedom, equality, and democracy all go hand in hand. A rightly ordered political world should evidence no conflict between these ideals. Enjoying the fruits of equality and freedom in a democratic system should naturally lead to economic success for the individual and the nation. Of course, the world is not perfectly ordered, and the failings and conflicts between these ideals are obvious. Perfect embodiments of ordered societies are impossible, but the increasing spread of knowledge among all socioeconomic subdivisions of the time convinced some that perfection, or something approaching it, was possible. Scientific positivism undergirded much of what the Progressives believed, suffusing it with a confidence that humans were naturally enlightened and given to understanding the common good. To the Progressives, social institutions outside of the church were more impediments to the public good than mechanisms to achieve it.[5] Materialism and self-seeking were two of the great enemies constructed in the Progressive mind, and they saw the machines as a symbol of the marriage of conspicuous consumption and democracy.[6]

In the late nineteenth and early twentieth century, the gap between the reality and the ideal grew large and these four ideals seemed to come into intense conflict. As one historian of the era writes, "Progressivism reflected a growing, if temporary, consensus among Americans that major changes in the late nineteenth century were producing unwelcome, un-American imbalances in their society."[7] Moreover, it was to solve the tensions between these ideals that gave birth to the Progressive movement and their acute desire to reform world.

To appreciate just what they got wrong, we must understand what they got right, and that requires us to consider the world in which they found themselves. Throughout the latter half of the nineteenth century, the United States underwent a remarkable social and economic political transformation. At one level, there was a breakdown in the traditional sense of community to which most Americans were accustomed. As the historian Robert Wiebe argued, "The great casualty of America's turmoil late in the century was the island community. Although a majority of Americans would still reside in relatively small, personal centers for several decades more, the society that had been premised upon the community's effective sovereignty, upon its capacity to manage affairs within its boundaries, no longer functions."[8] This breakdown in the power of local community gave an opening for demands for a more national response to problems. Progressives would exploit this opening in their electoral and party reforms.

But it was a changed (and changing) world. The country welcomed (or, to some, reluctantly accepted) millions of immigrants, and these immigrants were often from different places than previous immigrants: southern and eastern Europe. Many that came from the traditional northwest of Europe were the Irish, and they were Roman Catholic. The Catholic tradition of the new immigrants clashed with the Protestant ideals of most colonial-era arrivals. These were new people, with different cultural histories, and they arrived in great numbers. This frightened many Americans, quite a few of whom would become the core of the Progressive movement.

At the same time, the economy grew at a truly impressive rate. The best GNP estimate in the mid-1880s was $11 billion; that grew to $84 billion in 1919.[9] The country was without doubt much, much richer than ever before. People moved from farms to cities and became factory workers. New industries emerged—in railroads, oil, and steel production, to name a few. The technologies and products may seem quaint to us now, but people today probably feel a similar sense of anxiety over technologies upsetting the established order that people in the late nineteenth century felt. With this stunning increase in wealth came economic challenges. One of the most pressing was the concentration of wealth among a privileged few and a staggering gap between those rich and the working class, farmers, and the outright poor. (The wealth gap is yet another trend still a subject of intense focus today.) The inequality of the day led to intense political conflict and a fear that such conflict would lead to instability. James Weaver, presidential nominee of the People's Party in 1892, wrote with alarm:

> We are nearing a serious crisis. . . . If the present strained relations between the wealth owners and the wealth producers continue much longer they will ripen into a frightful disaster. . . . A bold and aggressive plutocracy has usurped the Government and is using it as a policeman to enforce its insolent decrees. . . . The corporation has been placed above the individual and an armed body of cruel mercenaries permitted in times of public peril, to discharge police duties which clearly belong to the state.[10]

The more restrained Herbert Croly (1965) clinically observed, "The net result of the industrial expansion of the United States since the Civil War has been the establishment in the heart of the American economic system of certain glaring inequalities of condition and power."[11] The decades that closed the century were marked by a significant amount of labor unrest and strikes—the Great Southwest Railroad (1886), the Haymarket Riot (1886), and the Homestead Steel Strike (1892), to name some of the most famous. Lest we think that economic problems existed only in the cities and in manufacturing, fierce discontent emerged among farmers, who frequently saw decreases in the price of commodities and brutal challenges created by the costs of getting their products to market. The tremendous economic expansion, with persistent periodic depressions, of the late nineteenth century, continuing into the new century, was creating alarming political and social problems. Whether the source of economic growth or contraction was the tariff, the gold standard, or a corrupt government was and still is a topic for debate. What is beyond dispute is that conflicting economic forces that made for perilous times rent the country.

The convergence of significant societal disruption and growing inequality clashed with the more optimistic view of human improvement and perfectibility that expanded educational opportunities and scientific advancement presented. The Progressives' ethical beliefs confronted the realities of the day, which likely only increased their righteous belief in social improvement through democratic reform.

Political Parties and Corruption

Dealing with these economic problems led some, such as anarchists and hardline socialists, to advocate for violence. Most of the leading politicians of the era at one time or another worried about unrest that led to riots and, conceivably, worse—revolution. Progressives wanted reform, yes, but structured through the classical ideals of democratic engagement and not in proletarian violence. In many ways what drove people to Progressive positions was not only a radical utopian future but also a conservative fear of instability. Thus, to Progressives the answer came in turning toward traditional politics and the ballot box. The question was, how best to make that turn? Of course, any embrace of politics would force Progressive-minded people to face the political parties and the party system. In their day, all American politics was party politics. The political party was, from the beginning days of the republic, the main mechanism through which citizen interest translated into collective electoral action. Parties dominated American political life, and not just in the urban realm. Everywhere, partisanship guided political activity even when it did not control said activity. Progressives saw parties as unavoidable at best, so should they become Democrats or Republicans or form their own third party? As it turned out, they tried all three paths. As one can surmise, though, in their turn to parties they were eternally frustrated. The parties they encountered appeared to them as barriers to reform—often populated by reactionaries opposed to the changes the Progressives saw as so necessary. Parties were, in reality, part of the problem as they saw it. That being the case, one might think that the best option was to create a third party not beholden to old ways of thinking; however, as they discovered (and it is a hard lesson for people to learn even today), America is a stubbornly two-party system. There were serious third-party moments in 1892 and 1912 (indeed, 1912 actually saw four significant parties, with the Socialist Eugene Debs winning 6 percent of the vote). Theodore Roosevelt's run for president as the Progressive Party candidate in 1912 simply led to a dramatic split in the Republicans that allowed Wilson and the Democrats to win an impressive landslide. The simple reality is the two-party system of Democrats and Republicans predates the Civil War and is, whatever the parties' flaws, remarkably durable.[12] The two main parties are inextricably intertwined with the American political order. So, seeing no alternative, most Progressives first fought to make their changes through the two major parties. Thus, there were Progressive Republicans and Progressive Democrats. *Progressive* was as much of an adjective to describe certain members of the two major parties as it was a noun to describe the party that formed in 1912 and again in 1924. So, as they worked to deal with the economic and social challenges of the era, they sought to reform the very parties themselves. If third parties did not work, the only solution was to radically alter the way the two major parties did business.

A new party was also important to symbolically reject the status quo. As noted earlier, the Progressives looked at history with a very selective eye. While they rejected Jacksonian ideas of spoils and strong partisanship, the Progressives were inspired by the knowledge that during Jackson's presidency participation rose. However, rather than seeing that success as due to the growing linkage between voters and parties, they saw it as driven by a public desperate to more directly participate in their politics.[13] The Progressives had confused the increase in participatory democracy under Jackson, in the guise of increased turnout, with a desire to have more direct democracy. That confusion would lead to great confidence among the Progressives that the public wanted fewer intermediary institutions and more direct policymaking decision points.

To better appreciate what the Progressives were doing, we need to delve deeper into what the parties were like at the time. To Progressives, parties were not merely barriers to reform, they were inherently corrupt institutions. The quintessence of parties was the large urban party machines. Frequently, the machines were Democratic, such as New York's Tammany Hall or the Cook County Democratic Party that controlled Chicago. However, there were Republican examples, with Philadelphia's Republican machine that ruled that city for decades and was just as notorious for corruption, in its time, as the infamous "Tweed Ring" of Tammany Hall. There were also tightly organized groups in small towns, old "courthouse gangs," and rural areas that were just as corrupt, in their own ways, as the urban machines were. In the 1890s, in rural Adams Country, Ohio, 90 percent of the electorate were paid to vote.[14]

What was the party machine like? To its critics it was an inherently unscrupulous organization that illegally and immorally profited from controlling the government. An all-powerful and wicked "boss" headed it. Theodore Roosevelt spoke the Progressive line when he wrote,

> The boss . . . is a man who does not gain power by open means, but by secret means, and usually by corrupt means. Some of the worst and most powerful bosses in our political history either held no public office or else some unimportant public office. They made no appeal either to intellect or conscience. Their work was done behind closed doors, and consisted chiefly in the use of that greed which gives in order that in return it may get. . . . If he is at one end of the social scale, he may through his agents, traffic in the most brutal forms of vice and give protection to the purveyors of shame and sin in return for money bribes.[15]

The machine was usually described in militaristic terms in its control of the government.[16] People "kicked up" work, bribes, and support in the form of a vote to the precinct captains, to the ward leaders, and then to the "boss." In return, down came the orders and, importantly, other benefits. To use one example,

> The Tammany machine, a juggernaut with its backbone in the local wards and neighborhoods. . . . Each of the city's three hundred forty election districts . . . containing about four hundred eligible voters . . . had its own Tammany captain and its local ten-member committee assignment to visit every single Democrat. The party provided each with $1,000 in cash for Election Day "walking around" money.[17]

We should note that, while there were some very powerful bosses, most cities were usually run more by a committee of machine leaders. One of the ways that machines committed voter fraud was with "repeaters," voters who voted several times in an election. (They would frequently grow beards and throughout the day strategically shave some to let one individual vote several times. The hirsute were a valuable resource for the machines.) The reality of repeaters in an age when preventing fraud was either not considered or impossible gave rise to the adage "vote early, and vote often." Along with this tight electoral organization, there was financial fraud that could reach epic proportions. The great symbol of the financial fraud exhibited by machines was the County Courthouse in New York City. Because of kickbacks to the Tweed Ring and to local contracts, the original construction budget of $250,000 was dwarfed by the more than $13 million eventually spent.[18] Even more sinister was the occasional violence used by machines. In Chicago, Mayor Carter Harrison (1879–1887) was unafraid to employ and defend brutal police officers who were prone to use violence, literally "cracking skulls" if necessary, even against women and children.[19]

As mentioned earlier, one of the most powerful benefits that the machine could bestow was a job—patronage. Across the country tens of thousands of jobs were the province of party organizations in power doling out positions to loyal partisans. The reporter William Riordan, who wrote a book quoting the Tammany Hall politician George Washington Plunkitt, wrote one of the most famous accounts of machine politics. The book is full of famous lines that often sound funny today—Plunkitt termed his tactics "honest graft," for instance. When it came to parties and jobs, Riordan quotes Plunkitt as arguing, "First, this great and glorious country was built up by political parties; second, parties can't hold together if their workers don't get the offices when they win; third, if the parties go to pieces, the government they built up must go to pieces, too; fourth, then there'll be h—— to pay."[20] In some ways, Riordan's quote would become a roadmap for Progressive reform. The ability of the great city machines to control and dispense thousands of jobs in return for support was essential to their control of city government. High-minded lectures about good government from reformers seemed absurd when families thought incessantly about making the rent. As one of the most perceptive Progressive reformers, Mary Simkhovitch, observed, "Compared with the sacredness of the job, what place does conscious civic principle hold?"[21] Of course, there were never enough jobs to give every voter a job.[22] That was never the goal. Nevertheless, each job given to one individual created a wider collection of family and friends who were grateful and likely machine voters. One estimate was that each patronage position produced ten votes for the machine.[23] Furthermore, patronage extended well past the local city bosses. The federal government had jobs to dispense. Woodrow Wilson spoke passionately about the evils of the spoils system, yet, when he became president, was quickly convinced of the necessity of patronage to get his legislative agenda through Congress.[24]

To Progressives this was not only ethically corrupt, it was a monumental assault on efficient government and a suppressive act against public participation. Progressives longed to create a scientifically efficient and accountable government (Roosevelt argued, "The State must be made efficient"[25]). They saw in the machine a horrible example of waste alongside the more morally and ethically unsavory aspects of urban politics. Furthermore, we cannot separate out the anti-immigrant, in particular anti-Irish, nature of the criticisms of many machines. The party machines were legendary as a means for newly arrived immigrants to make their way in the world and better their status and material comfort. In hindsight, we now see that the machines were remarkably effective socialization and assimilation entities for immigrants, educating them in the ways of American politics—corrupt though they could be in this era. Boss Tweed was a central figure in viewing the immigrants, particularly the Irish, "not as charity cases to pity"; he "respected them as voters to bargain with, to woo and court."[26] However, at the time, immigrants, particularly the Irish, were seen as highly dangerous in a political sense. The journalist Charles Nordhoff wrote in 1871, "The Irish immigrants to our shores display an extraordinary aptitude for misgovernment of cities."[27]

As the Irish played a prominent role in many urban machines, the machines were suspect on ethnic, as well as ethical, grounds. Many Progressives, generally, saw immigrants as lazy, corrupt, and unschooled in the ways of American democracy. Indeed, as one historian writes, "some immigrant groups—Italians, Jews, Slavs—were thought to be permanently unsuited to American life, having been prevented by 'race' from acquiring American culture."[28] However, we should note that other Progressives put great stock in the transformative power of education. Under the right conditions and with the right methods, people could be Americanized.

Even such a reformer and harsh critic of the machines as Theodore Roosevelt recognized their appeal. After the strong condemnation of machine corruption included in his autobiography, Roosevelt quickly admits,

> There is often much good in the type of boss, especially in big cities, who fulfills towards the people of his district in rough and ready fashion the position of friend and protector. . . . For some of his constituents he does proper favors, and for other wholly improper favors; but he preserves human relations with all.[29]

Mayor James Michael Curley in Boston told the story of a very proper "Boston Brahmin" lady campaigning for a reformer for a school committee position. Canvassing in the working-class neighborhoods in South Boston, she was asked by an Irish housewife if it was the case the candidate had a sister working for the school system. The campaigner assured the housewife that he was not the kind of man who would use his position to help his family. To which the housewife supposedly replied, "Well, if the son of a bitch won't help his own sister, why should I vote for him."[30] Reformers and the working class didn't speak the same political language, which was made worse by the reformers' tendency to talk down to voters. Thus, the city machines were frequently voted out of office and returned to power just as frequently. To many Progressives this was baffling, and only a myriad of corruptions could explain it. But to return again to Simkhovitch, the machine politician was a "job dispenser" who "is the same old 'Jim' that he used to be" who speaks and dresses the same way as those in the community (or maybe dresses a bit better).[31] When Richard Daley was elected as Chicago's mayor in 1955 there was talk of him moving to a home more befitting his new status; however, he remained in Bridgeport, the neighborhood he grew up in.[32] And, what of the reformer? Simkhovitch paints a portrait of an alien do-gooder unaware of the place he wants to reform and condescending in outlook:

> He [the reformer] comes from a different environment. His English is a different tongue from that of the people he desires to reform. . . . He is unfamiliar with all those elements that make up the great traditions of party loyalty. He does not sympathize with the traditions, even if he knows them. He is an outsider. He is working on the people, not with them. He wants them to be different from themselves and more like him. In all this the position of unconscious superiority is alienating in its effect. The people who listen to him may not doubt the desirability of the reforms which he mentions; they simply doubt *him*, and that is fatal.[33]

Both Theodore Roosevelt and Mary Simkhovitch were adamant about reform; however, they were neither simple minded nor condescending in their understanding of how the average person thought about politics or of the appeal machine politicians could present.

That said, the machines were certainly corrupt in many ways. They dealt in vice, bribery, and threats. Machines routinely looked the other way on issues concerning prostitution and the sale of liquor. Machine politicos could be quite menacing to people who didn't do their bidding. Simkhovitch tells the dark story of a popular saloonkeeper pressured into running for office by the machine. He doesn't want to run because of the time and expense involved; he is told, "If you don't run, we'll ruin your business."[34] In fact, he is eventually ruined by the expenses he has taken on without any compensatory benefits that the machine could, but didn't, bestow. Bribery was rampant, threats were real, and the machines themselves were often quite criminal or in business with criminals. "Big" Tim Sullivan, a Tammany Hall leader at the end of the nineteenth century into the twentieth century, was well connected to such underworld figures as Arnold Rothstein (the mobster reputed to have fixed the 1919 World Series) and "was part of a criminal syndicate supposedly collecting payoffs from every whorehouse, dice game, race course, and pool hall in the city."[35] In New York, for instance, well into the 1930s "the district attorneys were usually hand-picked incompetents designated by the Democratic Party's Tammany Hall Club," and this was specifically done to be friendly to organized crime.[36] In the 1950s the last Tammany Hall boss, Carmine DeSapio, was quite friendly with the famous mob boss Frank Costello.

However, when it comes to politics we must also look beyond the urban machines, as corrupt as they could be. Colorado Fuel and Iron operated much like a machine throughout the state, tightly controlling voting. "On registration and election day, company guards refused to permit anyone to enter these precincts [ones drawn to exist entirely inside company-owned land] who was thought to be a union member, an agitator, or a labor sympathizer. Foreign-born scabs who lived in the mining camps then were marched to the polls by company officers. Since many of the scabs were illiterate, they were given printed cards containing the letter R and illegally assisted by election judges."[37] Thus, electoral fraud was seen, rightly so, by many Progressives as endemic to the system—whether by corrupt party machines in the cities or by corporate malfeasance throughout the country. We should note that recent scholarship has cast doubt on the extent of such voting fraud—it was real, but not as widespread as many have thought.[38] Regardless, middle-class reformers of that era believed such fraud *was* widespread and that corruption suffused the entire system. There were enough documented cases of electoral fraud to understand how that view came to be widely accepted.

The Progressive Conception of Politics

From the settlement houses to meat inspectors, and from the newly educated to the meritorious civil service, Progressives undoubtedly sought to make the world a better place. Progressives were inveterate problem solvers and, at times, exuberantly or naively utopian. Many Progressives shared the belief that all problems could be solved if one applied proper thinking and science. Looking back, Walter Lippmann recalled believing "in the inevitability of progress, in the perfectibility of man and society, and in the sublimation of evil."[39] Most of the time they were pragmatic realists who looked at the world through clear eyes and tried to ameliorate problems. With such an optimistic view of human nature, the Progressives believed a modern incarnation of the Greek agora was close at hand, if only human institutions could get out of the way of human progress.

Like any great social movement, the Progressives made mistakes or pushed for controversial reforms that produced mixed results. To understand where they made their mistakes—which we contend were particularly concentrated in the introduction of direct primaries—we need to understand how they perceived politics. What did they think about democracy? What did they think about the relationship between the government and the people?

There were, of course, differences of opinion about how to improve that world among the diverse people who walked under the banner of "Progressive." For every Progressive reform proposed, there is an example of a Progressive who criticized it. To understand the disagreements among Progressives, one good place to start is Theodore Roosevelt. Roosevelt was largely seen as a Progressive president who clearly became more Progressive as he aged. He campaigned for president as the Progressive Party nominee in 1912 (after falling to secure, unfairly in the eyes of many, the Republican nomination) and many of his most reformist ideas came about just before and during that campaign. In speech given in Osawatomie, Kansas, in August 1910, Roosevelt laid out his new and most Progressive ideas. The speech, entitled "The New Nationalism," became the intellectual foundation for his 1912 presidential run. In that speech, commemorating the Civil War and the achievements of the Grand Army, Roosevelt lays out an analysis of what ailed the country and a set of proposals for dealing with those political ills. He strongly endorses the notion of equality of opportunity and sees the "destruction of special privilege" as a key to progress. When people are given true opportunity to advance, he claims, they and the nation will prosper. What stands in the way are those with special privileges. In addition, to deal with those barriers requires government action. Roosevelt envisions an activist government that passes laws regulating labor—workmen's compensation, outlawing child labor, guaranteeing sanitary conditions and safety for workers. He is quick to say that property must be respected but the state must step in to balance the interests of property holders and labor. The Progressives were critical of the political power of large corporations, though they were not anti-capitalist.[40] In fact, Progressives of the day rejected much of the Socialist rhetoric that other parties were advocating at the time. Still, Roosevelt clearly envisioned a national government doing things to make the system more harmonious. He seemed to believe that, under the right leadership pursuing good policies, the conflicts between labor and property would dissolve. In this sense, he harkened back to that old Republicanism of an earlier generation. One of the problems is that special interests, in the form of corporations, have too much control over government elections. Thus, he argues,

> If our political institutions were perfect, they would absolutely prevent the political domination of money in any part of our affairs. We need to make our political representatives more quickly and sensitively responsive to the people whose servants they are. More direct action by the people in their own affairs under proper safeguards is vitally necessary. The direct primary is a step in this direction, if it is associated with a corrupt-services act effective to prevent the advantage of the man willingly recklessly and unscrupulously to spend money over his more honest competitor.[41]

Roosevelt hearkens back to *Federalist* no. 10, equating all organized groups with factions. Thus, we should note that for Roosevelt the direct primary only makes sense in the context of other reforms. And this should give us pause in unabashedly endorsing it as an inherently good and democratic institution.

Any consideration of the Progressives and democracy must clearly recognize two assumptions they made: first, that the government should be more responsive to the people; second, that the people who counted should be restricted. Both of these observations force us to consider just what democracy is.

What all these reforms had in common were twofold. First, they intended to weaken the power of the corrupt machines. Second, they were designed to make the US more democratic and, in particular, to foster as much direct democracy as possible. The reality of such a physically large nation made the kind of deliberative democracy as practiced in a small city-state impossible (and it was probably undesirable anyway because of the limited intellectual capacities of most citizens). However, there could be ways to make our representative democracy more direct—even to make it a kind of participatory democracy. No one was seriously questioning whether the Americans would still have representatives in Washington or Topeka or Annapolis running most of the political show. However, citizen input would combine, at the state level, with initiatives and referenda. At all levels, citizens would directly influence politics by not simply ratifying the candidate chosen by party leaders but taking an active hand in selecting those candidates via primaries. Robert La Follette, another key leader in the Progressive pantheon, made the direct primary a key part of his agenda in the 1890s with his famous speech "The Menace of the Machine," and it became a central goal of his as governor of Wisconsin in 1900.[42] To such Progressives this was not exactly a new idea but one that resonated with our national traditions. The people must in some sense rule and they are capable, if not of the administration of government that must be left to leaders, of having direct input in who rules and what issues should predominate politics. Woodrow Wilson wrote, "when I hear a popular vote spoken of as mob government, I felt like telling the man who dares so speak that he has no right to call himself an American."[43]

However, there was a more ominous side to the Progressive faith in "the people." We cannot lose sight of the way many Progressives perpetuated racist and bigoted beliefs. Who counted as "the people" in any meaningful political sense was hotly contested. Woodrow Wilson's racism is widely known.[44] Other Progressives were more ambiguous—Roosevelt was fairly advanced on the subject, though even his record is mixed. When it came to elections, many middle-class and Progressive Americans viewed immigrants, in particular, with a great deal of suspicion.

> In the eyes of many old stock Americans, this mass of immigrant workers was an unwelcome addition to the electorate. Poor, uneducated, ignorant of American traditions, the foreign-born men peopling the nation's industries seemed to lack the judgment, knowledge, and commitment to American values necessary for salutary participation in elections.[45]

Progressives instituted various restrictions on voting for both legitimate (to deter fraud) and what we would today consider illegitimate reasons (to deter immigrants and minorities from voting). One of the most important was the creation of registration laws. They had existed in some places long before the Progressives (Massachusetts was registering voters in 1801); however, there was a dramatic increase in such laws in the late nineteenth and early twentieth century, and Progressives strongly supported them.[46] In some cases, registration laws were easy to follow and voting was not adversely affected. However, some places saw dramatic declines in voting. In Pittsburgh, the registration commission bragged about the stark decline in registered votes in its own minutes.[47] Thus, as with so many aspects of the Progressives, laudable reform ideas were often motived by other reasons, some of them disturbing.

The net result was that at the state and local level primaries quickly became the predominant method of party nominee selection. Primaries replaced the old caucuses and convention used throughout the nineteenth century. At the presidential level, primaries appeared in some states in 1912 but quickly faded in significance, as nominating conventions looked at them as advisory only. They persisted in some states from 1912 to 1968; they existed as a supplement to the traditional convention that still decided the nominees to lead the party. Some delegates were chosen via the primaries and they could be used to "test the strength and appeal" of candidates; however, the main business of nominating a presidential candidate occurred at those four-day summer affairs every quadrennial.

This leads us to consider what the Progressives thought the role of leaders was. What should be the relationship between leaders and the people? Despite their commitment to a more direct democracy, they hardly thought leaders were unimportant or that anyone could be a leader. The mass of people had a role, but this role was limited in many ways. What the Progressives really envisioned was an informed public, engaged in the political world, voting for a set of leaders to administer government. With their belief in social science and public administration, Progressives certainly thought that experts should be actually running government. This was not to be a world of the common person in charge of government. Indeed, one of the faults of the spoils system was that party loyalty trumped administrative skill in assigning jobs. The people should see two clear distinct policy agendas by the parties, weigh those options, and vote one party into power to do its bidding. The people also had a role, via primaries, in selecting the leaders—the candidates—of those parties. This would eliminate the corrupt nature of the backroom deals party bosses made in selecting candidates. It would also free many candidates (and later office holders) from the shackles that many bosses forged to control them, since party bosses often held less distinguished public office or no elected office at all, but always maintained a tight control over the nomination process. As Sidney Milkis rightly argues, "Roosevelt and La Follette formed candidate-centered campaigns that could appeal over the heads of the party leaders directly to public opinion."[48] And, of course, Roosevelt famously saw the office of president as that of a steward of the nation. Woodrow Wilson was hardly any less a believer in the role of leadership. He certainly saw his job was to educate the people—and his favorite pedagogical style was, in effect, the lecture.[49] He was not engaging in a freewheeling seminar of equals. Indeed, earlier in his academic career, Wilson had written, "It is the power which dictates, dominates: the materials yield. Men are as clay in the hands of the consummate leader."[50]

We see this attitude about parties illustrated in Woodrow Wilson's first inaugural address. He spoke about the Democratic Party being placed in power "for a large and definite purpose." His vision was of a party purged of seeking power for power's sake or distracted by minor things such as patronage. The mentality of the bosses had to go. Wilson was turning party politics completely around and rejecting the view of that famous Tammany Hall politician, George Washington Plunkitt, who said, "I know that the civil service humbug is stuck into the constitution, too, but, as Tim Campbell said: 'What's the constitution among friends?' " Both Roosevelt and Wilson, men who disliked each other intensely, agreed at least in their desire to purge this "go along to get along" political philosophy from civil life.

What the Progressives wanted were leaders who could work for the common good and convince voters of the wisdom of necessary reforms. Hearkening back to James Madison, they recognized that an enlightened political leader might not always be that helm; however, there was great hope that a better sort of thoughtful and inspiring leadership could move the nation forward. Progressives wanted change, but not revolutionary change. They wanted to both guide the public and listen to what most citizens wanted. In Madison's day, with their lesser commitment to democracy, the founders envisioned a limited electorate simply choosing the best men to run things. By the time of Roosevelt and Wilson, this was untenable. The new theory of politics required wise statesmen engaging in a dialogue with the mass public. However, to be truly democratic, party nominees need to speak to the concerns of most citizens and discuss the issues in ways that a solid majority thinks is fair and just. As we shall see, that did not quite happen. Instead of speaking to the great political center, where most of the voters are, they created a system that spoke to extremes.

Progressive Disruption

Instead of creating a political practice that valued reforms acceptable to all, the Progressive reforms were a profound disruptor of the American political system. Over time, they created a system that even dissolved a strongly held political science concept: median voter theory. Anthony Downs presented a view of the American voter in 1957 that assumed the electorate was distributed unimodally and evenly across a left-right spectrum.[51] The distribution of votes was thus a Bell curve (fig. 3.1). Strategically minded candidates and parties could thus plan to direct their efforts to engage with and attempting to earn the support of voters in the center.

Primary elections disrupt the centrist model of voting behavior. Instead of one single electorate where voters pool toward the ideological midpoint, primaries create two distinct electorates with medians well distant from the center, a W-shaped distribution (fig. 3.2).

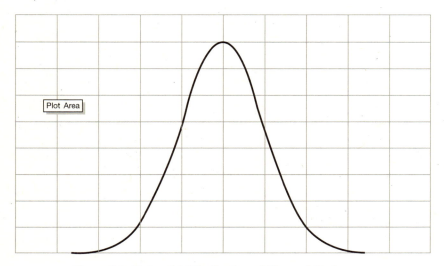

Figure 3.1. Unimodal Distribution of Electoral Preferences.

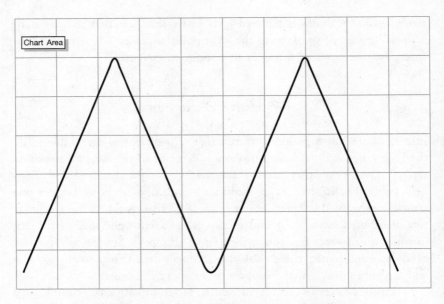

Figure 3.2. Bimodal Distribution of Electoral Preferences.

Primary electorates are distinct from their general election counterparts, because of the smaller voter pool and their intensity.[52] General election candidate pools may have an incentive to move toward the center, but they begin in a more polarized place that challenges candidates to pivot toward the middle. Few do so successfully, and over time, the electorate follow suit and become extreme themselves.[53]

Through bifurcation of the electorate and an incentive to start from an extreme ideological position, primaries have made politics more polarized. Outside groups are integral in the primary election, since the primary specifically and intentionally excludes the parties' organizations from the process.[54] Candidates follow those groups to the extremes, adopting ever more polarized and non-centrist policy positions.[55] The electorate follows the cues of elites in matters such as interest and candidates for office, as well.[56]

Primaries thus are the cause of changes within the electorate that make the basic policy compromises endemic to a republic more difficult or even impossible to achieve. The Progressives believed that their reforms would enable the democratic ideal of the highly engaged citizen, motivated only by the greater good. Instead, their creation has become a Frankenstein's monster: leading to greater polarization within the electorate, electioneering groups, and government. Voter turnout has declined. Faith in the government has plummeted, with approval ratings of elected officials at all-time lows. In sum, the Progressive direct democratic experiment in the guise of direct primaries has been a failed reform.

Progressives' Democratic Mistakes

Progressives held an abiding faith in the democratic ideal. The Progressive philosopher John Dewey is supposed to have said, "the solution to the ills of democracy is more democracy." A nice sentiment, but what did that mean in practice? For the Progressives it meant an idealized world where engaged and educated citizens had a greater say in politics and traditional parties were much weaker. An educated aristocracy populated by the common person was a paradoxical desire, but clearly, those two conflicting impulses guided Progressive efforts. It meant the drive to what we now call candidate-centered politics. It meant rooting out corruption and creating an efficient and responsive government. Nevertheless, we must grapple with the other things it created. The Progressive reforms restricted turnout, and the level of voting has never reached what it was before them. Today we are quite pleased if turnout reaches 60 percent of the voting-age population. Yet, in the nineteenth century, turnout routinely reached the mid-70-percent range and occasionally passed 80 percent. Furthermore, these were less educated voters, and research shows that education positively correlates with voting. How did those old, pre-Progressive parties get so many people to the polls? Have we missed something about the role parties can play in engaging and mobilizing voters?

The Progressives gave us the direct primary, where turnout is even more abysmal. In 2016, voting in the primaries was better than in the two prior cycles and yet it only reached 28.5 percent of the population.[57] Direct primaries have weakened parties and, thus, weakened the vital link between citizens and leaders. The trade-off has *not* been the democratic participation of mass citizens. On top of that, we are seeing a dangerous development in which primaries reward ideological activists who force both of the major parties further to the right or the left, squeezing out the moderate middle where most voters may actually be. If the goal of democracy is to foster a government of office holders who are more representative of the average voter, the primaries are not doing that. Political science has provided extensive examples of electoral polarization[58] and polarized governance.[59] Primary elections significantly drive that extreme push to the outer edges of ideological identification. That is not to say that all candidates are extremists; however, primaries are doing nothing to hinder that, and at times they reward ideological extremes. Simply put, primaries, whatever they may be in the ideal, are not fostering a healthy democracy in practice.

Chapter 4

Why the Machines Were Targeted

> There are many different ways to organize a presidential nominating system and almost all of them are more rational and orderly than the hodgepodge of systems that voters experience today.[1]
>
> —Elaine Kamarck

The Progressive Zeal for a Better Society

The Progressives were very much a product of their time, one of great change and advancement. The "modern day" of the late 1800s was one of rapid change and significant optimism about the future. Western expansion, economic growth, expanded literacy, and scientific and medical advances all combined to provide a sense of potential improvement or even perfectibility in humankind. At the same time, corruption was everywhere they looked—in government, during elections, and in business. Theodore Roosevelt was not alone in railing against the forces of "privilege and of special interests."[2] At the same time, there was a great sense of urgency to right the wrongs of the past. New advances in technology and knowledge, combined with an old moralism about creating a just society, drove Progressives to political action. It is telling, in this regard, that the historian Michael McGerr titles his book on the Progressives *A Fierce Discontent* and he writes, "the progressive middle class offered a radicalism at the center of American society, an ambitious program to halt the friction and conflicts of the industrializing nation."[3] This was an optimism impelled by burning desire to stamp out injustice. Whatever faults we may find with Progressive reforms, and we do, one must appreciate the nobility of their intentions.

This desire to create a better society meant that social and political efforts at ameliorating the world were often part of a seamless whole that necessitated an all-encompassing sense of reform. Progressives battled constantly and on many fronts. To take one example, prohibition was a vital issue to Progressives, and this crusade shows the way many Progressives easily combined religious beliefs (the immorality of drink and the way it destroyed families) with a political reform (that could be used to weaken the political power of local bosses who relied on the saloon as a base of operations).[4] The nation's westward expansion had brought women as equal partners on the journey and with it a sense that extending the franchise to women would bring more diversity of viewpoint and a more morally correct tone to politics.[5] Thus, gender equality was a good both in and of itself because equality was good, and also because it would help to transform politics and bring a larger portion of society's membership into the franchised electorate.

Further, the new Efficiency Movement pioneered by business but quickly expanding into many other segments of the economy promised to modernize processes and bring with it the scientific solutions to social problems.[6] Some in the Progressive movement supported the application of scientific methods to industry, finance, medicine, schooling, and even government.

Woodrow Wilson, before his entrance into politics while a professor of political science, keenly brought the scientific study of administration to the United States.[7] For Progressives like Wilson, the German administration, which "rested in hands of an extraordinary strong, professional bureaucracy," was a model to be emulated.[8] What was challenging, though, and particular to America, was how to do that democratically. "The good-government reformers were not entirely wrong in assuming that the incompletely democratized British and German cities were more honestly governed than their own."[9] While European intellectuals and reformers were well aware of corruption in their own countries, when visiting the United States, they were often shocked by the brazen and pervasive nature of unethical, and indeed criminal, behavior exhibited in American politics. As Wilson observed, "The poisonous atmosphere of city government, the crooked secrets of state administration, the confusion, sinecurism, and corruption ever and again discovered in the bureaux at Washington" must be replaced with a "science of administration" that will "purify its organization, and . . . crown its duties with dutifulness."[10]

However, American reformers had to accept—sometimes grudgingly, sometimes happily—the simple fact that democracy was assumed to be the ideal by which politics would be judged. Whatever failings democracy has as a concept, or whatever failings to live up to democracy that American politics exhibited, the democratic ideal had to be respected.

The Democratic Ideal

Passion for direct democracy is by no means an exclusive product of the late nineteenth century. The New England tradition of governance by town hall is well established as one of the guiding concepts undergirding the drive to independence. After self-government was secured, direct democracy was not only maintained by the northeastern states, but its elements were present in the small constituent-to-elected ratio of their state legislatures and much of the philosophy guiding the Anti-Federalists. The tension between proponents of direct and representative democracy never completely disappeared, though the most significant national effort at deploying direct democratic principles on a national basis did come via the Progressive reforms. Thus were born significant reforms that encouraged direct citizen participation in the way parties operated and the way government created laws.

The Progressive Era devotion to democracy once again brought into sharp relief the ambivalence Americans have always held toward parties. While parties were recognized as a natural element of American politics, the skepticism toward them encouraged anti-party sentiment to fester. The anti-party fervor was linked with a growing belief that representative democracy was inferior to something more akin to classical Greek-style direct democracy. Together, those viewpoints would shape the Progressive Era. Herbert Croly, one of the leading Progressive intellectuals, was actually critical of the direct primary, which he thought would "merely emphasize the evil which it is intended to abate."[11] However, despite his caution about many Progressive electoral reforms, his ideas about democracy reflected and informed a great many Progressives. There was a need to create a more democratic form of government than the one that existed. The political parties and representative government were now in a position to be radically transformed. Whereas great distances and ignorance made representative democracy a necessity, today the people can now assemble. This was, Croly believed, because

> the active citizenship of the country meets every morning and evening and discusses the affairs of the nation with the newspaper as an important interlocutor. Public opinion has a thousand

methods of seeking information and obtaining definite and effective expression which it did not have four generations ago.[12]

As Croly insisted, "Pure democracy has again become not merely possible, but natural and appropriate."[13] He knew that the New England town-hall meeting was not the answer and he recognized the importance of political parties. What was needed was a new set of institutions that recognized and furthered the simple idea that the people should rule. This was not about returning to Greek city state, whatever that could possibly mean. It was about believing that democracy was asserting itself in new ways. The old wine needed new bottles. Croly's solutions may have been unique to him, but his diagnosis of the times was widespread.

Progressives, Community, and the Parties

The Progressives were not simply anti-party. Once could imagine trying to dispense with parties altogether or creating a new pure type of party. But those were not the solutions proffered. Instead, they worked, for the most part, to reform and transform the existing parties. As Croly observed, the current system "carries with it an enormous prestige."[14] The Progressives believed, and fervently, that the answer to the corruption of the time was more democracy, in the Greek sense of being more direct and less mediated. In its own way, the Progressive movement was radically communitarian, not just political. The solutions to the nation's political problems were through a new understanding of the communal. As Frank Johnson Goodnow, the first president of the American Political Science Association, observed,

> We no longer believe as we once believed that a good social organization can be secured merely through stressing our rights. The emphasis is being laid more and more on social duties. The efficiency of the social group is taking on in our eyes a greater importance than it once had. . . . But we have come the conclusion that man under modern conditions is primarily a member of society and that only as he recognizes his duties as a member of society can he secure the greatest opportunities as an individual.[15]

These general pronouncements by men like Goodnow had already found practical form in the lives of everyday people. Farmers in the westward expanse instituted the co-operative agricultural model. While Benjamin Franklin is credited as having created the first co-op in the United States with a mutual fire insurance company in 1752, the model spread through agriculture as an antidote to the crop-lien system under which cotton farmers struggled during Reconstruction.[16]

A co-op, where common citizens unite together to store, market, and sell goods, was rooted in small communities just like the town hall of New England. Suffused in both the town hall and co-op is a sense that citizens thirsted to be actively engaged and that once engaged, those citizens made good things happen. For the Progressive ideal to work, the general public had to share that same zeal to collaborate and cooperate. The Progressives thus believed that the processes and structures of society kept that social capital from being activated and deployed. They had a great deal of confidence in the goodwill of the *people.* Thus, Progressives wanted to unleash the abundant energy of citizens *to be citizens.* We tend to forget that the ancient concept of citizen is not a passive given. The ancient ideal, best articulated by Aristotle, is that being a citizen means "ruling and being ruled over." In Aristotle's ideal, there is the very active "ruling" that required more than just exercising choice. Citizenship implies a shared sense of community where individual political decisions are collective and informed by deliberation and discussion.[17] The problem was that parties as vehicles for the goodwill of the people were terribly flawed in the eyes of Progressives. However, these institutions could be recast, at least theoretically, in a new mold that was more democratic.

The co-op and town hall also provide an example of what the Progressives believed politics would look like if those existing power structures were taken away. Communities of diverse but mutually respectful and thoughtful individuals would gather to constructively devise their shared future direction. That optimistic viewpoint suffused all of the Progressive mindset. The challenge was how to realize these optimistic dreams within existing institutional structures. How much remodeling was necessary, and could the foundation support the new political structures?

As we have already noted, wealth was exploding, not only among the already-rich entrepreneurs and trust barons but among the growing middle class.[18] Technological, scientific, and medical advancements were burgeoning faster than the typical person's ability to keep pace, suggesting that advancement and improvement were new constants.[19] A sense grew among Progressives that humankind was eminently improvable, if not perfectible. As individuals came to have more control over their own lives and prosperity, they came to believe that processes such as politics could be more controlled by common individuals and not self-styled political elites.[20] This moment of change was finally an opportunity to reinvigorate democracy in new ways.

The problem was that an inevitable conflict would emerge, as Progressivism itself was internally conflicted between radical individualism and communitarianism. Despite the community-mindedness of the typical Progressive, there was also a strain of strong individualism running through the philosophy of the time. Communities, to the Progressive, were collections of individuals more than organizations and institutions. Hofstadter notes that organizations had played a relatively minor role in the typical predominantly rural lives of most of pre-Progressive America.[21] Small communities were able, for the most part, to resolve differences within a loose governing structure allowing significant voice and influence from individuals. Few mitigating structures were present, approximating the more direct, freewheeling town-hall style of governance favored by many of the era.

The approach that suggested that humanity would be smarter, more collaborative, healthier, and more engaged was the hubris upon which much of the Progressive reforms were constructed. The confidence with which Progressives approached the future was indeed ill-founded, emerging from the striking progress of their time and believing that human society was changing in profound ways. That optimism was grounded in a sense of desire for greater control among the Progressives, who projected their desire for control into a sense that the general public shared their thirst for greater engagement in politics. By assuming that the rest of the nation wanted to take control of the ballot box as much as they did, the Progressives mistakenly grafted mechanisms that mimicked direct democracy onto American politics in ways that would prove more destructive than beneficial.

Part of what made the Progressives' failure was mistaking organization and institutionalization. Existing organizations were not serving the Progressives, especially the urban political machines of the day. The Progressive desire was to tear those organizations down and, in their place, individuals would emerge as the highly engaged citizen-leaders more common in the small New England town-hall setting. But as the population grew, forms of direct democracy would become ever more untenable. Some form of structure was necessary, but one which dispersed power more evenly. Handing control over things like primary nominations to the uninitiated was one of those mistakes. At the same time that the Progressives were rising politically, parties were beginning to adapt, albeit slowly. Even the urban machines were struggling to maintain the level of control they held over their communities. Population growth, new and changing public demands, and the collapse of numerous machines (such as Tweed's Tammany Hall) were changing the operational needs of party organizations.[22]

Parties were at a proverbial crossroads approaching the turn of the twentieth century. To maintain themselves, the parties needed to change. Publicly, pressure was mounting for significant change to limit the power of the party organizations or deconstruct them entirely.[23] The changes the country was experiencing were truly massive and conducive to an extending wave of change throughout society. Not only were the Progressives of a mind to experiment with social and governing structures, bent toward believing in the constant improvability of humanity, and possessed of an idealized view of civic engagement, an urgency borne of economic hardship was influencing the impetus for change. The wrenching depression of 1893 suggested to observers that the way of life common in the nineteenth century was not sustainable.[24] The only way to survive and take advantage of the new opportunities abounding was to change. This is an important point to underline—Progressives were confident in their ability to transform society; however, they were also fearful of a looming disaster if things didn't change. Collective strikes, which said to many that socialism was on the march, and individual bombs, which reminded people that anarchism was not just rhetorical, provided these middle-class reformers a necessity to act—at least in their minds. It also drove them to distraction when faced with their conservative opposition within both parties. Progressives were frustrated that their opponents, those devotees of the status quo, failed to see the dark horizons.

The intersection of these forces helped fuel the rise of the direct primary election. The direct primary would substantively change the way elections were conducted and how parties operated for the next century and into the foreseeable future. How the direct primary came to be one of the remembered cornerstones of the Progressive Era helps explain how it undermined the linkage role parties play in American politics.

Direct primaries were not, after all, the first or most aggressively promoted part of the Progressive agenda. The original push for change was reflected in the earlier Mugwump movement that sought to end the spoils system and usher in the development of a merit bureaucracy. However, that movement, while important at the time and key in helping in electing Cleveland in 1884, was rather narrowly focused on civil service reform and corporate malfeasance. Merit easily fed into the later, broader Progressive push for the widespread transformation of *both* politics and government. Everywhere they looked there appeared to be things that needed to be done.

The main first electoral reform thrust of the early Progressive movement was therefore the adoption of the Australian ballot.[25] Even though the term *Australian ballot* may be a misnomer, the adoption of a secret ballot in the US, which introduced the opportunity to split tickets and hide obvious cues to partisan observers, was the highest priority development to reformers during the rise of Progressive ideology in America.[26]

When thinking of the Progressive reforms, it is helpful to think of them not as a cohesive package of changes to the electoral system but as a series of battles in a longer assault on partisan power in America.[27] The Progressives were usually quite pragmatic in looking at problems as they appeared. A man like Herbert Croly, or a Woodrow Wilson, might develop a fuller philosophy of government and politics. But most Progressives had a general disposition and sense of direction that drove their immediate political thinking and suggestions for change. Not only did the Progressives successfully shepherd the secret ballot into the electoral system, but they were able to secure merit bureaucracy, win the adoption of nonpartisan local elections in many states, implement referendum and direct initiatives, and add the direct primary.

Noteworthy here is a response to Ware's assertion that the direct primary is more an artifact of partisan institutionalization than a successful anti-partisan campaign by the Progressives.[28] Taken as an individual reform idea divorced from the remainder of the Progressive reforms, Ware's case makes intuitive sense. As the country was growing in population and concurrently urbanizing, the predominantly rural method of elites selecting party nominees could not be sustained for much longer. But the parties did not simply accept the direct primary as readily as Ware suggests, nor was the direct primary an isolated concept. When the breadth of Progressive reform ideas is considered together, two primary guiding principles emerge: an avowed lack of faith in partisan politics as practiced in the 1800s, and a belief that everyday citizens were ready and willing to take on more of the responsibilities of self-governance previously supported by intermediary institutions like parties.

Besides the anti-partisan fervor of the Progressives, there were numerous reasons to suggest that some manner of reform was needed for selecting partisan nominations. Ware's institutionalization thesis, while not eclipsing the Hofstadter/Ranney perspective, does inform us of internal structures in need of adaptation within the parties themselves. The nomination of presidents at the time, for one example, was developed in a rather unsystematic way in response to the pressures of the moment. The Democrats held their first convention in 1832 in response to the increased popular demands and the realization that "King Caucus" was not going to work again.[29] Jackson therefore harnessed his own personal star power and formed a nominating convention of supporters at the local levels of power. This reveals the ad hoc nature of the American party system, particularly with regard to selecting candidates. The national convention was the logical evolution of state-level conventions, but even that evolved structure was ready for change. National nominating conventions in a rural and localized era were subject to location bias: Abraham Lincoln's nomination as president in 1860 was accidental. With seven ambitious hopefuls actively seeking the nomination, Lincoln was a largely agreed-upon vice-presidential nominee. So, the Republicans located their convention in Lincoln's home state of Illinois. When the other delegations became gridlocked over a nominee, the Chicago convention, heavily weighted in Lincoln's favor, placed his name into nomination not for the second spot, but for president, and he had enough favorable support to become the nominee.[30]

The national conventions simply mirrored the occurrences at the local and state levels. A tension has always existed within parties between their twin natures as elite-driven and mass-movement organizations.[31] While parties were initially built as electoral-support mechanisms for ambitious office-holders, those elite-driven institutions were unsuccessful without popular support. As the parties continued to develop at the federal, state, and local levels, that tension between elite incentives and popular sentiment began to grow. The era of machine rule empowered the elites to provide cooperation incentives (social welfare benefits, jobs, and public works favors, to name just a few) that kept the masses from revolting against elite rule, but that tension would continue to grow, and once the incentives were taken away by the erosion of machine rule, the masses wanted to exercise much more power over their parties.[32]

Concurrent changes nationwide were bringing the formerly laggard national party organizations into closer alignment with their more raucous and active state and local parties. Westward expansion and population growth were swelling the sizes of the national nominating conventions as well, making them more raucous and disorderly affairs. By the 1920s, the conventions were so chaotic that they dragged on for weeks and produced candidates that would prove disastrously incapable of competing in the subsequent general election. In 1924, the Democrats needed 103 ballots to arrive at the nomination of the hardly stellar John W. Davis.[33]

The Progressives were free to tinker with partisan structures because political parties are the least guided by constitutional rules among all American political institutions. As the Constitution's design was intended to prevent parties, all of the work of parties falls outside its guidelines. Since the Constitution tried to forestall parties' development at the national level, there was no method of reining in parties within the Constitution. If the great moral fault of the founders was their failure to deal with slavery, the great practical, structural, fault was the failure to imagine the rise of parties in managing politics. So tinkering and constant adjustment, a favored activity of Progressives, was easy to attach to the parties.

Thinking of primaries as part of the overall package of Progressive reforms, the lack of constitutional guidance may have been an even greater help to the advocates than was realized at the time. Merit bureaucracy (federally, at least, through the Pendleton Act of 1883) and the direct election of US Senators required federal legislative action. But the Australian ballot, nonpartisan local elections, initiative/referendum, and the direct primary were all reforms that could be won at the local level, where direct action had the greatest chance of success.

Initially the Progressives succeeded locally. As they earned more success, they expanded to state and national efforts. They closely followed advances underway at the time in Western Europe and adopted numerous policies, such as a transformation of banking through the Federal Reserve System's creation in 1913. Reformers felt that old-fashioned ways meant waste and inefficiency, and eagerly sought out the "one best system."

Disturbed by the waste, inefficiency, stubbornness, corruption, and injustices of the Gilded Age, the Progressives were committed to changing and reforming every aspect of the state, society, and economy. Significant changes enacted at the national levels included the imposition of an income tax with the 16th Amendment, direct election of Senators with the 17th Amendment, Prohibition with the 18th Amendment, election reforms to stop corruption and fraud, and women's suffrage through the 19th Amendment to the US Constitution.

The most notable Progressive reforms sought to enable the citizenry to rule more directly, circumventing machines and their powerful bosses. The institution of initiatives and referenda made it possible to pass laws without the involvement of the legislature, while the recall allowed for the removal of corrupt or under-performing officials, and the direct primary let people democratically nominate candidates, avoiding the professionally dominated conventions.

The March to Direct Primaries

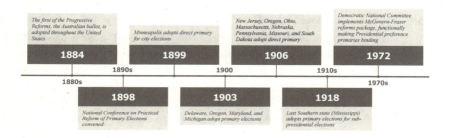

Support for primary elections expanded unevenly throughout the country for some time, but the impetus to formal reform began with the National Conference on Practical Reform of Primary Elections in 1898. The two-day conclave at the New York Board of Trade brought together reform-minded individuals from across the country to serve as a springboard for Progressive reform ideas to move from local and regional efforts into a cohesive national initiative. Noted supporters of direct democracy either addressing or in attendance including University of Wisconsin professor and labor historian John R. Commons, Philadelphia attorney and National Municipal League founder Clinton Woodruff, Chicago lawyer G. Fred Rush, and one of the more significant motive forces for direct democracy of the time, Bucks County (PA) Banking Commissioner B. F. Gilkeson, who advocated for more principles of direct democracy beyond the primary, including initiative and referendum, direct election of US Senators, and expansion of federal merit bureaucratic protections to the states.[34]

The transition from a party caucus nomination to nominee selection via the direct primary occurred simultaneously with the other Progressive reforms, most closely aligned with the spread of the direct ballot initiative and referendum process. Much like the direct primary, the initiative and referendum process was and is an experiment in expanding direct democracy. At times it was grafted onto existing state political systems. At other times, it was foundational to a state. Arizona was admitted to the union in 1912 with a state constitution that included the full set of reforms—initiative, reference, recall, *and* primaries—embedded in the document itself.[35]

The desire to infuse more elements of town-hall-style direct democracy into American politics is a common element of the Progressive mindset, evident not only in the primary election. The initiative and referendum process was of a piece with the direct primary, because many state legislators saw opening up the nomination process to the general public as a threat to their lucrative public offices. Nominations had been a closed system, giving officials comfortable with supporting the party line the ability to secure renomination easily. Putting faith in incumbents to limit their own ability to return to office was not a likely strategy for success, so the initiative and referendum can be thought of as "Plan B" in case they were not able to secure passage of their preferred reforms through traditional lawmaking processes. If the reformers were not successful in convincing legislators to vote for new rules that would go against their self-interest, the Progressives could always make direct appeals to the public to pass legislation directly, bypassing the traditional process.[36] This also allowed them to think of their project as less extreme. They were hearkening back to a golden age of engaged citizenry. Indeed, by pushing for primaries they could, with some reason, claim a reformist zeal and not a revolutionary one.

Thanks to the efforts of Oregon State Representative William S. U'Ren and his Direct Legislation League, voters in Oregon overwhelmingly approved a ballot measure in 1902 that created the initiative and referendum processes for citizens to directly introduce or approve proposed laws or amendments to the state constitution, making Oregon the first state to adopt such a system. U'Ren also helped pass an amendment in 1908 that gave voters the power to recall elected officials, and would go on to establish, at the state level, popular election of US Senators and the first presidential primary in the United States.

In 1911, California Governor Hiram Johnson established the Oregon System of "initiative, referendum, and recall" in his state, viewing them as good influences for citizen participation against the historic influence of large corporations on state lawmakers.[37] These Progressive reforms were soon replicated in other states, including Idaho, Washington, and Wisconsin, and today roughly half of US states have initiative, referendum, and recall provisions in their state constitutions.

Table 4.1. States with Initiative and Referendum

	STATUTES		CONSTITUTION
STATE	Initiative	Popular Referendum	Initiative
ALASKA	I*	Yes	None
ARIZONA	D	Yes	D
ARKANSAS	D	Yes	D
CALIFORNIA	D	Yes	D
COLORADO	D	Yes	D
FLORIDA	None	No	D
IDAHO	D	Yes	None
ILLINOIS	None	No	D
MAINE	I	Yes	None
MARYLAND	None	Yes	None
MASSACHUSETTS	I	Yes	I
MICHIGAN	I	Yes	D
MISSISSIPPI	None	No	I
MISSOURI	D	Yes	D
MONTANA	D	Yes	D
NEBRASKA	D	Yes	D
NEVADA	I	Yes	D
NEW MEXICO	None	Yes	None
NORTH DAKOTA	D	Yes	D
OHIO	I	Yes	D
OKLAHOMA	D	Yes	D
OREGON	D	Yes	D
SOUTH DAKOTA	D	Yes	D
UTAH	D & I	Yes	None
WASHINGTON	D & I	Yes	None
WYOMING	I*	Yes	None
U.S. VIRGIN ISLANDS	I	Yes	I

D Direct Initiative; proposals that qualify go directly on the ballot
I   Indirect Initiative; proposals are submitted to the legislature, which has an opportunity to act on the proposed legislation. The initiative question will subsequently go on the ballot if the legislature rejects it, submits a different proposal or takes no action.
I* Alaska and Wyoming's initiative processes are usually considered indirect. However, instead of requiring that an initiative be submitted to the legislature for action, they only require that an initiative cannot be placed on the ballot until after a legislative session has convened and adjourned.

The direct primary spread through two parallel and almost simultaneous processes. Those two processes were divided by geography and intent, though they achieved similar effects. The two parallel paths were followed on one side by the North and West, while the other was contained within the South. Each parallel path began for different reasons, but followed the same model. In the North and West, Progressive politics brought the primary forward. The South was no bastion of Progressivism yet still used the Progressive fervor toward primaries to install them in the Old Confederacy.[38]

Moving toward the direct primary happened concurrently and in many of the same states that passed initiative and referendum laws. The process had begun a bit before the Oregon initiative, and was met with limited success. The city of Minneapolis is credited with implementing the first direct primary in 1899, just eleven years after Minnesota became a state. Despite the state's youth, many of the ills ascribed to the "smoke-filled rooms" of politics were already present in Minnesota. Vote buying, not expressly forbidden in state law, was common. Physical voter suppression was common at the polling place. Earlier attempts had been unsuccessful at trying to exert influence over nominations, including state nominating convention regulations such as making the act of falsifying vote totals illegal. Other proposals that did not pass included the ability to add candidates to a general election ballot through petitions and a rudimentary form of ranked-choice voting.[39]

Minneapolis adopted its direct primary in 1899; the state of Minnesota quickly followed suit by adopting statewide direct primaries, becoming the first state to move entirely to nomination by election. They were not alone for long. Wisconsin, under the influence of Robert La Follette's aggressive Progressive agenda, immediately did the same. By 1903 Delaware, Oregon, Maryland, and Michigan moved to direct primary election nominations as well, though some of them only held advisory primaries while maintaining formal nomination power to caucuses and conventions.[40]

Notably, Minnesota concurrently implemented a voter registration system. As part of the desire to have a more ethical politics, voter fraud was a focus of the Progressive impetus for reform. While not as much an exponent of direct democracy as the citizen initiative or direct primary were, registration was part of that optimistic set of reforms that hallmarked the Progressive Era. The direct primary was no panacea, indeed failing in spectacular fashion with the election of A. A. "Doc" Ames as mayor of Minneapolis. Far from a reformer, Ames exemplified the worst graft of the machine era, including installing his unqualified brother as chief of police. Ames's administration was so corrupt that he became a fugitive of Minnesota law, fleeing to New Hampshire until his eventual arrest. Ames's brother was also arrested for corruption while still in the state. Of particular import to Ames's election was the fact that Minneapolis and Minnesota opened their primaries to those not affiliated with the party in whose nomination contest they sought to vote. Minnesota thus brought the "open" primary into existence, and immediately flaws in its intent showed through.[41] By going outside his own Republican Party's voters, Ames was able to bypass the safeguards that party elite nomination had previously provided. Thus, the first primary election of note displayed the same propensity for unintended manipulation seen commonly today in primaries.

Despite Minneapolis's cautionary tale, primary enthusiasm spread to cities and states across the country—not only in the more Progressive-aligned west and Midwest; primaries emerged on the east coast, where the parties held tremendous sway. By 1906, New Jersey, Oregon, Ohio, Massachusetts, Nebraska, Pennsylvania, Missouri, and South Dakota all decided partisan nominations with variations on the direct primary. Over the next decade, not only would most other states adopt direct primary nominations, but they would make the primary elections binding rather than merely advisory. The advisory primary was an effective way to introduce primaries to the public without overtly threatening the extant power of party elites.

The regional exception to the rise of primary elections was the South. The old Confederacy would be one of the last stalwarts to relent on adoption of the direct primary for partisan nominations. Within two decades, however, southern states would see the possibility of using primary elections to disadvantage African American citizens, which broke down the last barriers to national implementation of direct primaries.[42] The schism over black rights would continue to divide the South and its dominant Democratic Party for decades after Reconstruction. The one-party dominance led to a similar lack of accountability to that of the northern machines, and primaries were seen as a way not only to restrict the franchise but for minority factions to develop a power base to take the party over.

About sixteen states began using primary elections to reduce the power of bosses and machines. The 17th Amendment was ratified in 1913, requiring that all senators be directly elected by the public of their states. The motivation behind direct election of senators was to reduce the power of political bosses, who controlled the Senate seats by extension of their control of state legislatures. The result, according to political scientist Henry Jones Ford, was that the United States Senate had become a "Diet of party lords, wielding their power without scruple or restraint, on behalf of those particular interests" that put them in office.[43]

The direct election of US Senators, much like the merit bureaucracy, may seem tangential to the topic of primary elections, but is one of the contextual elements that help us understand the ambitious direct democratic scope of the Progressives. Corruption in government was one of the targets for the relentless desire to improve and/or perfect elements of human behavior, and what is quite remarkable about the Progressive Era was the scope of reforms they successfully passed. Most significant changes that occur in American politics occur in vacuums, where individual reforms stand uniquely alone during a particular time frame.[44] The Progressive reforms, though, occurred in relatively rapid succession. The Progressives were not content to pick their battles; they aggressively pursued passage of all their desired changes and would not rest until all of their desired policy changes were law. As the Progressives felt no need to cater to established norms of government such as compromise and gradual policy progress iterated over time, the reforms introduced two concepts into politics that persist into the twenty-first century: urgency and demand.

The Pace of Politics and the Role of Compromise

The politics of this time were predicated on a gradual pace. Many political insiders believed in a politics of deference and consensus building. This was not a bug, but a feature of the institutions of government. An example of the patience any elected official needed to show was the informal apprenticeship that all freshman senators were expected to take on. An ambitious candidate elected to the Senate may have envisioned the immediate ability to engage in debate and take the lead on policy issues, but that aggressive individual would have been thwarted by the norms that freshman senators took a few years to develop a portfolio of policy knowledge on a specific area and defer to more senior members of the party on floor fights.[45] A sense of urgency was unwelcome, not only in the Senate but in all politics of the time. Presidential nominees were still expected not to actively engage in campaigning, and the young, ambitious office seeker had to serve their own apprenticeship of sorts by campaigning on the party's behalf to curry favor with the nomination power brokers who ran their local party organization.

The Progressives took the notion of political patience and turned it on its head. Likely this stems from the moral certainty that undergirded their movement.[46] They also saw around them corruption sanctified by misplaced reverence of the past. As Wilson wrote in his famous article on administration, "the grandson accepts his grandfather's hesitating experiment as an integral part of the fixed constitution of nature."[47] With the passage of time the stifling effects of tradition would only grow stronger. A Progressive looked at politics as a system that needed not only comprehensive, but immediate, reform. Progressives looked at the pace of political time as something worth reforming at the same time that political processes were being upended.

The second concept the Progressives introduced that remains relevant today is demand, which is to say an unwillingness to compromise. Again, the norms of the time were diametrically opposite to the Progressive impulse. Along with what Progressives saw as an excessively leisurely pace, they saw both parties as going along to get along, compromising over issues where they saw no need for compromise because of their moral certainty. Progressives used historical examples such as the infamous Three-fifths Compromise as justification for why their cause was so righteous that opponents would need to either come to an agreement with them or be marginalized and defeated.[48] There was little room for traditional compromise in the Progressive agenda, and that belief system would extend from the movement into the politics of the day and become a new standard of expectation. Investing politics with a moral fervor was bound to make compromises difficult—a phenomenon we see all too clearly today. And, as Wilson and others made clear, the goal of Progressives was all about creating a "moral atmosphere."[49]

The urgency and unwillingness to compromise explain both the speed of success of the Progressive reforms and their scope. The direct primary spread quickly throughout northern states to a level of ubiquity. The reformist mindset found great public support as frustration with corruption at all levels of government aligned well with the comprehensive Progressive agenda. Primaries may have started in the North and West, but the southern reticence to adopt them would quickly fade. By 1918, every state of the old Confederacy had fallen into line with the northern and western states which had already adopted the direct primary.

Table 4.2. Adoption of Direct Primary Election for Partisan Nominations
Election Years in which the DIRECT PRIMARY has been specifically authorized re: Major Party nominations for Statewide and/or Federal elective office

STATE	STATE Direct Primary mandated	Post-Primary Runoffs utilized	PRESIDENTIAL PRIMARIES held
ALABAMA	1904	1914; 1932	1924–1932; 1940
ALASKA	1958		
ARIZONA	1912		1996
ARKANSAS	1910	1934; 1940	1976–1980; 1988
CALIFORNIA	1910		1912
COLORADO	1912		1992–2000
CONNECTICUT	1956		1980–1992; 2000–
DELAWARE	1972		1996
DISTRICT OF COLUMBIA	1971		1956
FLORIDA	1914	1930–2000	1904
GEORGIA	1918	1918	1912; 1920–1924; 1932; 1976
HAWAII	1959		
IDAHO	1910	1960–1962	1976
ILLINOIS	1910		1912
INDIANA	1916		1916–1928; 1956
IOWA	1908		1916 only
KANSAS	1908		1980; 1992
KENTUCKY	1912		1976–1980; 1988
LOUISIANA	1912	1912–1914; 1922	1980
MAINE	1912		1996–2000
MARYLAND	1911		1912–1964; 1972
MASSACHUSETTS	1911		1912
MICHIGAN	1910		1916–1928; 1972–1980; 1992–
MINNESOTA	1912		1916; 1952–1956; 1992
MISSISSIPPI	1902	1912	1980; 1988

STATE	STATE Direct Primary mandated	Post-Primary Runoffs utilized	PRESIDENTIAL PRIMARIES held
MISSOURI	1910		1988; 2000
MONTANA	1914		1916–1924; 1956; 1976–
NEBRASKA	1908		1912
NEVADA	1910		1976–1980; 1996
NEW HAMPSHIRE	1910		1916
NEW JERSEY	1911		1912
NEW MEXICO	1940		1972; 1980
NEW YORK	1914		1912
NORTH CAROLINA	1916	1916	1920; 1972–2000; 2008
NORTH DAKOTA	1908		1912–1932; 1984–1996
OHIO	1910		1912
OKLAHOMA	1908	1930	1988
OREGON	1904		1912
PENNSYLVANIA	1914		1912
RHODE ISLAND	1948		1972
SOUTH CAROLINA	1896	1916	1980; 1988–2000; 2008
SOUTH DAKOTA	1908		1912
TENNESSEE	1910		1972
TEXAS	1908	1918	1964; 1976
UTAH	1938		2000
VERMONT	1916		1916–1920; 1976–1988; 1996
VIRGINIA	1912	1969–1970	1988; 2000
WASHINGTON	1908		1992–2000; 2008
WEST VIRGINIA	1916		1916
WISCONSIN	1904		1908
WYOMING	1912		

Source: https://www.thegreenpapers.com/Hx/DirectPrimaryElectionYears.phtml

White Primaries: The South's Racist Experiment

How the South came to join in the primary craze has been the subject of some debate. Turner points to the one-party dominance of the Democrats in the South at this time as a motivating force behind the primary's adoption. In the absence of inter-party competition, primary elections became a way to introduce a modicum of competitiveness into the politics of the region.[50] But one unique southern element would define the expansion of the direct primary into the old Confederacy and expose the motivation behind its introduction there: the white primary.

Political parties are not only extraconstitutional entities; they are unique in politics as private enterprises. As such, parties were not subject to the same limitations and strictures established in the Constitution to which formal institutions of government must comply. The extraconstitutional nature of parties gave them the opportunity to be creative with their practices, sometimes to the detriment of entire populations. As such, the South adopted primaries in a counterintuitive fashion. While primaries in the North were imposed upon parties as a way to introduce direct democratic principles, the parties voluntarily accepted primary elections in the South, but not as part of the Progressive anti-corruption wave. The South adopted primaries to disenfranchise African American citizens.

At the same time that northern states were considering adoption of the direct primary, southern states were considering adoption of the primary as an extension of the post–Civil War Jim Crow laws, including the grandfather clause, literacy test, and poll tax. When the US Supreme Court invalidated the grandfather clause in 1915, southern whites looked for new methods to restrict the franchise to the exclusion of African Americans.[51]

The white primary only worked as a mechanism in the South because of the one-party dominance enjoyed by the Democratic Party at the time. The one-party nature of southern politics allowed the Democrats not to worry about limiting the franchise, as well as to bring some competition into the party structure. So, while the spread of primaries happened over the same time period in the North and South, they occurred for very distinct reasons.[52]

During the late 1800s and early 1900s, Populists were emerging to rapid success across the country. In states like Kansas, the People's Party even wrested majority control of the state legislature. Populism spread nationwide, and in the South a combination of emerging Populist success and a growing Republican base began to erode the Democrats' advantages. To stave off the upstarts, Democrats began considering different options to consolidate power. Most important to the Democrats at the time, African American citizens strongly preferred the Republican Party, so restricting their access to the ballot became a strategic priority for the Democrats.

In a basic sense, the white primary took the Democratic Party's ability to set its own rules as a private organization to an extreme. Primary elections were significantly different from general elections. In a general election, the 15th Amendment prevented such selective disenfranchisement. But primary elections were considered to be the province of party organizations exclusively, and thus not an election in the same sense as general elections. Restrictions on access to primary elections were therefore possible.

The party could determine its own rules of eligibility, so a primary became another method to restrict access to the ballot for African Americans. The southern Democratic parties adopted primaries but excluded non-whites from participation, hence the term "white primary." Primaries were simply another Jim Crow mechanism, similar in effect to the poll tax. Having primary elections be the mechanism for the racially restrictive practice would eventually leave the South with primaries alone, however.

White primaries effectively excluded African American voters from the primary ballot from their inception until the 1940s. Understanding the advent of primaries in the South is impossible without understanding the underlying racial motivations that eased support for the dominant party to turn nomination power of candidates over to the general public.[53]

The white primary's influence was significant, but stayed exclusive to the South. The earliest primaries, with white-only provisions, started in the mid-1910s in the South. The first challenge case, over Texas's 1923 statute installing white-only primaries for its Democratic nominations, was heard in 1927.[54] The decision in *Nixon v. Herndon* maintained the white primary, even after another challenge from the same plaintiff heard in 1932.[55] Another twelve years on, the white primary was finally defeated under a US Supreme Court more shaped by Franklin Roosevelt appointees in *Smith v. Allwright*.[56] To circumvent the 14th and 15th Amendment demands that no citizens should be denied the privileges of citizenship or the right to vote, Texas Democrats had simply claimed that they were a private club. Justice Reed, writing for the court in an 8–1 majority, wrote that "it may now be taken as a postulate that the right to vote in such a primary for the nomination of candidates without discrimination by the state, like the right to vote in a general election, is a right secured by the Constitution."

In this decision we can hear the echoes of the earlier Progressive Era. The Progressives had a checkered record on race, at best. However, the democratic notions of primaries underlay the position of the court. The 1944 Allwright decision ended the white primary, but not the primary itself. Only the racially discriminatory practice was overturned, and the legal status of a political party as a private entity was not fundamentally challenged. The parties were left with primary elections, but not for the reason they installed them. This malleability helped expose some of the inherent flaws in primaries.

What the Early Primaries Were Like

Primary elections tend to come in one of two types: a ballot election and a caucus. While we will later explore more of the effective differences between the two, at the time primaries were being adopted at the state level a push was on to separate from caucuses and install ballot elections as part of the primaries. Caucuses were seen by the Progressives as a holdover from the era of party machine dominance and thus something to be distrusted. The caucus system also consolidated electoral advantages among those already holding political power. Furthermore, reformers were predominantly from rural areas, and parties were reflections of urban interests at the time.[57] The adoption of the Australian ballot further pushed the faith of reformers toward the ballot instead of the caucus.[58]

Equally important to note is that the early primaries were installed and binding for state and federal office with the notable exception of the presidential nomination. While some states held primaries for their parties' presidential nominations, those primaries were nonbinding because the national party committees continued to set the parameters of their nomination contests. At the national level, party committees did not want to cede their power to nominate to the public, so binding presidential primaries would remain decades away from reality. To delineate the differences exhibited, we will use the term *binding sub-presidential primary* to discuss the era after which primaries were introduced until presidential nominations became subject to binding primaries in 1972, and *pre-primary* to discuss the era when party elites and caucuses had control over nominations.

As primaries emerged, the effect was similar to a dam bursting. Outsiders, reformers, and others who were passed over or rejected for nominations for sub-presidential offices in the party nomination era seized the opportunity to run for office in primaries, and often won. Ansolabehere and colleagues note some key distinctions in the early primary days. First, the South operated in a different environment than the rest of the country. Southern primaries were significantly more frequently contested and more competitive than those in the rest of the United States. Roughly two-thirds of all primaries in the South were contested throughout the first four decades of the binding primary era. Incumbents were successfully challenged more often in the South and victory margins for primary winners were narrow. A substantially smaller cohort of elections were contested in any of the other three regions (Northeast, Midwest, and West), clearly showing that unintended consequences dwarfed the initial motivation behind the southern primary adoption.[59]

The end of the white primary also had a suppressive effect on primary competitiveness in the South. Competition in northeastern, western, and midwestern primaries remained fairly consistent throughout the twentieth century, but after the 1944 *Nixon* decision, all measures of southern primary competitiveness declined. Uncontested primaries rose significantly in frequency, and incumbent success rates in primaries increased to over 99 percent. Notably, over this time voter turnout began to decline in general elections, leading to concerns about the representativeness of the primary electorate.[60]

Election competitiveness is a particularly difficult concept in American elections because of the two very different systems of elections conducted. The general election, for instance, is difficult to measure for competitiveness in the United States due to the binary nature of electoral choice between Democrats and Republicans. The two major parties dominate the electoral landscape, and often a given constituency is so dominated by one of the parties that the other party will fail to field a candidate.[61] Primary elections often allow more than a binary choice, but because candidates fall within a single party, they are usually similar in ideology and are selected by a much smaller and less representative portion of the electorate.[62]

Conclusion

Direct primary elections came mostly from reformers enamored of direct democracy and seeking to add more of its elements into American republicanism. While this was not universally the reasoning behind the introduction of the primary, especially in the South, direct-minded reformers concocted the idea of the primary and were its main supporters. Progressives believed that primary elections would activate the slumbering masses disenchanted with and disenfranchised by the party elite. A new wave of engagement would follow the introduction of the binding direct primary, so the argument went, that would circumvent the mischievous nature of parties as the Progressives believed, and in its place would be a new town hall. As we noted earlier, Progressives often saw solutions as solving many problems and reinforcing many good changes. Thus, direct primaries would simultaneously be a truer form of democracy and an institution that would cleanse the political temple.

However, from the beginning primary elections have been plagued by low voter turnout, which creates a cascade of problems. Primary electorates are less representative of the general public, are subject to manipulation by outside interests, introduce confusion among general election voters, and have numerous other issues we will explore as the book progresses. The proverbial genie, though, was out of the bottle. Primaries became a nationwide process by the 1920s, and while presidential election nominations were not binding, other races were being affected and changing the nature of the candidates as well as the parties.

Still, the direct primary did not encompass all American elections because most states had no primaries, or unbinding ones, for their presidential nominations. By 1968, only fourteen states held primary elections for partisan presidential nominations.[63] Especially for the Democratic Party, this maintained a significant power base for party elites. City, county, and state chairs were unburdened by consideration of popular will when choosing their preferences for their presidential nominee. The 1968 contest would be the last time, though, that Democrats would have that level of freedom to choose.

Chapter 5

The Early Primary Era

The people are inclined to be suspicious of any partisan organization. It suggests exclusiveness, possibly some sinister purpose and at least the chaining of big men to little or corrupt men. There is a loss of force in party action.[1]

—Frederick C. Howe to Robert M. La Follette

The convention system has its faults, of course, but I do not know of a better method for choosing a presidential nominee.[2]

—Harry Truman

Democracy, Conventions and the Chairman's Problem

Since the time of the ancient Greeks, there has been an ongoing debate about the extent to which politics should be democratic at all. There has been a line of thought that politics should be left to those who know something about how to achieve a just and well-run society—philosopher kings, experts who know how to guide the ship of state.[3] Pushing back against this idea is the notion that, in some sense, we are all equal and deserve a voice in deciding how to manage whatever community we are a part of. From one perspective, politics has always been, in part, about how to find a practical, workable middle ground between the rule of enlightened, educated elites and the unfiltered rule of everyone. Political parties present both a possible solution to this paradox and a complicating factor that can impede growing democratic impulses.

Both extremes have obvious problems. How can we identify philosopher kings and, if we could, might they eventually be corrupted by the power they are given? If the people rule directly, is the average person capable of making good political decisions about everything? How directly should the people rule? What is the mechanism for their rule? Should the people rule directly or through some mediating body? Exactly what role should parties play, and how much authority relative to the general public should they have in the selection of political leadership? The American constitutional system is an attempt to steer that middle course between those extremes. It must be acknowledged that there have always been democratic critics who view the Constitution, and the structures it created, as far too elitist and devoted to protecting the establishment. Nonetheless, the US Constitution has some place for mass participation, and there seems little doubt that the document has become more democratic over time.[4] And for many critics, there is a great deal of worry about the seeming evolution of the political system to ever more democracy.[5] Parties have traveled a parallel path, alternately becoming more insular and democratic over time, both mirroring and driving sociopolitical change in the United States.

These debates about how democratic versus how elitist the United States should be were complicated by the development of the party system. The failure of the founders to account for parties was a major problem or, more optimistically, an opportunity. Lacking a constitutional mandate, parties developed haphazardly and have always shown a remarkable ability to survive and adapt in surprising ways. However, that does not mean all the adaptations have been equally effective. As parties emerged they found their own ways both to be democratic and to recognize the demands of elite decision-making. In some sense, parties have tried to find, and reinforce, a working balance between the role of elites and the input of citizens. To use academic jargon, they created a system of peer review—political peer review that allowed for a reasonable system in selecting nominees.[6] The question has always been, though, how much the people should be involved in deciding nominees versus how much influence elites should have on that process. The question of what level of autonomy parties should have has hovered around the direct primary since its inception.

At issue is just what the role of the average citizens should be in the internal workings of a party.[7] In some ways, the French political scientist Bertrand de Jouvenel offered a powerful and simple diagnosis of the democratic problem in his playful essay, "The Chairman's Problem."[8] As Jouvenel observes, we all have a right to speak in theory, but in practice, how can we? Imagine a meeting with hundreds or even thousands of participants and a limited amount of time. Can everyone speak? No, the meeting would take weeks or months. So we have to think of how to create intelligible debates in a finite amount of time. Sadly, for ideal politics, "time is a scarce commodity."[9] Thus we need some mechanism for determining who should speak and why. Jouvenel focuses on the case of a meeting of some sort for the purpose of winnowing speech down to a manageable quantity. Jouvenel's thinking provides lessons for how to operate democratically in any large setting (as he surely intended). We want people to be able to participate but we want that participation to be informed, germane, and meaningful. For much of human history that meant simply limiting politics to a very tight elite. With the rise of democracy, in the modern world, it led to a system that was still largely controlled by elites but gave the people (however defined[10]) some role in ratifying who was in power among the elites. Large-scale democracy is simply hampered by the enormous number of people who, in theory, have a right to participate. But how can and should they participate? There will always be Jouvenel's "Chairman's Problem" to deal with: how to make political discussion meaningful but at the same time open to the many. One solution was the political convention.[11] While conventions of thousands of people don't allow everyone to speak, they are a process that makes some serious attempt to allow meaningful informed debate among political peers to select the best candidate for office. They are more participatory than the politics of "King Caucus" that preceded them, and seemingly less participatory than the primary system that has been firmly embraced from 1972 to the present. But the conventions did provide a balance point between the elite dominance of caucus-based nominations and the radically direct participation of a primary election.

In the nineteenth century the heart of that process was the political convention. In many ways this replaced and democratized the previous, much more informal world of elite politics that had dominated matters for the first quarter of the nineteenth century. Many historians have noted the deferential world that existed at that time. To give just one taste of that kind of milieu, the prominent Virginia planter John Campbell wrote to his son, in 1811, "I have heard with much pain that you have not recovered your health yet. Would a session in the legislature be of benefit to you?"[12] One should not generalize too much from an isolated example; nonetheless, American politics prior to the 1820s, at the earliest, was still marked by limited participation and deference to elites. Indeed, Margaret Conway reminds us that prior to the founding of the United States, in some New

England communities, a potential voter had "to prove that he met standards of good character."[13] Many states in the early republic had significant barriers to voting—most commonly property restrictions. Even when these restrictions were limited, turnout remained low.[14] That world was shattered in the 1820s and the rise of Andrew Jackson was both reflective of, and propelled by, his leadership in a new democratic age. Jackson led the way in increasing the role of the average male citizen in politics, and he was also instrumental in the adoption of the political convention.[15]

The conventions were the site of political conflict and political unity. They were the place where people came together to debate, to agree on principles to place before the broader audience of voters in the fall, and select nominees. National nominating conventions were arenas of real political action, hugely consequential, and often dramatic. Conventions had a sense of possibility with, at the outset, unknown outcomes subject to debate, deliberation, and, yes, intrigue. In short, a mechanism was created that was more democratic than what preceded it while at the same time maintaining a kind of pragmatic peer review that is central to making good political sense. A great deal always happened before the national convention met, of course. Potential candidates jockeyed for power; local counties and then states held conventions themselves. Nonetheless, nothing was fully assured until delegates met at some national convention.

From the contemporary vantage point, political conventions are seen as a mixture of manipulated media hype, archaic political ritual, and a candidate-centered pep rally designed to build enthusiasm among the party faithful for one person. To reformers throughout the twentieth century, they were seen as a site of corruption—a place of backroom deals, seemingly always suffused with cigar smoke, among party bosses trading favors with little concern for the national good. At their worst they were scenes of outright fraud. At their best they simply displayed the intense parochial demands of local leaders trading favors and forging some sense of compromised party message.

Yet nineteenth-century politics was defined by conventions, and they were seen as a positive and democratic institution. As Joel Silbey writes,

> The heart and soul of the mid-nineteenth-century political structure, its "indispensable mode of organization" . . . were the numerous regular party conventions held at every level of American politics., from local to nation. To the Americans of

the time, conventions were "the meetings where the power of the people was felt and made manifest." Andrew Jackson referred to convention delegates as being "fresh from the people."[16]

Politics by the middle to late nineteenth century was dense with meetings. "New York City's parties alone in 1880 held seventy-two primary elections and 111 conventions before deciding on their ticket for the general campaign."[17] The expanding quantity of elections was very much seen as part of growing democratic institutions and their almost ubiquitous presence in political life—with conventions at the local, county, state, and national levels—underpinned the legitimacy of the major parties.[18] Yes, they could be raucous affairs. The ideal was one of the arguments being resolved (importantly, though, the arguments had to be aired) and party unity being forged. And in reality, in large measure, parties strove to represent areas and peoples widely and respect the function of the delegate as "agents, or attorneys in fact, to whose care the business of the people is confided."[19]

Conventions truly brought more people into the political process and did give some real power to common citizens. At the same time, they also socialized those people into a way of political thinking. Delegates came together to bargain, resolve debates, agree on ideas, and then unite behind a set of candidates. There was a certain military air to this process and the idea of almost creating an army. "The enemy was always at the gates."[20] After the convention the debating must stop and the unity of the party was paramount. But this was also an ideal that was never fully realized. Dissent did happen.

These conventions became, in a way, an academy of politics, or a "campaign school" in modern political professional parlance. They taught the importance of collective action. As William Seward argued, "Every path must stand, not on the individual protestation of its members, but on the tendency of its corporate actions."[21] However, that corporate action was always a reflection of people joining together to discuss the issues. The image of bosses ordering their delegates around is not a baseless myth, but is much exaggerated. As James Reichley argues,

> Loss of control over nominations greatly reduced the ability of the party organization—in some cases, the "boss," but often simply the inner core of regulars who took responsibility for keeping the party running—to maintain a degree of harmony between

the branches and levels of government. If the organization could not punish dissidents, its capacity to achieve party unity on a given issue became, at most, advisory.[22]

Their value, which has been largely lost today, was their role in making their participants see the twin values of principle and compromise. Conventions steeled delegates and observers to the realities that have always defined politics: that we have ideals, but we live in the real world where human interests and ideals vary. The nominating meetings also fostered a sense of communal purpose, loyalty to an organization beyond the nominee of the moment. Furthermore, conventions made the eventual nominee more committed to the organization of the party itself. This would, as we shall see, foster a more cohesive governing party than what we have today. Conventions did, at their best, teach people to be political in the highest sense and that, as Aristotle reminds us, people must both rule and be ruled over.[23]

Critics of the Conventions

However, the critics of the parties as they came to function by the late nineteenth century were not deluded in thinking something was amiss. There were flaws in the convention system. It was never the case that conventions were truly representative of all of the people. Although they sprung from a desire and a claim to be more democratic than the older caucus system, they were not particularly faithful to democratic principles. There were simply too many people at the conventions to be fully deliberative. As Austin Ranney pointed out, in the twentieth century political scientists actually pushed for a more restrictive convention in terms of numbers.[24] A group of a few hundred might conceivable engage in the give-and-take that is the hallmark of actual deliberation. However, as conventions grew larger in numbers of delegates, the real action increasingly receded from the convention floor. This is not to suggest that conventions were ever some sort of scholarly ideal of deliberation and discussion as seen in the seminar room. But the input of common delegates became less and less important as the conventions moved to include thousands of delegates.

Corruption was real and the ideal just presented was less and less apparent. Party bosses did exist and they did all the unsavory things critics feared and, at times, party leaders engaged in acts ranging from unethical to criminal. Yes, conventions and caucuses in many places could be in the control of those bosses, and this made a mockery of the democratic claims made by their defenders. The method of selecting party nominees seemed less and less democratic and more beholden to defending the status quo, and this defense seemed less and less about defending the status quo because it was good but rather because it simply was the status quo. Those who had gained power simply wanted to hold their stations rather than use that power for particular policy-related purposes.

Starting in 1912, and continuing through 1968, the major political parties began a striking experiment in how they nominated presidential candidates, with the first presidential primaries. In many states those presidential primaries followed suit with the primaries for state-level and congressional offices. The primaries forged a kind of hybrid system that included primaries that allowed citizen participation in the nomination process; however, they continued to use conventions to make the final determination of party nominees. These conventions allowed party elites a great deal of say over who became the party standard-bearer. These conventions were not the televised pep rallies of today, orchestrated by a presumptive nominee preparing his general election campaign and awaiting a final legal stamp to his candidacy.[25] Those conventions were lively, dramatic affairs where the outcome was far from certain. Conventions often went through multiple ballots to determine the nominee. During this time five Democratic conventions went beyond the first ballot (including the infamous 1924 marathon that included 103 ballots), as did four Republican conventions. Even conventions decided on the first ballot were not always foregone conclusions.

Of course, such a history of brokered conventions had been the case throughout the nineteenth century. What was new, and would eventually change the process entirely, was the inclusion of primaries to select delegates to the convention. Prior to 1912, virtually all delegates to the national conventions were selected by state conventions, which often reflected even lower-level county caucuses. There was often, usually at the county level, involvement of party regulars to selected delegates to some high-level conventions. But those delegates, once chosen, were free to vote as they like. As Alan Ware writes, "In its standard form this type of nominating system permitted delegates to a convention to vote for them they wanted when they attended; they were bound neither by party rules nor law to do otherwise."[26] An enormous amount of variation in practices existed. Local customs ruled the day and were deferred to by almost everyone. Of course, there were powerful local and statewide party leaders who had a great deal of influence. But diversity or, to be more critical, chaos ruled the day. As

Ware observes, "the most conspicuous feature of the 19th century party nomination procedures was their informal and decentralized nature."[27]

This informal, customary way of nominating people was also problematic for two reasons. First, there was a growing sense that the system was corrupted and a new, better, more systematic way of nominating candidates should be found. There was a sense that the American democratic ideal needed to be restored. Robert La Follette, one of the first prominent politicians to really push for primaries, had argued in his speech "The Menace of the Machine" that while parties were necessary, they had been taken over by the nefarious machine that was "its own master" and a form of despotism.[28] The real threats were not the colorfully notorious bosses, such as Tweed. No, the real threat was "this invisible empire [that] does its work so quietly." The political processes that, in Jackson's view, meant that delegates were "fresh from the people" were now sullied—the wellsprings of democracy were now a fetid stream owned by concentrated and corrupt powers.[29] Indeed, La Follette saw that the party men who ran the convention "had artfully violated every principle of honor." This stands in stark contrast to the very notion of honor that underpinned the idea of conventions from early decades. In the view of that time, any rejection of the convention "should be regarded as a kind of minor treason."[30] By the end of the century it was very nearly the opposite—the machines and the convention system they devised were inherently un-American. "Abolish the caucus and the convention. Go back to the first principles of democracy. Go back to the people," La Follette thundered. Adopt the direct primary and "destroy the political machine, [this] will emancipate the majority from its enslavement."[31] Inherent in La Follette's words were the core conflation problem that hallmarks primaries today: believing in primaries as a method of direct democracy rather than expanding participatory democratic practices such as making the conventions open to more participants.

To LaFollette, there was no way to effectively reform the caucus and convention system.[32]

> The caucus, delegate and convention system is inherently bad. It invites manipulation, scheming, trickery, corruption and fraud. Even if the causes were fairly conducted the plan of this it is a part removes the nomination far from the voter. . . . The convention under the most favorable conditions are anything but a deliberative body. Its work is hurried and business necessarily transacted in confusion.

La Follette's argument is that the machine controls the convention and corrupts the convention. Even if the machine were defeated, "the opportunity offered by the caucus and convention plan would simply restore the old or build up a new machine in its place." This fit with La Follette's other concern about the power of corporations and the unholy alliance between party bosses and corporate interests.[33] Conventions were the linchpin that held this insidious structure in place. There was nothing deliberative or democratic about conventions, in LaFollette's argument. They only got in the way of the citizen voter. The only answer LaFollette would accept was to remove this deceitful method and replace it with the direct primary. As Austin Ranney observed, "La Follette also believed that the direct primary would strengthen the parties by purifying them."[34] The convention, which had distorted the will of the people, would no longer be a barrier to true democracy. Parties would still serve some purpose as, one supposes, ideologically driven organizations that united people under a common banner. But the interplay of ideology, practical issues of organization, the need to create winning coalitions, accommodate ambitious politicians, and forge a common sense of communal purpose—all the things beyond policy and ideology—would cease. Still other Progressives, such George Norris, saw the opposite and were glad. Norris thought the primary would weaken the parties and "increase individual independence. . . . It lessens party spirit and decreases partisanship."[35] The general sense of the primary's advocates, then, was not that the public needed different or reformed participatory systems but rather that the public was a sleeping giant simply waiting to be awakened without the need for any linkage institutions.

We should note, at this point, that La Follette may have been a great champion of the direct primary and deserving in credit for its greater adoption; however, he was not its creator. Rather, it appears that direct primaries were begun when the Democratic Party of Crawford County, Pennsylvania, adopted the method in 1842. From there it spread to other counties in the western part of the state and in eastern Ohio. Later still, they began to appear in various southern and western states. People migrating may have brought the idea with them or it may have been "discovered" at various places at various times. It certainly appears that some writers in the late nineteenth century were not aware of Crawford as the birthplace.[36] (It is also possible that some further historical research will find an earlier example. The documentary records are rather incomplete.) Still, contrary to the views of some commentators, the direct primary was not created de novo with Progressives. Rather, it was an uncommon, but not unknown, system being used in a number of states for a variety of offices from the middle of the nineteenth century. Direct primaries (sometimes referred to, in the 1880s, as the Crawford County System) already had momentum behind them when Progressives like La Follette took up the cause. Whatever the provenance of direct primaries, it is certainly true the Progressives added much energy in pushing the direct primary forward. Without the champions provided by the Progressive movement, primaries may have been a geographical local party oddity and nothing more. The Progressives also provided the intellectual justification for immediate adoption of the direct primary. It is possible that someone in Crawford Country in 1842 made an impassioned speech full of references to democracy urging its adoption. More likely it was a pragmatic decision about how to organize politics at the county level. It would take men like La Follette to transform the pragmatic actions of the people of Crawford county into direct democratic principle.[37]

Second, party leaders saw the system as uncertain and prone to fostering unnecessary conflict, especially in the North and West. Thus, the story of the late nineteenth century, with regard to politics and elections, was actually the convergence of a practical desire by party leaders to create a more certain system of nomination and a strong desire on the part of reformers to purify the system and return to democratic ideal that had seemingly been lost (and that in reality had never really existed in practice). We see in the history of primaries something that James Morone has identified in the creation of public policy and the state. Morone writes,

> At the heart of American politics lies a dread and a yearning. The dread is notorious. Americans fear public power as a threat to liberty. . . . The yearning is an alternative faith in direct, communal democracy.[38]

If only all the impediments to the people's participation—the corruption, the bosses, the party structures, the ties that bound party leaders—could be swept away, "a unitary, discernible public interest, stretching beyond factions, and even politics itself" would reemerge.[39] Progressives believed in Rousseau's concept of a popular will, but it could only be discerned through wide-ranging popular participation. That Rousseau's concept of the general will almost certainly precluded the very idea of parties does not seem to have occurred to them. Instead, Progressives wanted to use them in some form—to reach the idealized notion of participation of Rousseau's concept without accepting the very real impracticality of it.[40] The gap between the direct democratic impulses of the Progressives and the reality of participation is where the direct primary has come to undermine the very progress and reform it initially symbolized. And, we should emphasize, this communal, public-spirited, and moral world was there. It was not lost and in some ways it didn't need to be created; it had to be freed from the shackles imposed by the party bosses and machines.

Alan Ware forcefully argues that the usual narrative of Progressive reformers battling old-line party regulars and leaders was false. The rise of primaries satisfied a great deal of people in many different camps. In the southern states, one-party dominance allowed a new burgeoning sense of participation, for instance. Thus, primaries were increasingly adopted as a way to systematize a chaotic process and bring order to the way parties nominated candidates. By the 1920s, Overacker noted that "the presidential primaries have also served the purpose given the states which provided them an amicable and certain way of deciding between various party factions."[41] While there are definitely places (New York for instance) where reformers and establishment party leaders did battle, in most places the rise of the primaries was peaceful. In the 1880s to the early part of the twentieth century this occurred at the state level and involved the selection of statewide offices and congressional candidates. Finally, in 1912, primaries were adopted as significant method of selecting delegates to the national conventions for nominating presidential candidates.

Conventions and Primaries—The Hybrid System

As primaries were seen as a solution to a number of problems it was not exactly clear how to use them. Primaries were rapidly adopted at the state level for selecting almost all nominees for office. There were some exceptions to this and some states found ways to use conventions for nominating candidates for statewide offices. But that increasingly became uncommon. But the more challenging question was, how should they be used at the presidential level?

The way parties nominated candidates from 1912 until the early 1970s was in part a result of Progressive reforms. However, it was only partly this way, because many of the old practices continued. What emerged was a hybrid system that used primaries largely as Progressives envisioned combined with the more traditional methods that favored the parties themselves, as opposed to the mass of voters. Progressives believed in a rational system to manage things but, as is so often the case in American history, a confluence of differing actions, the complexity of a federal system, and the power of party organizations meant that nominating presidential candidates changed but the new system was far from systematic or neatly logical. In short, we did as Americans often do: we muddled through to a new way of doing things.

One logical solution could very well be a national primary. Indeed, Theodore Roosevelt and the Progressive Party adopted that very ideal in its 1912 platform.[42] And, in Woodrow Wilson's first address to Congress, he argued for them:

> I feel confident that I do not misinterpret the wishes or the expectations of the country when I urge prompt enactment of legislation which will provide for primary elections throughout the country at which voters of the several parties may choose nominees for presidency without the intervention of nominating conventions.[43]

But the synchronous national primary was never seriously considered, for a number of reasons. How would vice presidents be chosen? Who should be allowed to vote in these national primaries? Southern states would have fought such a movement as an attempt to end-run around their Jim Crow efforts to continue the suppression of African American suffrage. In the main, the nature of the American party system was highly decentralized and it is hard to imagine states willing to give up their influence in such a system. State parties may have seen adopting primaries within their own states as a defensive fallback position to prevent the national primary idea from taking hold and even further usurping their power. The idea of a national primary raised the issue of what defines a party, and this has always been a vexing question not easily resolved.[44] Instead, what occurred was sixty years of finding a place for primaries, which some changing collection of states adopted, while keeping the convention as a meaningful body to decide matters.

Although a handful of states had adopted primaries for selecting delegates early in the twentieth century, 1912 was the first presidential election where primaries truly mattered. There was a significant increase in the number of primaries held by each party—twelve states for both parties.[45] That year both parties had dramatic nomination fights with the outcome in doubt. As an incumbent, William Howard Taft was wounded, but still a formidable candidate. That year also saw some more open campaigning by candidates than ever before. Prior to Theodore Roosevelt's emergence, presidential candidates did not campaign at all, even if Mark Hanna's subsidized train trips to William McKinley's front porch came conspicuously close. The primaries fit into this emerging campaign reality, though candidates also appeared at state conventions to make direct appeals there. Whereas earlier, the few primaries that were held took place in smaller states, in 1912 large states such as Illinois, Pennsylvania, and Ohio held them and they were integral to Theodore Roosevelt's drive to take the nomination away from Taft. They also underscored Roosevelt's claim to a kind of democratic legitimacy. Where the common people could vote, Roosevelt earned 52 percent of the vote to Taft's 34 percent and Robert La Follette's 14 percent. Roosevelt won nine of twelve primaries, La Follette two, and Taft one. Of course, Taft won control of more states using traditional delegate selection models and ultimately won the nomination fairly easily. His control also rested on controlling the party delegate process in southern states, which was very suspect. The Republican Party in the solid Democratic South meant that Taft's support rested on nearly dormant party organizations in the region with states almost certain to go for the Democratic nominee in the fall.[46] On the Democratic side, primaries were also used, and a spirited race developed largely between the Speaker of the House, Champ Clark, and the reformist governor of New Jersey, Woodrow Wilson. Here the race was closer, with Wilson winning around 45 percent of the total vote to Clark's 42 percent. However, to many observers at the time, Wilson's overall performance in the primaries was less than stellar—he needed more wins to impress the more conservative elements in the Democratic Party and he simply had not done well enough.[47] In particular, Wilson had engaged in much personal effort to win the Illinois primary, yet Clark defeated him there by a wide margin.[48] This was an early example of the power of primaries to act as expectation-setting structures.

Initially, many predicted that the primaries, used extensively but not exclusively in 1912, would sweep the nation. The *Boston Globe* confidently predicted that "there can be little doubt that by 1916 practically every state will have a well worked out presidential primary act." Such views were echoed in leading papers in Maryland, Ohio, Illinois and California.[49] Many of these writers said that 1912 would be the last of its kind—a convention that was dominated, despite the existence of many significant primaries by the old political order (Taft beat back Roosevelt's challenge, after all). And indeed, 1916 saw an increase in the number of primaries held by each party to twenty and, for the first time, more than 50 percent of the delegates in each party were selected via primaries (see table 3.2.) In that sense, these early commentators were correct. Primaries would never go away after 1912; however, sweep the country they did not. The initial enthusiasm for them at the presidential level quickly waned.

What might seem remarkable to us today is that after their earlier use in 1912 and 1916, the primaries were viewed with some suspicion. Frank Lowden, the Republican governor of Illinois, who was a serious candidate for president in 1920 (he actually led the delegate count as late as the eighth ballot—Harding was nominated on the tenth), spoke for many when he said of primaries that they were the "most demoralizing departure we have ever made from the principle of representative government."[50] And it took some time for the system to fully develop. In 1920, an editorialist in *The Oregonian* was led to write,

> The outstanding lesson of the primary is that the presidential primary law as it stands is a burlesque and a contradiction. It should be so changed that no delegation to any national convention will be under binding instructions to any candidate unless he shall receive a majority of all the votes.[51]

One could only imagine what the editors of *The Oregonian* would think about the process we employ today. In some way, things are similar. One can see parallels between William McAdoo's promising efforts to win the Democratic nomination in 1924 undermined by his connection to oil interests and Hillary Clinton's recent problems being associated with Goldman Sachs. One very early scholar of the new use of primaries, Louise Overacker, astutely wondered in 1926 about the emerging role of films and radio to bolster candidates.[52] It is not hard to see that echo through the decades to the present-day obsession of the power of social media. Overacker's prescient insight about the new technologies led her to foresee the possibility of multi-primary days (not common then) resulting in the importance of "the personal tour" by the candidate "to be displaced by the radio and the movie or by a combination of the two."[53] At the same time, the role of money in politics prior to the convention was more and more evident. The modern term to describe the pre-primary phase, "the money primary," can be seen as an extension of the warning Overacker provided in the early days of the direct primary experiment. The new money flow wasn't exclusively for primary expenses, but it is tied in part to their rise. Simply put, running a campaign in a primary demanded an organization and that had to be created, maintained, and done much in advance to be of any use. As Lewis Gould observes,

> Wilson was learning what would become evident in other primary campaigns in the decades that followed. To be a viable national candidate with serious organization in key states demanded larger amounts of money than had been required under the older system of party conventions. In essence, the campaign was running a dozen statewide elections all over the nation simultaneously.[54]

Also, not surprisingly or coincidentally, the beginnings of campaign professionalism emerged at the same time as direct primaries were spreading and allowing extra-partisan entities more access to the apparatus of campaigns.[55] What was noted quite early has only become painfully obvious: democratic politics, in a large society, is going to cost a lot of money. And that would raise the specter of corruption, as we must ask where that money is coming from. The direct primary introduced an unintended threat that could nullify its reform value: by bringing in outside interested money, the primary promised not to eliminate corruption but simply replace the beneficiaries of corruption with other new beneficiaries to a different type of corruption.

At this early stage, as well, primaries were already seen as exposing internal divisions both within the individual campaigns and within parties. "An elaborate machinery of national and state managers may be wrecked if there is friction between the different parts of the machinery."[56] Already, according to some accounts, Leonard Wood's failed attempt to win the Republican nomination in 1920 was a case study of a faulty campaign whose conflicts became quite public.[57] The drawn-out nature of the primaries also allowed public debates between candidates to persist and, in some cases, deepen into intense animosities. The very first year of extensive primary use, 1912, saw the Republican Party shattered and Roosevelt bolting from the Republicans to run as a minor party candidate after he failed to wrest the nomination from Taft at the GOP convention. We can never know what would have happened under a different nominating system, but the fact that Roosevelt won so many primaries gave him an air of democratic legitimacy that hardened differences at the actual convention. Furthermore, the show of great support for him those primaries convinced him and his followers he was popular enough to possibly win the general election and encouraged his flight to another party. Of course, the opposite could also could also be the case—decisive defeats in primaries might very well convince some candidates that they simply lacked a compelling case to be the party's nominee.

One effect of the direct primary that was very clear from the beginning was that primaries had not led to a dramatic and sustained increase in voter participation. Although turnout was fairly impressive in 1912, that has not been the general case since then.[58] Turnout remained stubbornly low, although it could increase dramatically in certain years and in certain primaries. Those booms were brief, followed quickly by a return to the equilibrium state of lower turnout. Indeed, the overall trend was not for a great deal of actual citizen involvement and it clearly fell short of the flourishing democratic ideal of its most ardent supporters. Already by the mid-1920s Overacker had noted the dramatic decline in turnout in comparison to voting in the fall in the same states, after the initial excitement of 1912.[59]

At this early stage—by 1924 they had been used in only four presidential election cycles—primaries were still experiments, and their long-term effects on the democratic system were not yet fully evident. There was clear evidence that direct primaries could generate excitement among voters, but only in specific races during specific times. The flood of participation presaged by La Follette had not emerged. In fact, quite the contrary: there were many cases of very low turnouts. Whether candidates should contest them or not was still a strategic issue during a time when professional advisers were few and far between. The confusion led to candidates second-guessing if they should enter primaries at all, enter all of them, or enter just some. Overall, it was quite apparent that primaries would have a role to play in the process of nominating party candidates; however, the nature of that role was still being debated. Given the federal nature of the country and the highly decentralized nature of parties, there was a great deal of experimentation. In many cases, primaries were non-binding to delegates. They were used to allow voters to register their opinion, but not to actually require the delegates to vote for a certain candidate. Other states did make them binding.[60]

For the next several decades primaries played an increasing role in the nomination process. While the conventions still dominated the nomination process, primaries would not be completely rejected. In 1916 Charles Evans Hughes got the Republican nomination without competing in a single primary. Harding won the Republican nomination in 1920 while only actively competing in two primaries—winning his home state unimpressively and polling poorly in Indiana. Often candidates would use them to make a show of strength in certain places, as Franklin Roosevelt did in 1932. FDR did not personally campaign in primary states but used surrogates and did make a number of important addresses that brought national attention to his campaign.⁶¹ In 1944 Wendell Wilkie campaigned furiously in the Wisconsin primary in an effort to regain the Republican nomination that had come to him so shockingly four years earlier. His reasoning goes a long way to explaining how primaries worked at this time. He needed to show strength in the Midwest—the heartland of the Republican Party. In his discussion with party leaders, many indicated that the results from a midwestern primary, such Wisconsin or Nebraska, would weigh significantly in their minds. Finally, Wisconsin had a certain legacy—going back to La Follette—as a Progressive state. Wilkie embarked on vigorous thirteen-day campaign, giving forty speeches. The outcome was a disaster. He failed to win a single delegate.⁶²

Four years later, though, another failed nominee, Thomas Dewey, more effectively used a primary to regain the nomination. Dewey won the hotly contested Oregon primary and this was key to dispatching rival Harold Stassen and convincing party leaders he was still a popular figure among voters. Of equal note, by the 1940s candidates were not only competing in primaries, they were doing so in person.⁶³ FDR's detached approach was a thing of the past. Primaries were becoming a useful tool in helping with the nomination but were far from being his only or even the most important one. Primaries could serve as a way to win some delegates, show strength, appeal to voters directly and, not so subtly, signal to party leaders (bosses?) that one was a serious candidate. Of course, some candidates were by definition serious and may well have believed there was no reason to "prove" anything.

A Settled Peace—Primaries and Conventions

Competing in primaries was sometimes useful and sometimes not, and was largely contingent on unique factors for each election cycle depending on the position of a candidate. "Primaries were secondary in the naming of the nominee, but they were not always unimportant."⁶⁴ There was even a kind of convention wisdom that running in the primaries was a sign of weakness—candidates needed to overcome some perceived disadvantage by running around the country convincing voters and party leaders they were worthy of consideration.⁶⁵ This view is hard to imagine today. While today primaries seem the only legitimate way to select nominees, for decades they were seen as something far less than legitimating—although the argument that they were meaningless misses the mark.

Some candidates pursued an entirely "inside" strategy trying to appeal to party leaders (Stevenson in 1952, Johnson in 1960, and Humphrey in 1968—two successful). Others attempted an "outside" strategy of winning primaries and forcing themselves upon the party through the sheer impressiveness of public wins (Stassen in 1948 and Kefauver in 1952 and 1956—neither successful). Finally, some employed a mixed approach that combined some primary wins while still working on convincing party bosses that they were the best candidate for president (Roosevelt in 1932, Taft in 1952 and Kennedy in 1960—two successful).[66] In 1948, Truman was seen as an extremely weak candidate by many Democrats and a number of prominent party leaders wanted him to bow out.[67] There was much talk about drafting Eisenhower as a candidate to save the party. However, the general decisively declined the idea. Although he was the incumbent president, Truman was still very weak and his victories in the primaries—along with no significant primary challenges—meant that the primary stage was an overall plus for him.[68]

On balance, there was an apparent settled "peace" that allowed primaries a secondary place in the political world of presidential selection. Wins in primaries could help bolster a candidate's appeal—most memorably by Kennedy's wins in 1960—or sink a candidate, such as Wendell Wilkie's earlier defeats in the 1944 primaries.[69] Of course, primaries remained central in the nominations of other offices below that of the presidency.

Primaries and Conventions: Balancing Ideology and Winning

We should note, contra some critics of the convention system, that the system was not shut off from outsiders. There are, in this period, a number of successful efforts by those looked on with skepticism by party regulars. Conventions were emphatically not automatically controlled by the "establishment." We can see that by highlighting three cases: Wendell Willkie in 1940, Dwight Eisenhower in 1952, and Barry Goldwater in 1964. In each case, a political newcomer or, in Goldwater's case, someone actively hostile to part of the Republican Party establishment seized the nomination. The important point is that while the convention system constrained choices and was hardly prone to radical actions, it is not the case the system was closed. The hybrid primary-convention system was quite susceptible to popular pressure, and party elites were governed by practical demands in considering what the various factions in the party wanted and how to making that appealing to a broader public. Of course, only one of the three cases mentioned here resulted in a presidential victory. Nonetheless, they represented sincere and reasonable attempts at honoring the wishes of the party base within reason.

In 1940 the Republicans had been in the political wilderness for eight years and suffered a string of fairly brutal defeats in election after election, although they had scored impressive gains in the 1938 mid-term elections. With Roosevelt nearing the end of his second term they looked forward to the presidential election with justified hope. But the party was beset by internal struggles that needed to be resolved. Since Republicans had so dominated politics from the 1890s to the early 1930s, the devastation wrought by the Great Depression was clearly seen as their responsibility. In response to this, some Republicans responded to Roosevelt's New Deal with criticism, but not outright rejection. They saw it as a flawed, but not irredeemable, set of policies—policies to be tempered and better managed. Yet there remained a still powerful old guard that saw the New Deal as an anathema to all that was good and American. The way forward was to find someone reasonably acceptable to these factions. The Republican convention was the scene of a contest largely between Wendell Wilkie, Thomas Dewey, and Robert Taft. Wilkie, who had actually been a Democrat until just the previous year (though he had voted for Alf Landon in 1936), had started as dark horse but had a creative grassroots campaign and was supported by much of the East Coast intentional wing of the Republican Party—and the convention organizers, who loaded the galleries with Wilkie supporters. The incessant chant of the alliterative "We Want Wilkie," combined with a broader momentum building before the convention, propelled him to the nomination on the sixth ballot. Wilkie had benefited from a smart media campaign and, in many ways, he did represent what many Republicans wanted. Here was the consummate outsider—popular, and ideologically complex—seizing a convention. But, in some ways, the events of the convention made dramatic what had been going on within the party. As Wilkie himself said, "I represent a trend, or am ahead of a trend."[70] Furthermore, even though Wilkie lost to Roosevelt, his energetic campaign in the fall reenergized the Republican Party and showed a way forward in maintaining a sometime contentious, but often successful, moderate-conservative alliance in the party. If the Republican convention did not pick a winner that year, it found a way reimagine itself. In the long run, that can be a sign of a healthy party and a successful convention.[71]

Twelve years later, the Republicans once again turned to someone outside the traditional ranks of politicians and nominated Dwight Eisenhower. After losing five straight presidential elections, many Republicans faced 1952 with a mixture of confidence and fear. Certainly, five successive defeats were sobering. In particular, the stunning Truman victory in 1948 loomed large in their minds. However, Truman's first full term had not been terribly successful. His domestic agenda had been almost completely stymied. Only in the area of foreign affairs was he more successful—particularly in cementing the western alliance—but Truman had also led the US into the Korean War with no end in sight. His administration also had a number of scandals that increased his vulnerabilities. Truman was seen as a formidable candidate, but not unbeatable. In the event, however, Truman decided not to run.[72]

That is the backdrop against which the Republicans fought the 1952 nomination phase. On one side was Robert Taft—Mr. Republican. Taft epitomized the midwestern conservative, isolationist roots of the Republican Party in that region. For many Republicans and those sympathetic to the party, this was dangerous.[73] Much of the opposition was based on a desire to firmly align the party with a more internationalist approach. There was also a fear that Taft was just too conservative on domestic policy to make an appealing candidate in the fall. Thus, a concerted effort was made by eastern Republicans—led by Thomas Dewey, Henry Cabot Lodge, and Sherman Adams, among others—to entice Eisenhower into running. By all accounts Eisenhower was truly reluctant, but eventually he was convinced to run out of a genuine sense of duty. Nonetheless, despite seeming inevitable in hindsight, the nomination process was complicated one and by the time the Republican convention convened in Chicago in July, Taft was seen as clearly ahead, though short of the needed delegates. Then, through either a series of blunders by the Taft forces or a series of clever moves by the Eisenhower forces, Eisenhower was nominated.[74]

The 1952 Republican convention was a good example of how the era worked. Primaries were held in thirteen states and the results were mixed. Eisenhower won a number, as did Taft. Furthermore, other "favorite son" candidates—Stassen in Minnesota and Warren in California—won their states. Taft, however, through his long tenure as a party leader, worked assiduously to win over delegations through state conventions and caucuses well before he convention occurred. That is why he entered the convention a favorite.

One might with some justification question whether the various machinations and maneuvering at a convention should decide the fate of a party nominee. But how does that compare to the importance of gaffes in debates, the role of momentum out of the Iowa caucuses, or the ability to fundraise in determining nominees today? The 1952 process narrowed the field to the exemplary conservative voice in the Republican Party versus a more moderate, internationalist war hero. Each represented important factions in the Republican Party and the party did have a serious debate about how best to proceed in challenging the Democrats. Eisenhower easily won in the fall, and while we will never know how Taft would have done, he was a more-than-plausible candidate if the party wanted to emphasize a more rightwing perspective. The desire to finally win back power versus a need to represent a coherent conservative philosophy are just the sort of appeals that parties need to balance, and a reasonable balance was struck with Eisenhower.

The Eisenhower years were, for the Republicans, a confusing time. The president made repeated calls for a new "modern" Republican Party. But many were not sure what that meant. Clearly it meant some commitment to an international perspective, an engagement with allies and the world. Domestically, Eisenhower had a general skepticism about too much spending, but he saw any effort to repeal the New Deal as foolish and politically suicidal. By the end of his administration, many old Taft supporters and newcomers like Barry Goldwater were getting restless, and a new conservatism was about to emerge. However, the party still had a significant East Coast establishment that looked forward to a more Progressive Republican Party. Such figures as Nelson Rockefeller, the governor of New York, loomed large. Again, the party was balancing various factions and trying to win elections while at the same time finding its way forward as an ideological force.

Finally, we come to 1964 and another battle over the direction of the Republican Party. We should first remember that Republicans faced a steep uphill battle going into 1964. Even before Kennedy's assassination, Democrats were favored to win. The economy was going well, and while there was the concern of Vietnam on the horizon, the country was at peace. As had been the case for some time, civil rights threatened to tear apart the Democratic coalition. Of course, with Kennedy's tragic death, Johnson ran in 1964 as a popular president and upholder of a martyred leader's legacy. Any Republican would have faced likely defeat—but the Republicans seemed to court an epic trouncing with the nomination of Barry Goldwater. How did that happen and what does it say about the health of the party at that time?

Although we have presented the Republicans as balancing matters from 1940 to 1960, for Goldwater and a great many conservatives, that period was about the complete domination of the Republican eastern establishment. All the presidential candidates—Wilkie, Dewey, Eisenhower, and Nixon—no matter where they were from originally, seemed to be reflective of that view. For a young Patrick Buchanan, the Eisenhower years had been like wandering in an "arid desert." Goldwater, and in particular his book *Conscience of a Conservative*, was like being "hit like a rifle shot."[75]

Surprisingly, even with the availability of primaries, Goldwater did not choose them as his primary route to the nomination (though he did compete in New Hampshire, and lost, and more importantly in California, where he won). Goldwater's appeal inspired an extensive grassroots movement that actually worked through traditional channels to capture state organization. F. Clinton White, leader of the Young Republicans, worked with other activists and some party leaders in doing this and started as early as 1961 in seizing the nomination.[76] This movement was not officially endorsed by Goldwater, but he was the key beneficiary of this conservative takeover of state parties. These machinations were all done in the expectation that Goldwater would be the preferred candidate, but these activists were first conservatives. And they clearly didn't want Nelson Rockefeller (a "New York Republican," which effectively meant a liberal Republican). At this time, there were a number of conservative groups working on a number of fronts—taking over the Republican Party at the state level, fostering a general move in a clearly conservative direction for the party as a whole, and trying to draft Goldwater as the candidate to lead them all.[77] When Governor Scranton of Pennsylvania made a late push to stop Goldwater, one his aides recounted making efforts to get establishment figures to support the governor: "We called all the old names, but they weren't there any longer. . . . It was if the Goldwater people had rewired the switchboard of the Party and the numbers we had were all dead."[78]

In the end, despite a great deal of effort by the moderate wing of the Republican Party, Goldwater sailed to the nomination on the first ballot. At that convention, Goldwater made it clear he would run an unabashed conservative campaign. And, as was expected, President Johnson crushed Goldwater, winning over 61 percent of the popular vote to Goldwater's 38 percent and overwhelming the senator in the Electoral College 486 to 52.

Of course, from the ashes of that defeat many commentators have traced the eventual triumph, sixteen years later, of Ronald Reagan and a conservative agenda he embodied. Nonetheless, the defeat was total and at that moment, in 1964, the party and conservatism seemed routed.

Can we say, though, that it was some mistake on the part of the party? There is every reason to think a person like Scranton would have done somewhat better against Johnson. But he most likely would have lost. Furthermore, in no way are we suggesting that ideology is an unimportant part of a political party. The Republican Party always had a conservative wing and it makes sense, as the parties began to sort themselves out ideologically, that a fully conservative candidate would emerge at some point. Goldwater was a prominent, elected Republican official who spoke for an ascendant conservative movement. His supporters worked to gain control of the party and were successful. Yes, they displaced the previous leaders—but they did so by appealing to a conservative ideology, to pragmatic businessmen who recognized a kindred spirit in Goldwater, to old-line Taft supporters and young new voters who were filled with passion. If anything, his capture of the Republican Party showed that, even if older leaders were being displaced, the system itself could accommodate the outsider and that a new establishment could be formed. The electoral defeat of the Republican Party in 1964 was very real, but it hardly meant that the party was dead (though some may have thought so in 1964).

Furthermore, Goldwater's rise predated the binding presidential primary era that we posit as the pivot point where polarized candidates became common. Goldwater could be used as a counterexample, since extreme candidates were possible prior to the McGovern-Fraser era. But Goldwater was an anomaly. The fact Goldwater stood out is evidence that extreme candidates were possible, but far from likely. Candidates of Goldwater's relative ideological extremity are now much more common. Also noteworthy is that Goldwater and his allies had a strong cadre of allies within the Republican Party leadership, so his nomination is much more consistent with the "party decides" thesis than post-1972 party nominees.

Conclusion: A Working System

Overall, these political arrangements were viewed as well-functioning and fair. Writing in 1963, the political scientist Gerald Pomper concluded, in his accounting of the overall nomination process,

> The present system has the final advantage of tradition and legitimacy. The nominating process is well-known in the nation, and both the electorate and party politicians can plan their actions in accord with accepted procedures. The decisions of the convention are widely regarded as authoritative.[79]

Thus, all seemed well *and* predictable when it came to nominating presidents. There was little reason to expect major changes. But the 1968 presidential election would shatter that uneasy peace and usher in a new era in the evolution and advancement of the direct primary. The apotheosis of all of the concerns about participation, linkage, and reform brought about by the rise of the direct primary was about to emerge.

Chapter 6

The Pivotal 1968 Democratic National Convention

Parties from *principle*, especially abstract speculative principle, are known only to modern times, and are, perhaps, the most extraordinary and unaccountable *phenomenon*, that has yet appeared in human affairs.[1]

—David Hume

The subject [election of the president] has greatly divided the House, and will also divide the people out of doors. It is in truth the most difficult of all on which we have had to decide.[2]

—James Wilson, speaking at the Constitutional Convention

The convention had not yet begun, and already the talk and reporting was of the clash, the violence, the showdown. This language was used to refer to the convention itself, where Humphrey forces were meeting McCarthy and the peace delegates, but also to the thousands of demonstrators and police in downtown Chicago.[3]

—Mark Kurlansky

We believe that popular participation is more than a proud heritage of our party, more even than a first principle. We believe that popular control of the Democratic Party is necessary for its survival.[4]

—McGovern-Fraser Commission Report

Politically the 1960s commenced conventionally along well-established lines. True, the new president was a Roman Catholic, as no president before had ever been. But the way he was selected was traditional and would not have seemed odd to Franklin Roosevelt or Herbert Hoover a generation earlier. Primaries for the presidency occurred as they had been conducted since 1912; however, the majority of delegates were chosen by state conventions or other methods controlled or influenced by party elites ("bosses" to their detractors). As a political scientist at the time observed, "whatever the particular mechanism involved, the fundamental fact is that the rank-and-file voter is either two or three steps removed from the choice of delegates to the national convention."[5] The delegate allocation system was also not nationalized, with state or local elites in control of delegate selection. Indeed, the national parties, generally speaking, were rather weak entities overshadowed organizationally by the fifty state parties. The parties did, however, come together every four years in a convention that mattered. National conventions were still lively affairs where uncertainty often prevailed. Party leaders from the various states met and bargained with each other and whatever candidates had declared themselves (or not, in some cases). The possibility of multiple ballots of the delegates to reach a consensus candidate was still on the minds of many.

While it is true that John F. Kennedy won on the first ballot in 1960,[6] it was a close run.[7] Richard Nixon, as the vice president, was more easily expected to be the Republican nominee—but even among Republicans the processes worked in their customary ways. In 1964, Lyndon Johnson, now president, was easily acclaimed the Democratic nominee, as any sitting president would be.[8] (There were, however, civil rights issues raised that particularly concerned the seating of the Mississippi delegation that can be seen as a portent of conflicts among Democrats to come.[9]) On the Republican side, there was a more intense battle between the very conservative Senator Barry Goldwater and more moderate candidates such as Governor Nelson Rockefeller of New York and Henry Cabot Lodge of Massachusetts. In the end, Goldwater won; his campaign combined the use of primaries (though he did not win them all) with a sophisticated plan to energize activists to win delegates in non-primary states by either challenging or converting state parties as they allocated those delegates. The plan was to win with supporters running for precinct and county party positions and thus to take over the machinery of the party locally, and then use that mechanism to control delegate selections in largely non-primary states. We should further note that Goldwater's nomination saw an influx of what have been called "amateurs," as opposed to party regulars, and in some ways gave a glimpse of the world that would emerge later.[10] These amateurs believed that "the parties would become sources of program and agents of social change" rather than "neutral agents which mobilize majorities for whatever candidates and programs seem best suited to capturing public fancy. . . . The amateur asserts that principles, rather than interest, ought to be both the end and motive of political action."[11] This contrasted sharply with the "professionals," who believed in "maintaining the party as an ongoing organization and not simply as an instrument for accomplishing certain policy objectives."[12] Of course, amateurs and professionals are stereotypes that don't quite perfectly describe any one individual.

Overall, the 1960s looked to be a continuation of the world forged in the early part of the century. Party elites were largely in control, and the hunt for nomination occurred in "the underground battle for delegates," as *New York Times* reporter James Reston aptly wrote in 1968.[13] Nonetheless, primaries assigned some delegates and also, more importantly, functioned as important indicators of popularity for some candidates who felt the need to contest them. Indeed, the primaries might be said to have two audiences: voters in the primary state and party leaders around the country. Winning over the first audience was essential, but only as a step in winning over the second audience.[14] As Theodore White observed, about the 1960 Democratic contest,

> For John F. Kennedy and Hubert Humphrey there was no other than the primary way to the Convention. If they could not at the primaries prove their strength in the hearts of Americans, the Party bosses would cut their hearts out in the back rooms of Los Angeles.[15]

In Kennedy's case, his religion was at issue and he had to win primaries to show party leaders that he could appeal to voters, particularly in a Protestant-dominated state, to prove his bona fides to those leaders. Thus, for Kennedy, winning the West Virginia primary was absolutely essential—there were few Catholics in West Virginia. To underline just how subtle the entire system was, Kennedy had a month earlier won the Wisconsin primary. But he had lost all the key Protestant counties in the state, and this caused party leaders in other states to hold off their support until he won the West Virginia primary.[16] Still, other candidates felt free to bypass primaries altogether. Then-Senate Majority Leader Lyndon Johnson was a serious contender for the Democratic nomination in 1960, yet he made no effort to compete in any of the fifteen primaries that year.[17] Indeed, in some ways competing in primaries could be seen as a sign of weakness—an imperative to offer evidence to party leaders that one was popular enough to win an election. Some candidates, such as Johnson, believed that he didn't need to offer such confirmation of electability.[18] Besides, Johnson expected "that other candidates would kill each other off in those primaries."[19]

Democrats and Democracy in Turmoil

By the end of the decade, however, this political world would be shattered and transformed in stunning ways. With the reforms adopted in the early 1970s, the selection of presidential candidates would never again give primacy to party professionals in their capacities as gatekeepers to potential nominees and consolidators of political support. The parties themselves would be altered into something radically new. Candidates would turn their attention to the voters—if not exclusively, then close to it—rather than other party leaders. Party elites would no longer control the nomination process and the voters would decide the allocation of delegates and determine whom each party would nominate. The Progressive dream of a more direct democracy would reach its logical conclusion. Voters would firmly take center stage and party professionals receded in importance. While the methods of selecting candidates for president held steady through the sixties, events culminating in Democrat Hubert Humphrey's presidential nomination in 1968 led directly to significant reforms that would shape the era of the 1970s to the present day.

Despite the apparent normality in which the decade began, discontent was in the air. In 1960 college students and political activists created Students for a Democratic Society (SDS). The very name of the organization underlines both the political and democratic yearnings of many. In 1962 that group issued its famous manifesto, *The Port Huron Statement*. It was a central document in the rise of the New Left that so animated politics in the 1960s. Largely written by the activist Tom Hayden, it opened with the observation, "We are people of this generation, bred in at least modest comfort, housed now in universities, looking uncomfortably to the world we inherit."[20] The discomfort they felt was based on what they perceived as political apathy and rampant materialism in American life. There was a strong critique of what they saw as the failings of capitalism and the consumerism that obsessed Americans. They were particularly upset by the engineered apathy created by those in power—"Apathy, we came to suspect, was what the administrators and power technicians actually desired," as Tom Hayden later wrote.[21] They saw problems, such as civil rights and the Cold War, not being addressed. Just as important in their analysis was that they saw the problems as linked—the Cold War, poverty, and racism should not be seen as distinct policy problems to be dealt with individually. The solution, so reminiscent of the Progressives half a century earlier, was more democratic participation by the people. More democracy will solve the problems of democracy. The underlying assumption of *The Port Huron Statement* was that the people desperately wanted to be political but they were thwarted by the system.[22] Echoing the ideas of John Dewey, the philosopher of twentieth century democracy, the manifesto insisted that "the search for truly democratic alternatives to the present, and a commitment to social experimentation with them, is a worthy and fulfilling human enterprise, one which moves us and, we hope, others today."[23] The new political world the SDS envisioned was one of a highly participatory democracy—"we seek the establishment of a democracy of individual participation."[24] Indeed, participatory democracy was not just a good method of politics—politics itself was essential to finding meaning in life. *The Port Huron Statement* comes close to Aristotle's observation about man being a political animal. The authors write, "politics has the function of bringing people out of isolation and into community, thus being a necessary, though not sufficient, means of finding meaning in personal life." And they were interested in spreading democracy far beyond selecting officials to run the government. They wanted to reform not just traditional politics in a more participatory, democracy way. They wanted to change corporations, college campuses, religious institutions. In short, they wanted democracy everywhere and to create "decentralized decision-making, remaking the world from the bottom up."[25]

One of the barriers to that possible new world was the political parties themselves. The Democrats and Republicans were major contributors to the problem—in large measure because they led to a political stalemate that stubbornly refused to offer real change. They did not offer meaningful choice and they remained fixed to old ideas and ways of doing things. While we do not suggest that all, or even most, college students were so politically engaged, *The Port Huron Statement* was indicative of the tenor of the times and a harbinger of things to come.[26] As political scientist Samuel Huntington wrote, "the 1960s witnessed a dramatic renewal of the democratic spirit in America."[27] And this renewal was based in part in questioning traditional authority in many American institutions—including the political parties and their customary ways of doing things. Furthermore, many of the figures associated with *The Port Huron Statement*—most notably Hayden—would figure prominently in later events of the decade, most famously for the events addressed here: the 1968 Democratic Convention. He was there "bringing the war home" to American and the establishment.[28]

Of course, it wasn't just students and activists who had complaints about how the system worked. James MacGregor Burns observed at the time,

> Behind the fascination with political personalities and election gladiators there is in this country, I think, a vast boredom with politics. Because it had failed to engage itself with the problems that dog us during our working days and haunt our dreams at night, politics has not engaged the best of us, or at least the best in us. If people seem complacent or inert, the cause lies less in them than in our political system that evades and confuses the real issues.[29]

For Burns, the problem in particular was the unresponsive nature of the two-party system—which was really four parties housed in two. Burns believed that our system was strikingly "static" and resistant to change.[30] Other academics, such V. O. Key, saw a system where the "voters are not fools"; Key discerned "an electorate moved by concern about the central and relevant questions of public policy, of government performance, and of executive personality."[31] But Key's voice was drowned out by the much louder voices criticizing the system as inherently undemocratic.

The decade was, of course, rocked by tragic events—President Kennedy's assassination, the slaying of his brother Robert, and of Dr. Martin Luther King. The Civil Rights movement grew in intensity and, under King's leadership, employed nonviolent protests to great effect. However, those frustrated by the lack of progress often employed violence, ignoring King's admonitions of peace. There were numerous riots, and they were most intense in the wake of King's murder. At the same time, the US was embroiled in an apparently intractable war in Vietnam that divided the nation. The twinned issues of the Vietnam War and civil rights shook America in fundamental ways and made the decade dramatic, tragic, *and* hopeful. Many people, particularly the young, were frustrated but engaged. After the political somnolent '50s, the '60s was a decade of intense political activity—possibly too intense for some. It is against this complex political and social background that the Democratic Party found itself facing the 1968 election.

There are a number of reasons we look primarily to the Democratic Party, as opposed to the Republicans, in this chapter. We should recall that at this time the Democrats were clearly the dominant party. If realignment theory is correct, the country was aligned Democratic and had been since the election of 1932.[32] It was not that Republicans couldn't win, but all things being equal (which, of course, is never the case) the Democrats were more likely to control government. From 1932 until 1968 the Democrats had controlled both chambers of Congress thirty-two out of thirty-six years and the presidency twenty-eight out of thirty-six years. Only a war hero such as General Dwight Eisenhower could apparently break the Democrats' control of the White House. The Democrats defined the political agenda and the direction of the political world, and the Republicans were usually in a reactive mode. Even if one is skeptical of realignment theory, the Democrats entered 1968 in control of the presidency and both chambers of Congress (and by fairly comfortable margins). Furthermore, they had won the 1960 and 1964 presidential elections—1964 itself had been an epic landslide and a seeming repudiation of conservatism. Among the general populace, voters were much more inclined to identify as Democrats than Republican. In 1968, for instance, 55 percent of Americans identified as either "strong Democrats," "weak Democrats," or "leaning Democrat." The corresponding total for Republicans was 33 percent. The remainder were independents. (In 1964, the split between the parties was even starker: 60 percent to 30 percent.)[33] We also focus on the Democrats because, as we shall see, events in that party, along with its efforts at self-reform, initiated changes in both parties. The Democrats led the way (not always wittingly) in creating the political world that exists today. Furthermore, "state legislatures, in revising their statues to bring them into conformity with national Democratic Party rules, frequently adopted the same or similar rules for both Democrats and Republicans."[34] The Republicans, thus, largely followed suit whether they really wanted to or not.

That said, Democrats convened in Chicago in 1968 a party at war with itself. Vietnam led the issues that divided the party, though civil rights was also highly contentious.[35] President Johnson's decision not to run for reelection had thrown open the field, and Senator Eugene McCarthy (who had actually challenged for the nomination before Johnson decided not to run) and Senator Robert Kennedy had crisscrossed the nation battling it out in state primaries. McCarthy, an early and vehement opponent of the war, was joined by Kennedy, a somewhat later entrant to the race, and both established themselves as candidates of peace.[36] Altogether, five different people won primaries in 1968, but the real battle in the primary phase was between Kennedy and McCarthy. All the while, in the background Vice President Hubert Humphrey, after President Johnson made his dramatic decision to not seek reelection, chose not to contest the primaries and sought the nomination via convincing party leaders in various states to back him. He felt no need to get delegates via primaries. For instance, Eugene McCarthy received almost 72 percent of the vote in the Pennsylvania Primary. However, the Democratic State Party Committee awarded Humphrey two-thirds of the state's delegates.[37] Humphrey was also part of the administration and, thus, tied to its war policies. His private requests to separate himself from the administration's war positions were emphatically rejected by President Johnson.[38] In fact, Humphrey's attempts to distance himself from the war infuriated the president and made him doubt that Humphrey was even fit to be president. Robert Kennedy's assassination on June 4th, the night of his triumph in the California primary, fractured and wounded the party even further.

It is far from clear what chance Kennedy actually had for the nomination—he was behind Humphrey in most contemporary delegate counts. Humphrey had benefited by strong support from the unions and many important state party leaders; AFL-CIO president George Meany and United Steelworkers union president I. W. Abel endorsed him immediately after he announced his candidacy.[39] Still, had Kennedy lived, it seems likely the convention would have been more closely contested. In the event, Humphrey easily won the nomination on the first ballot and had the support of almost three times the delegates of his nearest rival, Senator McCarthy.

However, to say that Humphrey won the nomination easily is both literally true and fundamentally inaccurate. What transpired in Chicago that August is now the stuff of political legend. As Norman Mailer later wrote, in his account of the convention, "It was possible that one was at the edge of that watershed year from which the country might never function well again."[40] Anti-war protesters, along with radicals and protesters of many other stripes, converged on the city and entered what was virtually an armed camp. The convention hall was encircled by barbed wire. Democratic mayor Richard Daley was openly hostile to the protesters, putting the city's police and members of the National Guard on alert. Daley was virtually a textbook example of the old-school big-city boss (and, in actuality, one of the last of a dying breed).⁴¹ "As long as I am mayor of this town there will be law and order in Chicago," he declared.⁴² One historian has written that the way the mayor handled the convention "was a last cry of the old, crude, boss-dominated, national politics Daley represented."⁴³ And the case can be made that, while protesters would have shown up no matter where the Democrats held their convention, the mayor and his method of politics were particularly disliked by many and acted as a magnet.

> Nothing rallies a political movement like an appealing enemy, and Daley seemed to be the perfect embodiment of the establishment that the anti-war moment was fighting. . . . As boss of a machine that thrived on patronage, corruption, and voter theft, he stood for everything they disdained about the old political order. . . . And Daley's authoritarianism was the antithesis of the libertarian spirit that animated the anti-war movement.⁴⁴

The fact that Daley was actually against the war mattered little—he was, to the protesters, as much a symbol of what was wrong with the country as anything else.

Protesters were limited to Grant Park, which incensed them, and the city was the scene of frequent clashes between the police and demonstrators. Things grew quite ugly when the Democratic Party, after a raucous debate, came out in support of the administration's position on the war and a clear rejection to proposals by the more "peace" oriented delegates. As word reached the amalgam of protesters in the streets of what had transpired at the convention, confrontations between police and demonstrators erupted.⁴⁵ A later federal commission that investigated the events termed what happened a *police riot*.⁴⁶ Inside the convention hall things were also rancorous among the delegates, if less violent.

> Delegates literally fought each other for access to the microphones stationed around the floor, as credentials and platform battles spun quickly out of control. Party officials grabbed reporters and vented anger about this or that injustice. . . . The convention organizers tried in vain to keep order.⁴⁷

For all the drama outside the convention hall there was chaos inside as well. Much of this can be traced back to the impossible situation Humphrey was in. He was supported by many, but enthusiastically by few.

Southerners didn't like him, though he was preferable to what they saw as the more extreme candidates. Until almost the end, Humphrey feared President Johnson somehow reentering the race. The vice president wanted to distance himself from the war, be loyal to the president, appeal to the old guard but find a way to talk to the younger generation. The task would have taken a political magician of the first order and Humphrey, for all his many skills, was not at that level.[48]

The 1968 Democratic Convention in some sense brought together a number of forces that simply overwhelmed Humphrey the man and the Democratic Party as an institution. On one level, the broader policy questions were the war and civil rights. But on another level these conflicts were met with intense debates about political procedure and party structure. There were numerous battles over rules and credentials. The unit rule, which required a state delegation to vote together, was subject to debate, and Humphrey chose to be silent on the question. (It was about the future, and Humphrey was more concerned with securing the nomination now.) Eventually the convention adopted the minority report from the Rules Committee that ended the unit rule and called for changes in the nomination process in the future. (This led directly to the McGovern-Fraser Commission.) At the time, the importance of this was not recognized, and Walter Cronkite deemed it "a technical matter."[49] As we shall see, it was much more than that.

More dramatic was the fight in the Credentials Committee. Humphrey could afford to ignore future rules, but he needed votes in the present. McCarthy challenged a number of delegations. The 1964 convention had, when faced with a fight over the Mississippi delegation, said that for future conventions, states had to have delegations that were formed "regardless of race, color, creed, or national origin." The Southern delegations in 1968 certainly did not reflect that ideal. The problem was that Humphrey couldn't allow all those delegations, a base of his support, to be disqualified. However, he couldn't be seen as rejecting the ideal. Humphrey's forces on the committee did agree with the challenge to the Mississippi delegation and were willing to reach on a compromise concerning Georgia. But they held firm on the other delegations and won the floor fights on those delegations.[50] Humphrey's wins on credentials solidified his control of the convention and showed that he was in control. But these wins also revealed fissures in the party that would have to be dealt with at some point.

In the end, Humphrey secured the nomination. Yet, as he was being nominated by African American Mayor Carl Stokes of Cleveland, NBC cut back and forth to footage of the riots in the streets. What Humphrey, a supporter of civil rights since the 1940s, had hoped would be the wonderful symbolism of a black elected official nominating him to the highest office was ruined. As Theodore White wrote, "and Stokes' dark face is being wiped from the nation's view to show blood—Hubert Humphrey being nominated in a sea of blood."[51] As author Rick Perlstein aptly put it, in his acclaimed work *Nixonland,* "Hubert Humphrey wins the Democratic nomination. But is he leading a party, or a civil war?"[52]

The anger felt by political activists at being shut out of the nominating process—again, recall that Humphrey had not contested a single primary—led to a call for reform. To his critics, Humphrey would always symbolize how liberalism chose "opportunism" over principle.[53] "In fact, 25% of the delegates to the Democratic convention in 1968 had been chosen in 1967," as Kamarck points out.[54] The impetus for change had actually started before the convention. In June of 1968, McCarthy got only nine out of forty-four delegates, under the normal processes, in Connecticut. Those nine and others met and worked on a plan to challenge what they believed was an unfair process of selecting delegates. In haste they created what became known as the Hughes Commission (for then Iowa governor Harold Hughes, who chaired the commission). Although this was a private commission, they were able to put together a report—*Democratic Choice*—and have it published prior to the convention and have its findings presented to the Rules Committee of the convention. Many party leaders immediately saw the danger this report posed to the traditional ways of doing things; however, they were not able to stop it.[55] Still, later, the Hughes Commission report would remain a key resource for the McGovern-Fraser Commission in its work on reform.[56]

One normally would not expect a nominee to accept changes to the method that got him the nomination; however, that is exactly what happened. Largely to mollify critics and unite the party, Humphrey had not opposed proposals to change the way delegates were selected, and the convention approved a report that called for such reforms. "Many people thought this was the way to throw the liberals a bone, plus the fact that nobody understood it," Democratic Party activist Anne Wexler observed. Wexler was the primary author of the Rules Committee minority report—based in large measure on the Hughes Commission report—that recommended changes to the way delegates were selected. The minority report was actually adopted by the full convention.[57] Delegates in Chicago probably didn't think they were approving major changes to the system.[58] They most likely thought they were changing the so called "unit rule"—the rule that meant a majority vote in a state delegation bound the entire delegation and created a unanimous state vote—and not much else. In reality, the other part of the report, calling for a more democratic process in selecting delegates, was much more important.

Depending on your outlook, it is fitting or ironic that this last hurrah for the traditional way of doing things transpired in Chicago, the last true haven of machine politics. Mayor Daley, one of the last and fiercest of the old type of party bosses, presided over the death of one kind of politics and was present at the conception of a new form of politics (though he was probably not aware of either the death or the conception). What shape that new form would take was still quite unclear, however.

After the election, Senator Fred Harris, from Oklahoma, chair of the Democratic National Committee, appointed a committee to make recommendations for reforming the system and this led to changing much, much more than the "unit rule." The resolution that called for reform and established a Commission suggested

> to study the relationship between the National Democratic Party and its constituent State Democrats Parties, in order that full participation of all Democrats, regardless of race, color, creed or national origin may be facilitated by uniform standards for structure and operation.[59]

This charge from the convention seems to be largely about dealing with race and ethnicity. Even defenders of the Democratic Party structures knew that such issues needed to be addressed. Little did they know the issues of race would be overshadowed by a demand to reconstruct the Democratic Party entirely.

Officially, this group was titled the Committee on Party Structure and Delegate Selection. However, it came to be known by the two men who led it—Senator George McGovern of South Dakota and Representative Donald Fraser of Minnesota. Hence, one of the most consequential reforms in party history and one that, effectively, gave birth to the arrangements by which both parties now select presidential nominees came to be known as the McGovern-Fraser Commission.[60]

Reforming the Democratic Party (and Everything Else): The McGovern-Fraser Commission

All of the machinations for reform at the convention might not have led to anything. Calls for reform might have ended up a dead letter. However, that was not to be the case. Various groups with different motivations—

overlapping but distinct groups of pro-McCarthy, anti-Vietnam, pro-reform, and anti-Humphrey activists and others had found each other during the convention and saw a chance to change the Democratic Party in fundamental ways. It may have been nothing more than a sense that if they couldn't get the Democratic Party to stop the Vietnam War they could focus their energies on reforming the party. Still, some were genuinely committed to finding new ways of doing politics. Whatever their initial motivations, they came around to reaching for a new goal: participatory democracy in the nomination process. This is quite striking since, as Philip Klinker points out, there were serious policy issues that could have been considered.

> Instead of implementing a policy response that might have reached out to the ten million people who voted for Wallace for ideological reasons, the Democrats focused on a procedural response that would accommodate that portion of the three million McCarthy voters who had stayed home or voted for Humphrey's opponents because of their dissatisfaction with the nomination process.[61]

It was not that ideology or policy meant nothing to the reformers. Many had strong policy beliefs; however, they coalesced around the need for procedural reforms as the key answer to the question—how should the party respond to the 1968 defeat? As a key staffer for the commission, Ken Bode, remarked, "Almost every argument made was based on 1968."[62]

In some sense this is not surprising—discussing policy was inherently divisive in a party that had members with such widely different takes on key issues. Further, appeals to democracy have great rhetorical power in the US and resonate with fundamental values of most Americans. As Geraldine Joseph, vice-chair of the Democratic National Committee, said of the reformers, "They had all the good words. They had all the things we say we believe in."[63] Almost thirty years earlier, E. E. Schattschneider had argued that "democracy is not to be found in the parties but between the parties."[64] Such a statement would be anathema to the reformers.

The commission that changed the Democratic Party felt a deep sense of concern. The very comforting perception of the legitimacy of the nominating process that Gerald Pomper had seen in the middle of the 1960s was now emphatically less clear. In guidelines prepared for the commission, Yale law professor Alexander Bickel and University of Chicago historian Richard Wade wrote with alarm that "the chief danger to the continued stability of the American political system is the erosion among some groups . . . of a sense of the legitimacy of the system's decisions and choices."[65] This sense of urgency provided the backdrop against which the commission did its work. We should not forget that the reform movement was radically transforming a party that had nominated Franklin Roosevelt, Harry Truman, John F. Kennedy, and Lyndon Johnson.[66] The Democrats had suffered a very disappointing loss in 1968, but cooler heads might have looked back on a run of success that started in 1932.

What is even more important to understand is that the commission selected by Harris was strongly inclined to make significant changes to the nomination process. Furthermore, the staff who did the research and presented the proposed changes were even more emphatically reform minded.[67] Indeed, staff members were suspicious of any deviation from a complete overhaul of the party. Senator Harris himself was viewed almost as the enemy. This is all the more striking when one considers that the directive they had from the 1968 convention was less than clear. What kind of authority did the commission have to make demands that the party change itself? Should they study, recommend, urge, or frankly demand changes to how the party operated? However, despite some debates about these issues among commissioners, in the end they charged ahead with sweeping demands that the party reform itself. In fact, the report claimed it was authorized by the 1968 convention to do its work; thus, it did not need approval from the DNC or any other party apparatus, and its changes in how delegates would be selected were mandatory for state parties. (It is one of the hallmarks of conventions that they held a kind of sovereignty over the party as a whole. Hence, the commission claiming authorization from the convention meant it did not feel beholden to follow the wishes of the national committee.) The greatest transformation of the nomination process since the development of the conventions themselves in the 1830s occurred in a few short months.[68]

Their task was made easier because the one force that might stand up for the old way of doing business—labor, which had a seat on the commission—effectively bowed out of the commission early on after rightly perceiving that the final product would be hostile to labor's interest.[69] This is quite striking, since unions had been a foundational force in the Democratic Party going back decades and had done extraordinary work in boosting Humphrey's chances in 1968. They believed, probably correctly, that it was labor that held the party together in 1968, almost delivering a victory in trying circumstances. But to the commission staff, labor and the traditional party were seen as the enemy. As one staff member recounted, "There was much more enmity toward the DNC than toward the Republicans among the reformers."[70] We will never know for sure, if labor had stayed active on the commission, what might have happened. It seems unlikely that the unions could have stopped the overall thrust of the reforms—too many commissioners and virtually all the staff were too committed for that. But they might have softened and modified some of the proposals.

In the end, the report called for numerous changes. But the most important and controversial ones involved taking affirmative steps to represent blacks, women, and youth in state delegations; taking steps to eliminate "closed caucuses" and making such meetings open to the public; ending the unit rule; forbidding ex officio delegates in caucuses and conventions; ending proxy voting; and requiring primary states to "identify the presidential preferences of candidates for delegates."[71] The main thrust of those changes can be summarized in three points:

1. Grassroots participation in the process of selecting delegates
2. Proportionality in the allocation of delegates
3. The supremacy of the national party in setting the rules

What is immediately striking is that the original call from the convention had, arguably, focused on issues of exclusion based on "race, color, creed, or national origin." Yet the staff, while certainly cognizant of this, largely focused on participation and their own notions of what democracy should look like.[72] When the staff's ideas were presented to the commission there was pushback on this and a deeper concern about issues of race, and importantly gender, but this didn't stop the overall focus from being on a more participatory system of selecting delegates and on the need to end winner-take-all primaries, which were quite common.[73]

In fact, a focus on highly participatory processes was bound to favor the middle and upper classes, which had the time and wherewithal to involve themselves in such lengthy proceedings, and which were whiter than working-class people.[74] This problem seemed to cause more consternation among the commissioners than among the staff—the latter saw it as regrettable but no reason not to forge ahead with their preferred abstract theory of proper democracy. They were in the thrall of Achen and Bartels's "folk theory" of democracy and held the belief that the "cure for the ills of democracy is more democracy."[75] In the end, the commission decided that certain targets concerning race, gender, and age should be kept in mind as future state delegations were created. When the report moved toward the implementation stage, the issue of demographics would reemerge, and women's groups in particular fought for stricter requirements for representation in delegations that would eventually prevail.[76] Still, a strong case can be made that while the new process had the potential to be more democratic, it was more likely to result in the replacement of one elite with another.[77]

We should also note that what the reformers wanted was participatory caucuses—not the closed caucuses that party regulars used to control delegation selection *and* not primaries. This may be surprising given the rise of primaries, but that was not the intention of these reforms. The simple fact was that participatory caucuses would benefit the types of people—middle- and upper-class whites—who had the time to engage in lengthy caucuses and the policy inclinations that the reformers liked.[78] Of course, the staff would probably defend themselves by arguing that the quality of participation in caucuses was inherently superior to simply pulling a lever in state primary.[79] This again harkens back, consciously or not, to the notions articulated in *The Port Huron Statement* about the true nature of democracy. The hope, which never materialized, was high-minded debate about the issues and thoughtful deliberation about which candidate was best. This would occur at the local and state level and culminate in the utopia of a thoughtful national convention.[80] This would best be achieved in a new kind of robust caucus system and not primaries. Primaries do nothing to perpetuate the kind political dialogue, the almost Aristotelian version of politics, that so many reformers wanted.

The third point, on having national rules, followed logically from the first two. If real democracy, in the terms the commission wanted, was to exist, then states had to fall in line and follow national rules. The decentralized nature of the parties had to end. In some ways this was the biggest change and challenge to the commission. Heretofore, the national Democratic and Republican parties had actually been the creations of the states' parties, who were largely allowed to do as they pleased. In some ways, one could view the national conventions as meeting of the confederation of Democratic and Republican state parties. With the suggested reforms the power would shift emphatically to the national party.[81] This shift was later sanctioned legally by the Supreme Court in *Cousins v. Wigoda*, where the court held, "The states themselves have no constitutional mandated role in the great task of the selection of the Presidential and Vice-Presidential candidates."[82]

We don't mean to suggest that the commission and staff were in fundamental disagreement. However, as Bryon Shafer makes quite clear in his definitive account of the commission, *Quiet Revolution*, the staff largely drove the agenda and brought the commission to its point of view more often than not. If Shafer is right, the McGovern-Fraser Commission is virtually a textbook case of the power of staff under the right circumstances. In this case, the commissioners all had other things to do besides their work on the commission and could only give it some of the attention it deserved. The staff was permanent and focused intently on only the matters at hand. Furthermore, the staff was largely made up of people who believed in a theory of participatory democracy and, just as important, held no affection for the customary ways of doing things.[83] They had a vision of what they wanted, and the actual commissioners rarely seemed to think about how that would affect the party as a party.[84] They were a cohesive group that pushed relentlessly for wide ranging reforms and with little to no regard for anything that deviated even slightly from their theory of democracy. This was, to use James Q. Wilson's terminology, the triumph of the amateurs. As Wilson astutely observes,

> political amateurs in this country . . . are vitally interested in mechanisms to ensure the intra-party accountability of officeholders and party leaders. They are concerned with repealing the iron law of oligarchy as described by Michels, and for his reasons: unless party leaders are responsive to the party rank and file, they well be corrupted by the rewards of office and compromised by their participation in the government. . . . The concern for policy implies a concern for mechanism, such as intra-party democracy, to ensure that the correct policy is followed.[85]

All through the document were demands that party officials, particularly state officials, not have ex officio status as delegates. (The staff wanted to go as far as simply banning party officials altogether from the convention, and this became a continual source of conflict between the proposals and the party regulars.) It is quite striking that Wilson's point that good policy would simply follow democratized party procedures seems to be implicitly accepted by reformers.[86] On this point they were both right and wrong. They were right that eventually the party moved to adopt solidly left policy positions. They were wrong, though, in the party's ability to then win over enough voters to take the White House. The Democrats would lose, in landslides, four of the next five presidential elections. This possibility seems not to have occurred to reformers but is something the old party establishment would have considered more closely.[87] Of course, the reasons for these losses are open to much debate, but it does seem that the reforms may have contributed to those losses—and certainly didn't help.

The upshot of their way of thinking led to the rather bizarre aim, embodied in the report, "at isolating the party itself from what was . . . the party's nomination."[88] One party regular from Pennsylvania, Joseph Barr, said with obvious disgust, "They agreed to let us sit with the delegation, if we weren't elected. Can you imagine that? They, people who had never given a damn for the party, were telling us we could sit with our party."[89] One can be outraged by the obvious abuses that occurred under the old system and still understand party regulars like Barr being offended by the arrogance of the reformers. Throughout the process many of the reformers were suspicious of anyone with long association with the institutional structures of the Democratic Party, pushed for the most extreme changes, and grew almost paranoid when things slowed down during implementation. Ironically, sometimes in the implementation stage, where states were trying to rewrite their rules to be in compliance with the new national reforms, the reformers would engage in the kind of practices they derided (for instance holding meetings where opponents to reform would not be able to attend).[90] In hindsight it is quite apparent that reform was moving inexorably forward and any caution that occurred was quite normal in trying to balance the various forces and centers of power within the party. In fact, one should actually be impressed by the speed and scope of the reforms rather than be concerned by the caution and deliberation that did manifest.

Reform was undertaken by people who were, at best, weakly loyal to the party and, at most, actively hostile to it. For many on the staff, it is probably the case that they saw the Democratic Party as a convenient vehicle to further their ideas about democracy and, eventually, certain policy preferences. The virtues of moderation and compromise that the party had once held were derided by the reformers and seen as vices.[91] Tom Hayden wrote that *The Port Huron Statement* envisioned "the realignment of the Democratic Party into a progressive instrument."[92] This was to be the realization of the Progressives' ultimate goals—and if the details were different, the reforms undertaken were certainly "in the spirit of the earlier Progressive reforms."[93] The notion that a party could be anything more than ideologically oriented (if we include a devotion to participatory democracy as an ideological stance itself—which is some sense it surely is) appeared *relatively* unimportant to many on the commission and alien to virtually all of the staff. There is also the fact that three of the commissioners—Senators

George McGovern, Birch Bayh, and Harold Hughes—were contemplating running for president in 1972 and had to be seen as sympathetic to reform. In the case of Senator Hughes, the sympathy for reform was not calculated in any way—he was enthusiastically in favor of it. And Jamie Sanchez Jr. argues that to a significant degree most of the commissioners were, in their own way, fearful about the legitimacy crisis the Democratic Party faced and the need for serious reform.[94]

More broadly, it should be noted that the political environment in which all this took place provided fertile ground for reform. Democratic National Committee official Geraldine Joseph said, "You have to remember that mind-set for reform. . . . Those who feel most strongly about the thing are those who will get out for it. Those who were against it weren't really, *really* against it."[95] Press coverage, though not extensive, tended to be pro-reform.[96] However, the press, as is their normal practice, looked for conflict, found it, and exaggerated it to show that reform might not prevail.[97] There were, of course, the adamant reformers we have discussed. Members and staff of the commission had numerous allies—of varying degrees of intensity—throughout the country. We should also not forget that in doing its work, the commission found numerous examples of disturbing behavior by state committees. They held many hearings around the country and received testimony that could make even party regulars blush. The commissioners heard, for example, of a precinct meeting that had been adjourned before normal wage earners could attend; they learned of a district meeting that had been held in the locked basement of a local party leader; they even encountered a precinct caucus that had been convened on a moving bus.[98]

There were also states where no duplicity needed to be used—the rules simply allowed remarkably undemocratic procedures in creating a delegation. In Georgia, for instance, the state party chairman, with the consent of the governor, just handpicked the delegates.[99] And no one, party regulars and conservatives included, wanted a replay of the 1968 convention. That convention had seen an enormous number of credential fights over seating delegates. Even party regulars saw the need for some reforms and standards so has not to have those fights recur in 1972.

So, the makeup of the Democratic Party at large, in 1970, was probably a significant minority who were very strongly in favor of reform; another minority group who were decidedly hostile to reform, but could rarely decide how exactly to fight back; and a plurality who were less enthusiastic about reform, but at least saw the need for something to be done. Of course, the specifics of that something was open to debate; however, there was little chance of nothing happening in the efforts to reform the Democratic Party. The anger among Democrats was palpable in the country and, just being quite practical about matters, people were not contributing to the party and finances were dire.[100] The financial situation was so urgent the party actually held a telethon to raise funds.[101] The only question was how extensive these reforms would be. The report was, overall, pushing the more extensive end of the spectrum when it came to change—although, even with that, there were activists who thought the report was not radical enough.

Of course, issuing a report, even one that claims the authority of party law, is only one step. The demands or recommendations (never quite clear to anyone, except most of the commission and its staff, who saw their report as binding on the states as soon as it was published) needed to be implemented. And for the next year that was a source of much debate among the various stakeholders—the commission itself, the Democratic National Committee, various state parties, and activists throughout the country. There was a great deal of back and forth between the national party and the people associated with the McGovern-Fraser committee and the various state parties. As one would expect, there were fifty-five unique responses (fifty states, Washington DC, and four territories). Furthermore, in many cases any reforms had to deal with state laws and could not simply be imposed by party command. Some states, such as Minnesota, were eager to comply, and others, such as Texas, were actively hostile to reform.[102]

Central to implementing these reforms was the fact the DNC, and its head Larry O'Brien (who returned to replace Fred Harris in March of 1970), were in favor of reform. And, despite the belief by some that the commission did not need the approval of the DNC, the reality was that the DNC was necessary to enacting these suggested changes. O'Brien may not have been as zealous as the McGovern-Fraser Commission and staff were; however, he did back reform, and his actions, and the respect he had from party regulars, were key in getting things done. Throughout the process of implementing the commission's proposals, O'Brien was extremely adroit in his maneuverings and perceptive about what arguments would sway the different factions within the party. Whatever else he thought, O'Brien was keen to unify the party, thought reform was necessary, and decided that the best way to do that was to support the broad thrust of the McGovern-Fraser recommendations and work to bring party regulars aboard.[103]

Reform was further helped along by the 1970 midterm elections, which brought a net gain of eleven new Democratic governors. Governors are almost always seen as the leader of the party in their state, and many of these new governors were either pro-reform on principle or saw a political value in being perceived as pro-reform.[104] Finally, reform was helped by how relatively quiet the established party regulars were. When the DNC adopted virtually all of the proposed changes, R. W. Apple, reporting in *The New York Times*, wrote, "The party conservatives said nothing as the McGovern proposals were approved."[105] Throughout the process of adopting the McGovern-Fraser Commission proposals, the conservatives (in the sense of defending the traditional party, not necessarily connected to policy outcomes) won various battles but lost the war and lost it decisively. In part, it is probable that it was a combination of not realizing how great were the changes pending in the reform proposals and the belief that party customs would soften any potential great changes when put into practice. As Joseph California, then a key staffer for the DNC, later wrote,

> But even those Democratic party leaders involved in the presidential quest believed that the newly established McGovern-Fraser Commission procedures would be of little significance. They assumed that the rules of the presidential nomination game would basically be the same. . . . Their failure to appreciate the depth of the procedural revolution reflected in the new rules left them standing, mouths open, shocked into political impotency during the pre-convention and convention rites in Washington and in Miami in 1972.[106]

The old party was barely breathing by 1972 and would be dead before the 1976 campaign began. For some that was the whole point. The idea was to destroy that old guard and to move the party forward into becoming a more democratic and inclusive party. It is certainly true that new people became central to the Democratic Party. Whether that actually enhanced democracy itself is another question.[107]

So, the Democrats reformed their party. And for a variety of reasons, the Republicans largely, though not completely, followed suit. In many ways, both proponents and opponents to these changes were not sure what would happen. And, as we shall see, while the McGovern-Fraser commission achieved its goal of changing the party, it most certainly did not lead to the creation of what they hoped for. Instead of participatory caucuses, primaries became the main vehicle for selecting delegates; states that used caucuses never predominated. Furthermore, while some caucuses do provide some sense of citizen participation as envisioned by the reformers, they had hoped for so much more in the way of citizen involvement. Their model of democracy required not just talk, but political deliberation, and few caucuses exhibit that—though they do provide a public forum for hints of it.

Voters moved to a more central role in selecting nominees. The result, sadly, was not deliberative democracy but a transformation of the parties into new types of institutions that fostered the ideological divides between the parties and weakened them in their traditional role of conducting peer reviews of the candidates. As we shall see, the power of money, the importance of the media, and the necessity of momentum became important in ways they never had been before. Whatever the good intentions of the reformers, the results were far from ideal.

Chapter 7

What Direct Primaries Have Done

In 2018, a little-known candidate, one who was not heralded by media pundits as a "rising star" in Democratic politics, shocked observers by beating an established three-term incumbent, Joe Crowley. Indeed, prognosticators had not mentioned Alexandria Ocasio-Cortez's name even as a dark horse in her campaign against the established Crowley.

Crowley was not only a member of Democratic Party leadership in the House, he was also called "the last of the party bosses" in a nod back to the nineteenth century's political machine era and the likes of Boss Tweed.[1] New York's unique and arcane rules still provide a bevy of positions one can pursue, giving the appearance of a remnant of the machine era if one only looks at an organizational chart. After all, if there are more than a thousand party committee positions available in one New York borough alone, then an observer may take on the impression that the party in question is robust. But Crowley's defeat at the insurgent Ocasio-Cortez's hands was a signal that despite the strong numbers of positions up for election in any given cycle, the party organization is a shadow of its former self. Robust parties would have either strongly contested elections for such seats or an autocratic control mechanism that doled them out to party loyalists. But many of the candidates for these offices had no idea that their party organization had even nominated them.[2] That same party organization, which Crowley ran before and during his time in Congress, was credited with getting him in office and keeping him there. But Ocasio-Cortez's dominant win showed that the party organization that Crowley controlled was not enough to overcome the power of the direct primary. The "Queens machine" was anything but a machine in 2018.

Ocasio-Cortez's upset win shows us the state of the modern party. Despite a significant structure within party organizations, they are meaningless when an individual candidate can build a larger, more motivated, better supported, or simply more effective organization of their own outside of the party. Donald Trump's ascent to the presidency can also be viewed as a companion piece to Ocasio-Cortez's win, as a form of hostile takeover of a political party. Trump was a popular figure, one with great name recognition among the public but with no history of candidacy for office and almost no bona fides within official GOP circles. Trump was able to leverage open primaries, where voters need not even hold allegiance to the party for whose nominee they are voting, to win the Republican nomination.[3]

Trump is in ways an even more salient example of the impact primaries have on parties, because Trump as a candidate was the only candidate for president in thirty-six years to have a net negative evaluation in polls of party leaders. Trump was the most hated of all presidential hopefuls from 1980 to 2016. And yet, the primary system allowed Trump to wrest the nomination from insiders and party preferred candidates like Jeb Bush and Marco Rubio.[4]

Ocasio-Cortez and Trump also exemplify the weakness of the modern party organization, because by winning a primary each went instantly from being outsiders to having control of the party's organization and electioneering mechanisms. Such was especially true of Trump, as the GOP nominee is given the authority to hand-select the chair of the Republican National Committee during their candidacy and presidency. Trump truly went from outsider to party leader overnight. Ocasio-Cortez wrested more control over time, but was in the difficult position of being a party's nominee despite the efforts of the party organization for which she became the nominee.

Trump and Ocasio-Cortez may be as ideologically divergent as two modern-day American political candidates can be, but both share a common role as the disruptor in party politics. And both emerged as disruptors because the mechanism for party nomination decisions, the direct primary, allow them to do so.

Disruption and Decline

With a century of history concerning sub-presidential primaries and nearly fifty years of binding presidential primaries, a detailed picture of the longer-term effects of the direct primary becomes possible. Thus, we turn to examining the effects on American politics generally and political parties as linkage institutions specifically.

First, we should understand the effects of the direct primary on the undergirding philosophy of increasing elements of direct democracy in the United States. Recall from earlier chapters in this work that a unifying philosophy behind the Progressive reforms was the belief that the American public yearned for more opportunities to participate more directly in the governing process. Progressives saw parties, machines, and in-power entities as actively suppressing the governance potential of the general public.

The Progressives did not accept the idea that the constitutional design of American government and the principles of direct democracy are incompatible. The adoption of the direct primary occurred often simultaneously with that of initiative and referendum, especially in the reformist West. Initiative and referendum are not the only exponents of the direct democracy mindset of the Progressives, but they are the most obvious. Taken together, the primary election and initiative/referendum movement violate some of the foundational concepts of American constitutional democracy: the balancing of majority rule with minority rights.[5] They also struck at the heart of shared leadership by elites—ideally, if never perfectly, rational and dispassionate. The framers envisioned a leadership that was responsive, but not beholden, to the people.

We note here first that *majority* and *minority*, in this discussion, simply refer to the number of people on one side or the other of a given public policy issue and not as a substitute for considerations of race. Pure majoritarianism is problematic in any society because that majority can become tyrannical. The designers of the Constitution were very careful to introduce multiple elements of balance between majority rule and minority rights to avoid falling into the autocratic trap, in no small measure because unfettered minority rule was as dangerous to them as monarchy. Demagoguery, violent swings in policy, and corruption were, to the Constitution's authors, part and parcel of unchecked majority rule. The oppressive quality of tyranny was the most obvious threat the framers wished to defeat; however, the impulsive and unpredictable nature of such politics was part of its tyranny and to be avoided at all costs. *Novus ordo seclorum*—a new order of the ages—meant that the capriciousness of tyranny, as much as its potential cruelty and injustice, was to be replaced with a reasonable and fair politics.

Furthermore, the US is a diverse nation. Diverse societies require the consideration of minority interests or risk alienation to the point of homogeneity. Minorities of number (or any identity) must be accommodated and have some modicum of power for heterogeneous societies to operate peacefully. Direct democratic reforms such as the primary, where the public has full and unfettered majority rule, thus represent a violation of those deeply embedded republican principles such as separation of powers and federalism.

Direct democratic reforms also subsume the deliberative, long-term processes of governance to whims of the majoritarian moment. Just as state constitutions with initiative can be changed within a single election year while amending the federal Constitution takes multiple years at least, primaries allow majorities of a moment to upend a generation of incumbent officeholders and eliminate a decade or more of strategic positioning, recruitment, and messaging on behalf of a party's candidates. Direct democratic reforms allow for a more decisive and swift-moving government but at the same time are prone to rash decision-making that can sacrifice long-term stability for momentary passions.[6] The framers of the Constitution were probably aware of numerous examples from the ancient world. The Athenian assembly was famously swayed by the charismatic Alcibiades to launch the disastrous invasion of Sicily. Indeed, although the historical record is debatable, direct democracy has a legacy of, at times, impulsive action that gives pause. As Hamilton asked in *Federalist* no. 6, "Are not popular assemblies frequently subject to the impulse of rage, resentment, jealousy, avarice, and other irregular propensities?."[7] The framers were not ignorant of direct democracy—they explicitly rejected it.

Republican democracy buffers the government from the violent swings of opinion which minorities are prone to take. Having seen oppression of minorities, most of them religious, the Constitution's designers knew that unfettered majority rule of the direct democracy kind would threaten the longevity of a self-governed society. To see the results of direct democracy's failings, one need look no further than California. The US state has become a poster child for the excesses and failures of direct democracy, from the constant threat of recall votes to a flood of initiatives and referenda that confuse voters, suppress turnout, and bloat budgets to crisis proportions.[8] Certainly those ills are not the product of the direct primary alone, but the same philosophy that produced them has put the modern-day political party in a similar position of jeopardy.

The distinction we made earlier regarding the difference between direct and participatory democracy also bears note here. The Progressive advocates for the direct primary did not differentiate between direct and participatory democracy, which led them to believe that increasing the number of direct democratic initiatives would ipso facto enhance participatory democracy.

However, the significant difference between the two has been exposed over time. Participation has not increased commensurate with participatory opportunities, and in fact the increased participation for which the Progressives hoped has not emerged. Furthermore, it is highly debatable whether that participation has been any more rational and deliberative than the earlier system.

Taking the Parties Out

The Progressive reforms did many things, and at a significant cost of unintended consequences. Just as initiative and referendum created problems for republican democracies, so the direct primary went well beyond weakening or ending the urban political party machine. The scope of the Progressive reforms was so great that they affected the entirety of the political party structure, not just the machines. The spillover effect did achieve its intended results of marginalizing the party machines, but it did so at the larger cost of weakening parties themselves for the long term.

Parties are vital linkage institutions in a republican democracy. A functioning and active political party creates the intermediary encouragement to participate that a representative citizen government requires. The Progressives, in their anti-partisan fervor, thought that parties were an impediment to participation rather than one of its main drivers. Thus, the Progressive mindset was not simply to reform parties, but to minimize them. The import of direct, as opposed to participatory, democracy is vital. In a direct democracy, since all citizens participate in decision-making, no intermediary institutions such as parties even need to exist. Progressives thus believed that parties did not even rise to the condition of a necessary evil. Even when parties could not be legislated away, they believed they could be regulated and restricted enough to render them basically useless. And as more direct democracy such as the initiative and referendum took hold, the parties would be gradually seen as a relic of the colonial era and fade into oblivion.[9]

The assumption was based on the idea that parties were expendable, a casualty of the process of evolutionary improvement of human society to which the Progressives strongly adhered. Some of that assumption may derive from the relative youth of parties as well. American political parties, as we understand them today, really didn't exist at the beginning of the republic, and only emerged after the 1820s. Prior to that they were coalitions among elites that, while real, were highly fluid and subject to continual shifts in membership. So, party-based politics was still a reasonably new development at the time of the Progressives. Because there was not a strong extant party culture in America, Progressives saw them as fully expendable.[10] There was always a sense among Progressives that parties were a perversion of the founding itself.

Parties may have been a necessary intermediary during the founding of the Republic, thought the Progressives, but the belief in human progress toward higher ideals would guide the parties slowly to extinction. One of the iconic characters of the era, Theodore Roosevelt, exemplified the Progressive attitude toward direct public participation when saying, "To neglect . . . political duties . . . shows either a weakness or worse than a weakness in a man's character," and admonished listeners to "not become too fastidious, too sensitive to take part in the rough hurly-burly of the actual work of the world." To conclude, Roosevelt admonished the listener, "if you are too timid or too fastidious or too careless to do your part in this work, then you forfeit the right to be considered one of the governing and you become one of the governed."[11]

Roosevelt's point was twofold: first, that the public should generally be more involved in the day-to-day participation of government, and second, perhaps more subtly, that participation in the work of one's government is arduous and difficult, but a prerequisite of a functioning democracy. Relying on intermediary institutions and self-interested others to execute the daily work of political engagement was distasteful, and to some an abrogation of the social progressivism that the movement embodied.[12] To such as Hartz and Weinstein, a more radical democracy was the unattained promise of the Progressive Era.[13]

The Progressive reforms embraced a gradual evolution to direct democracy through the intermediary step of weakening the primary linkage mechanism available to the public—the political party. Weaken the linkage, and the rough-and-ready New American will adapt to the greater participatory needs of governing and improve. The reality of the direct primary, though, would never live up to the promise and expectation of the ideal Progressive society embodied in it.

Effects on the Parties

Political parties are unique in politics, but as organizations they are subject to the same challenges and stimuli that confront any collective group.

Collective action problems, variable leadership, participation, membership, intensity of support, funding, and public sentiment all influence the strength of an organization, and parties are no different. For organizations that had lived with relatively little regulation, though, the major American political parties struggled under the changing environment that the Progressive reforms created.

Leading up to the Progressive Era, partisanship within the electorate was incredibly strong even though it was fairly new to the political milieu.[14] The term *independent* was loaded, as a citizen self-identifying as such was seen as corrupt, willing to sell their vote to the highest bidder: constantly swayed not by higher principles but the whims of the times and the appeal of individual candidates. The first great defender of political parties as a good (as opposed to a necessary evil), Martin Van Buren, argued that without parties politics would be "overrun with personal factions."[15] With luck and skill, the great parties had bound together voters who valued a commitment to something more. They fused together a sense of solidarity with higher principles to forge a team that connected elites to voters. The electoral public were highly loyal to their party and willing to vote. Even accounting for the voter fraud that invariably occurred in this era, voter turnout was high and driven by strong electoral partisanship. Yet there is no doubt the drive to win corrupted Van Buren's ideal image of parties. The party organizations used this loyalty to their advantage, shirking accountability and in part inviting the scrutiny and greater regulation of the Progressive Era. Parties were not ready to adapt to their new environment. As much as the nineteenth century was the era of party-based politics, the twentieth century is the story of American partisan decline.

The term *machine* was certainly apt in describing the partisan politics of the nineteenth century. Strong partisanship, driven not only by ideological loyalty but by employment prospects in government, kept loyalty and mobilization high. That guaranteed turnout also minimized the accountability mechanism that voting provided. Party organizations at the local level were the linchpins of machine politics, so they were as strong as mostly local entities could be. With strangleholds on all government positions of employment, the local party government would have been one of the city's more prominent employers. National parties were such in name only, except for the quadrennial presidential campaigns for which they would ramp up. Parties were strong, but local. In fact, you could argue that we didn't actually have a two-party system. America was defined more by two broad alliances of dozens of state parties. The local machines could fundraise from a tithe of sorts from their employees with vested interests in funding a successful campaign if for no other reason than job security. Loyalty within the party kept things moving, but prevented the influence of outside forces. The parties as a closed system, with internal elites determining the candidates for office the parties would put forward, helped keep the parties unified in message. Party strength owed more to the conditions of which the machines had taken advantage than to a natural connection with the electorate. All of the components of the political landscape combined to build a strong party-based politics. Party machines, and thus the party organizations in which they were embedded, were a means to an end. When the conditions changed, so did the strength of the party machines.

The Progressive reforms, as a package, comprehensively eliminated the conditions upon which the machines were built. The machines, in short, were a combination of spoils-distribution bureaucracy, growth of government as an employer, and electioneering body. Without the ability to dole out jobs from which they would then fundraise, the machines were weakened. Equally important was the reduced power role that internal elites held as the nomination power was taken away. The machines faded, but the parties themselves could have maintained much of their power—perhaps even continued to thrive—had they been able to continue with some of their abilities such as the freedom to nominate candidates.

Machines did fade in the early twentieth century and, with the notable exception of Richard Daley's Chicago, seemed to disappear entirely. Daley's machine was, in reality, just an extraordinary curtain call for a show that was closing. But with the functional eradication of the machines there was a slower aftereffect on the parties as well: gradual weakening. Most of the Progressive reforms focused on internal government operations, such as initiative or merit protections. The one Progressive reform that directly impacted the electorate was the primary election. As such, the direct primary is unique among the Progressive reforms, as it had the most significant effect on elections. In other words, while the party may not have been able to provide jobs any more or serve as an ersatz welfare state, it could at least provide meaningful and consistent slates of candidates to the public. The loss of nomination power took that ability away as well.

The Progressive reforms exposed the inherent weakness of the American party system, leaving piecemeal local organizations with none of the support structure they needed to serve the intermediary role that had built their strength. Parties did not weaken overnight to the level seen in the twenty-first century, of course, but gradually the old vestiges of party politics eroded. Evidence of the gradual decline of parties abounds.

The "Meaningless" Party

An initial sign of the gradual weakening of American parties is found in the study of significant elections throughout American history. Burnham's work on realigning elections provides a sign of party weakness in its discussion of those historically pivotal contests. As Burnham describes, periodically the preferences of voters shift significantly enough that their partisan supports change accordingly. After one or two generations, those micro-level shifts aggregate into a large enough change to move the power balance from one party to the other. Burnham notes 1800, 1828, 1860, 1896, and 1932 as these significant "realigning" elections.[16] The last recorded realigning election was in 1932, providing nearly ninety years without a realignment, a period in which at least three realignments should have occurred.[17]

Why has no realignment occurred since 1932? The parties, and the changes that the direct primary foisted upon them, are the important variable disrupting the historical flow of realignments. A realignment is predicated upon the idea of strong party loyalty, which occasionally shifts from one to another. What realignment theory did not account for was what happens when partisans turn away from their parties. By taking the parties out of their core linkage role, their value decreased to the typical voter. With no value, there is no loyalty. Dealignment then is a preventive force against realignments.[18]

Put another way, realignment (and machine) era politics were predicated on the vast majority of the electorate identifying with their party in a reasonably strong fashion. If one became frustrated with one's party, the only viable option was to shift that loyalty to the other party. But since the direct primary cut across both parties' power structures, once one cut ties with one party the transition to being a partisan of the other party was no longer a given. Thus, the rise of the illusory "independent" voter.[19] The term *illusory* is intentional here, because the voter who self-identifies as an independent has not truly abandoned a political party, since they tend to vote for one party over the other. However, that does not mean that the voter is still as loyal to their party as they were in the pre-primary days.[20] The modern-day "independent" voter is actually a marginally engaged individual whose partisan ties are not strong. That individual may even have an allegiance to a party, analogous to a fan of a sports team who cheers for that team to win but does not go to or watch the team's games. An individual citizen may see themselves as a "fan" of the Republicans or Democrats, be excited about their electoral prospects, but not participate in the voting process that puts them in office. On occasion that marginally engaged citizen may go to the polling place, but they are inconsistent bordering on unreliable. That kind of inconsistency would be unheard of (and would likely cost a person their job or status within the party) during the nineteenth century. But today, the parties lack any enforcement mechanisms to ensure voting, so they must use less-effective carrots instead of the sticks that were available to them prior to the primary era. Whereas the machine-era voter would never have thought to split their ticket in an election, the weak partisan today is quite comfortable not only with splitting tickets but with rolling off the ballot for races in which they are not interested or engaged.[21] This latter phenomenon strikes at the heart of a party as a collective governing institution. Party loyalty and the benefits voters derived from that loyalty went away as primaries spread and the dissonant voices within the party that were once kept behind closed doors became fodder for campaigns. This marginalization of the meaning of party to the voter is one of the most significant exogenous shocks delivered on parties anywhere in the world. Had the parties been more institutionalized, generally speaking, when the direct primary was introduced they may have withstood the shock better.[22] Put another way, having no constitutional basis, parties could not rely on their origins to protect them from exogenous shocks of electoral reform.

The Party in Government Retreats

Within Congress, the party had taken hold as part of the gradual institutionalization of the legislature.[23] Committees were a functional element of institutionalization, but the emergence of stable and active leadership was key and, in that area, party was vital.[24] Leadership was particularly important in the early work of a one-party Congress, but as a true two-party system developed in the 1820s the parties' role in advancing a growing and more complex legislature became more necessary.[25] Opposing parties required more structure and development, advancing the legislative parties.

During the machine era, parties in government were paramount, especially at the local level. Party government was the backbone of the machine in the cities. State legislative parties were also important players in the machine era, often conspiring with local leaders or taking bribes to ignore the excesses of the local machines. Those state legislative parties also nominated and selected US senators, who could block any reform efforts at the federal level.

Throughout the nineteenth century, party power within Congress was high. Parties organized Congress, were able to command loyalty from partisans in their votes, and consolidated power in the Speaker of the House. Much like among the electorate, party was the driving force of government at the time. But that would change during the time of the Progressives.

The direct primary thus had the effect of weakening party government at every level, not just in the cities. Concurrent with the rise of the direct primary was a revolt against strong partisan leadership in Congress.[26] Party strength in government reached its peak in the late 1800s under Maine's Thomas Reed, who controlled every aspect of House business from committee assignments to the calendar. Discontent with the intermediary power of party leadership fermented until the 1910s, when rank-and-file Republicans ousted Speaker Joseph Cannon.

After Cannon's departure, the party in government became much less significant and powerful. Seniority began to emerge as a controlling factor in committee assignments over party loyalty and those committee assignments became paramount. Committees replaced party as the controlling force in Congress, further weakening the linkage function parties serve in American politics.[27] In some ways, Congress entered an era of political feudalism with weak central leadership but many fiefdoms located in committees with powerful senior chairs.

Throughout the remainder of the twentieth century until almost the very end, committees and seniority were the congressional markers of power. Party was much less influential. Indeed, the party in government of this era was marked by the "conservative coalition," where northern Republicans and southern Democrats controlled most policymaking in Congress.[28] The conservative coalition era marks an important pivot point in this history of party in government. Under the machines, party in government was paramount. Nomination control by party elites provided the opportunity to maintain party discipline within government. All members of a party's coalition in government were expected to comply with the party's platform and agenda under threat of not being renominated in the future.[29] Moreover, the party's power over elected officials was ubiquitous regardless of level: state legislatures were as dominated by the parties as the national legislature.[30]

The direct primary took away elite nomination power, and with the it only mechanism the parties had available to them to keep discipline within the party's electeds. Losing the power of nomination introduced the freedom for nomination-seekers and electeds to buck the party's agenda in favor of one's own, which allowed for a cross-partisan coalition to guide policy making and render the party in government much less powerful, indeed ineffective.[31]

The core reason driving the rise of committee and seniority as power markers in American legislatures during the twentieth century was the growing weakness of political parties. Particularly the loss of nomination power under the direct primary provided individual legislators more freedom to vote outside of their party's mainstream and leadership without consequences at the voting booth. While the Democratic Party held majority control of the House for half of the twentieth century and the Senate for nearly as much time, that era was marked by the party's relative inability to force rank-and-file members to comply with the party's platform. One-party control did not equate to one-party dominance.[32]

Party did become more powerful in Congress for a brief period in the 1990s, as a compensatory development against the increasing loss of party power throughout the century. During the 1980s, after decades of stable Democratic majority control of the House, Republicans began organizing their own quasi-party organization. Known as GOPAC, the entity was the brainchild of Delaware governor Pierre du Pont in 1978. Du Pont believed that the Republican national party structure, in both the party in government and national committees, was not as strong in support of candidates as it needed to be. The GOP's weakness as an electioneering support entity was the key to du Pont's vision, as he believed the state of the national Republicans hindered the ability of GOP candidates to effectively run campaigns and win office. The direct primary's damage to the party in government was such that the existing structures were inadequate to maintain the party's core.[33]

The changes of the 1990s began a new phase in Congress that appears—at least on the surface—to suggest that partisan strength has been increasing: a new era of polarization. Whether one looks at increased ideological polarization,[34] electoral inputs,[35] the changing nature of the electoral connection,[36] changing internal norms,[37] social media,[38] identity politics and realignment of voters,[39] or executive-legislative conflict,[40] political polarization within Congress has increased over the last three decades. But one must not conflate polarization with party strength. As Martinez and colleagues note, party leadership gained no more influence even at times while party unity voting was on the rise. We will discuss the polarization paradox in greater depth in chapter 8.

Weakening the Party Organization

In the classic V. O. Key tripod of party structure, the party organization stands out as the leg on which the most change has occurred. The party in the electorate and government are fairly well delineated, but the party organization has always been more difficult to categorize. While partisan development in the electorate and government have been well documented and understandable according to theories of ideological attachment and the self-interest of elected officials, the party organization's history has been significantly more haphazard.[41]

Party organizations are thus difficult to discuss. Some argue that in the United States, party organizations exist in name only.[42] Especially when compared with other countries, American political parties have remarkably minimalist organizational structure.[43] The decentralized nature of American parties and the variable robustness of their local structures suggest that the party organizations were the most susceptible to the Progressive shock of direct primaries.

Political party organizations as stand-alone organizations are an anomaly, an institutional buffer created functionally for the electoral ambitions of one individual: Andrew Jackson. Party caucuses existed within government prior to Jackson's emergence on the national scene, but they were not formalized and were subject to factionalization.[44] Local party organizations before Jackson emerged during election periods only, disappearing between campaigns. National party organizations outside of the congressional caucus were nonexistent.

The most significant pre-Progressive disruption to the American party system was started by Jackson, the very person whose legacy the Progressives sought to dismantle. As a transformative figure, Jackson is easily one of the most significant in American history not only in the presidency but in the nature of American partisanship. Jackson, with the organization help of Van Buren, remade the National Republicans into the party now known as the Democrats, but did much more to the party system.

Jackson was the pivotal figure in transforming American political parties from elite-driven cadres to a mass movement. Jackson arrived at a time when the United States was becoming more unified than its prior amalgamation of semi-sovereign states. Mobility, the spread of news, franchise expansion, and a growing sense of power among the electorate combined to elevate the dynamic firebrand Jackson into a national spotlight. Jackson used that spotlight to pursue the presidency, and in that pursuit the beginnings of his transformation of the American partisan landscape would emerge.

Presidential nominations were, at the time he first aggressively pursued the office in 1824, driven strongly by the caucuses of the parties in government. Only one party, the Democratic-Republicans, was competitive at the time, the twilight of the Era of Good Feelings. Factionalism had emerged within the Democratic-Republicans, with no fewer than five splinter groups emerging within the party caucus. The preferred candidate of most caucus members was John Quincy Adams, but Jackson also had his name placed into nomination along with William H. Crawford, Henry Clay, and John C. Calhoun. At the time, nominations were not even formal affairs: splinter caucuses could emerge around individual candidates at their behest (as was the case with Crawford and Jackson) and place their name into nomination. No rules were established, since the parties had no national organization of which to speak. The system was fluid and informal. Yet, since it was centralized among elites, who knew and generally understood each other, it was not initially chaotic. There were understandable patterns and rituals that held sway for a time. However, over time, the democratic impulses meant such a closed system could not persist.

Even after Calhoun's withdrawal, the presence of four candidates on the ballot was enough to divide the electorate in November, with the result a brokered election that would be decided in the House of Representatives. Complicating matters was the steadily growing number of states holding advisory public votes for the president. Prior to the 1820s, few states held any presidential-level public votes and those that existed were merely advisory for their state's Electoral College voters, who had ultimate autonomy in choosing for whom they would vote. Jackson was a runaway winner in states that held popular votes, but even electors within those states did not follow the wishes of their states' populations in some instances. Jackson believed that, as the popular vote winner, he should have had the presidency. Instead, the brokered Electoral College vote thrust the final decision back into the hands of the House of Representatives. Per the 12th Amendment, only the top three vote-getters in the Electoral College round would be eligible to be considered in the contingent election of 1825 that would decide the president. House Speaker Henry Clay, who finished fourth among electoral vote recipients, thus was excluded. The next president would be Jackson, Adams, or Crawford.[45]

Through deal-making and loyalty trading, Adams emerged as the president-elect. Clay, a Kentuckian, ignored a directive from his state's legislature to allot the state's votes to Jackson. Personally, and professionally, Clay disliked and distrusted Jackson. Clay's machinations meant that, even though Jackson won the initial popular vote by 10 percent and took a plurality of electoral voters in the first round, Adams would be the victor as finally determined by the US House.[46] Whatever Clay's motives or actions, what he did became known as the "corrupt bargain."[47]

Jackson was enraged, seeing himself as the winner in 1824 of both the popular and electoral votes. However, even though Jackson did take a plurality of electoral votes, he secured less than 40 percent of the Electoral College votes. The 1825 contingent election in the House selected Adams, but Jackson believed that the presidency had been stolen from him by corrupt vote-traders in the House of Representatives. The internal caucus system of nomination worked against Jackson, and he became determined to strip "King Caucus" of its ability to prevent outsiders from ascending to the presidency.[48]

Thus, Jackson immediately began a campaign for 1828, but not in the traditional sense. Jackson and his supporters immediately disavowed themselves of the Democratic-Republicans. The split in supporters would cause the party to change its name to the National Republicans, while Jackson and his supporters split off into a new Jacksonian-focused entity. Eventually Jacksonites adopted the name Democratic for their new party.[49]

Jackson also supported efforts in the states to expand the franchise to nearly all white males regardless of landholding. Between 1824 and 1828, four states that had allowed their legislature to select electors handed that power over to the popular vote. With Adams firmly in place and having the National Republicans aligned behind him, no nominating caucuses were held in Congress for 1828. Jackson would win the presidency in 1828 and fully end the practice with one of his significant changes to American elections and partisanship.[50]

Jackson knew that, with Adams gone, the National Republicans would likely revive the nomination caucus for their candidate in 1832. Further, Jackson did not want to rely on the nomination process that had caused him to title it "King Caucus" before. For 1832, Jackson called for a national nominating convention, and to plan it created the first semi-permanent party organization at the national level, the Democratic National Committee. The birth of the DNC marks a transformation of party organization in America, as a first attempt at providing structure. However, the DNC was created for the purpose of organizing the nominating convention, and so even the standing committee was barely extant outside of election years for some time.[51]

Local party organizations existed prior to the DNC's creation, but—also dissimilar to other industrial democracies—the creation of a national organization did not subsume the local party entities under the national party's umbrella. The federal nature of the government was, in a sense, recapitulated in the formation of parties. The local party organizations remained highly sovereign, in kind with Jackson's populist views. Elites, who had exercised dominance over politics, would be overrun with the new American electorate, and the party structure accommodated that bottom-up philosophy.[52]

Not all local party organizations were created equal, however. Local electoral strength often fed organizational dynamics within the local parties, making for some very robust party organizations and some that were nearly or completely nonexistent.[53] Jackson's love of the "spoils" system would invigorate local party organizations and indeed help them develop into the machines that the Progressives detested.[54]

Embracing Jacksonian spoils politics helped urban party organizations institutionalize, but that development was not universal. Rural areas in particular had less patronage on which to rely, inconsistent leadership, and little support from their urban-minded state party organizations.[55] While the brunt of the direct primary may have been focused on the well-organized urban machine, it had a disproportionate effect on the unready-to-respond party organizations of smaller communities.

As primaries spread and party organizations struggled, every element of the party organization began to suffer. Without institutional structure and permanence, every level of party organization was confronted with an adaptive challenge for which they were not prepared.[56] At the national, state, and local levels, party organizations faded into obscurity and irrelevance. Stripped of their ability to nominate candidates, the local party organizations that had at least been able to claim some successes in state and national conventions had nothing upon which they could justify themselves.

Critics of the belief that party organizations were negatively affected by the direct primary point to the organizational resurgence that the national party committees experienced from the 1970s to 1990s. However, the nature of that "revival" is actually further evidence that parties were not robust enough as political entities to withstand the shock delivered by the direct primary. In reality, party leaders acquiesced in changes they didn't quite want or fully understand.

As parties were both accidental products of the American political system and still very young entities, they were not prepared for grafting the direct primary onto their operations. As the Progressives stripped away not only nomination but every power upon which the parties had built themselves, the parties were not institutionally developed enough to maintain most of their strengths as linkage institutions. So, the party organizations in particular shrunk against the force of the direct primary throughout the twentieth century until the 1970s.

The twin party natures of informality and confederality contributed to the parties' inability to recover from the shock of the primaries. National party committees, for example, were not at all prepared for the coming technological, geographic, and societal changes of the twentieth century. National party committee membership and leadership were sporadic and mercurial. With no set national headquarters, irregular meetings and communication, and uncertainty about how clearly the party should articulate its vision, leaders gradually devolved into a passive role that weakened the public's perceived value of party.[57]

Beginning in the late 1970s, the parties did enjoy a brief period of resurgence. National committees built Washington DC headquarters just steps from Capitol Hill, raised money with direct mail, institutionalized leadership and staff, and began building the kind of infrastructure that stable organizations require.[58] The national committees were so successful with their new institutionalization that they began to help their state counterparts, who were also struggling to adapt to a system that had adopted and embraced primaries.[59]

Using agency agreements, issue-based advertising, and aggressive messaging from stable leadership, the national parties were able to build not only themselves but many of their state counterparts.[60] The joint revitalization of party organizations led to some theories, notably those of Schlesinger, who saw the party as transforming into a pivotal electioneering entity, one where the party organization was the central nucleus of a scattered and yet coordinated system of campaign players including the candidates themselves, a network of aligned interest groups and campaign professionals, media companies, and the voters.[61]

The view of party organizations as having reversed the trend of decline over the twentieth century stemming from the organizational advancement of the 1970s to 1990s is an incomplete one. The parties became, in effect, service-providing organizations that helped candidates but had relatively little influence over them. There was nothing like the nineteenth century's party-defining institutional loyalty. For the improvements to become a long-term resurgence of party organizations, they would have to withstand exogenous shocks in ways they did not during the initial era of primary adoption. The era of resurgence, though, was relatively brief because the parties only made piecemeal improvements in their processes but were not able to institutionalize their newfound strength enough to maintain it once a new shock occurred.

Throughout the 1990s, the party committees began using unlimited donations for what the FEC called "party-building activities" for purposes beyond their original intent of buying or building headquarters and paying permanent staff. Republicans especially began to use the party-building funds to run issue-focused ads that did not engage in express advocacy but functionally were attacks against candidates of the opposing party. The unlimited party-building funds, termed "soft money," were upheld by the US Supreme Court as constitutional in 1996, encouraging both parties to aggressively expand their use of comparative ads. Instead of spending soft money on its intended purposes of infrastructure building and party recovery, the parties expanded their electioneering efforts.

The soft money era would be very short-lived. By 2002, Congress passed the Bipartisan Campaign Reform Act (BCRA), which outlawed soft money spending. Soft money had partially subsidized the false dawn of party resurgence by making the parties central players in the electioneering process, but its removal just as swiftly marginalized parties in the electioneering realm.[62] By removing the central coordinating force in election campaigns, BCRA and subsequent court rulings such as *Citizens United* and *SpeechNow* dealt parties another blow against which they were not prepared to defend.

As party organizations shrank from their electioneering role, other entities emerged to fill the void. Organized interest groups, most notably, emerged to take prominence in the electoral arena in the absence of parties.[63] A problem emerges by extension, however. Parties make sense as a coordinating body within the campaign milieu. Parties are the only true linkage institution, with purely electoral motives. Only political parties run candidates under their banner for office, so parties are focused on winning as many elections as possible. The period of resurgence worked partly because parties were simply returning to the role they had once ably held. SuperPACs, a byproduct of BCRA, were merely organized interests with less accountability for their spending. These outside groups did not coordinate; they just increased their power and influence. But they did not serve campaigns as well as the parties did in their coordinating role.

As interests and other players rose in prominence, the parties were returned to their marginalized position as they had been prior to the direct-mail-fueled days of resurgence. Since organized interests have agendas which are ideologically more extreme than the parties, the campaign environment post-BCRA (and especially post–*Citizens United* and *SpeechNow*) has followed them away from the center.[64]

Despite a brief period of resurgence, American political party organizations have never recovered from the damage done to them by the advent of the direct primary. As few other countries have adopted the direct primary, it is difficult to say whether a party system exists that could maintain its linkage role under a primary regime. Party organizations in America were certainly not strong enough nor adequately institutionalized to withstand the strain of the direct primary. As the party lost its linkage role, the electorate lost its connection to political engagement.

Electoral Partisanship Morphs and Declines

Electoral partisanship emerged in the nineteenth century for reasons purely of an accidental nature. Constitutionally, parties were not supposed to exist at all. But the parties that emerged regardless of such prohibition only became strong when they began to provide tangible benefits well beyond voting.[65] Indeed, the first parties in America only found electoral success by "swilling the planters with bumbo," providing free food and drink on haycarts that would travel from polling place to polling place. Riders on the carts would enjoy the food and drink as long as they cast ballots for the sponsoring party at each stop along the circuit.[66] Machine-era politics brought social welfare and employment into the benefits portfolio for a voter.[67] Ideological alignment was not adequate to maintain connection between the voter and the party.

As the direct primary advanced throughout the states, slowly a new type of candidate emerged. The new style of candidate no longer extolled the virtue of their party, but instead stressed their own qualifications and capacity to lead. Indeed, they often ran against "the establishment," a nebulous charge that often included a mythic strong party organization at its center. (Bernie Sanders's most loyal followers and the candidate himself profess, at times, a deep hatred of the Democratic Party. And they believe that the all-powerful DNC robbed him of the 2016 nomination.) These new candidates often diverged from the platform of their state or national party, creating a significant dissonance in the voter's mind.[68] American political parties were powerless to push back against the "maverick" candidate because they had no other mechanisms to encourage voter loyalty. If the electorate wanted to upend the entire party's structure and ideology, they were free to do so. Even the resurgent party organizations of the 1970s to 1990s were unable to counteract this growing division between the voters and the parties.[69]

Among voters, identification with a political party is a direct measure of partisan strength. Parties that adapt to changing environments would notice little, or brief, disruptions in electoral loyalty under an external imposition such as the direct primary. Both in choosing a party and in the strength of one's identification, we can see how much partisanship imbues itself into the political lives of its people. Voters choose a party, and their loyalty to that party over time is another measure of party strength.[70] In that sense, party strength in America has significantly declined.[71] By any measure of partisan identification strength, American parties have struggled. While data prior to 1952's American National Election Study does not exist to elucidate the first years of the primary's effect on parties, the six decades of data collected since show that by almost any measure party identification is significantly weaker than in the early or mid-twentieth century.[72]

Partisan identification has declined significantly since 1952, with important points of punctuation during a period of general decay of voter attachment. From the 1960s until the 2010s, an era of growing dissatisfaction with parties led to an explosion in the number of voters who did not identify with a political party or merely "leaned" toward that party. In 1952, less than 20 percent of voters in total identified as independent leaner or purely independent. By 2002, that number had doubled to nearly 40 percent. Parties went from having majorities or near-majorities of voters identifying with them in the 1952 iteration of the poll to a near-majority rejecting both of the political parties as stable ideological homes.[73] Even though the 2010s saw a decline in independent voters, still roughly one-third of the American electorate does not identify with a political party. Electoral partisanship has in no way recovered from the parties losing their ability to impose discipline on their candidates and thus their ability to organize the ballot for the electorate.

The rise of sporadically loyal independent "leaner" voters may not, by itself, mean that parties have declined, but other data points further suggest the damage done by the direct primary. Importantly, split-ticket voting has increased significantly in America since the advent of the direct primary.[74] Such a development is not surprising, but the correlation between the loss of loyal voters and split-ticket voting suggests that partisan decline contributed to the development.[75] With more cognitive noise emerging during primaries, voters are prone to become confused regarding the positions of candidates because there is no consistency between candidate and party. Candidates were free to violate their party's norms and platforms in seeking office, contributing to the confusion, and as a result voters chased those divergent views to candidates more so than their party. Research has shown that while voters can learn the policy positions and ideological leaning of presidential candidates from primaries, at the lower levels that learning does not occur, suggesting that they are making decisions that violate the basic assumptions of citizen knowledge.[76]

The partisan decline thesis is further predicated on the larger-perspective behavior of the American electorate. Should voters lose some of their informational advantage or shift their partisan loyalties more often than in prior elections in isolation, the end result would not be as deleterious. However, the larger trend in voter participation over time is highly salient to this discussion. Voter turnout during the machine era was remarkably high, reaching into the 80 percent range throughout most of the nineteenth century. The high number is illusory, because we also know that the party machines engaged in rampant fraud that inflated voting rates.[77] Yet, there is every reason to believe that, even if the official numbers are inflated, the level to turnout was much higher than it is today.

Over the course of the twentieth century, voter turnout declined precipitously. Some adjustment to the turnout rate is expected, particularly with the introduction of another Progressive reform, mandatory voter registration. However, the overall effect of registration on voting is estimated to be no higher than 5 percent, much less than the nearly 30 percent decline noted over the course of the century of direct primaries.[78]

Indeed, voter turnout has plummeted since the arrival of direct primary elections. The primaries themselves did not cause the decline in turnout in a vacuum, but they did weaken the political party linkages that make for strong patterns of voting participation.[79] In a multinational study over the last half of the twentieth century, the greatest contribution to turnout decline over the scope of eighteen industrialized nations was lack of mobilization by party organizations.[80]

As noted earlier, even during this era of steady-state decline in party strength and partisanship, a curious and counterintuitive development has occurred. One would expect that in an era of partisanship decline, the intensity of electoral identification with the parties would also decline. Until the 2010s, such was the case. But the twenty-first century has evinced a seemingly contradictory development: the continuing decline of parties *and* an increase in the intensity of partisan identification. Self-identification in the ANES as a strong Democrat or Republican has increased by an aggregate of ten percentage points since 2004.[81] As noted above, partisan polarization has increased dramatically over the last decade and a half. It is important to note that increased polarization is not a sign of the partisan decline trend's reversal, but rather a new development in the process. It is an unanticipated but not illogical outcome of the reform era.

The concept that parties are simultaneously polarized and in decline is not self-contradictory. In fact, the two forces are likely interrelated. While the number of people identifying as partisans has declined, the intensity of party loyalty of those remaining has grown. As weaker identifiers have spun off from the parties, those that are left tend to be the most ideologically extreme and committed supporters.

Since 1972, when the effect of the McGovern-Fraser reforms was to make presidential primaries binding just as lower-level election nomination contests were, voter turnout in those primaries has been incredibly low. Ballot primaries have ranged from high levels in the low 30 percent range for early-calendar primaries such as New Hampshire to lows of 2 percent for caucuses. Overall, voter turnout in primaries has hovered near 10 percent nationwide since the McGovern-Fraser binding presidential primary era began.[82]

The extremely low turnout rates for primaries and caucuses have a number of important effects. First, only the most motivated choose to participate, especially in caucuses.[83] Those highly interested individuals are also more ideologically extreme and thus more polarized.[84] Furthermore, the extra primary elections lengthen the campaign calendar and introduce campaign fatigue, which itself suppresses subsequent general election voter turnout.[85]

The Twentieth-Century Decline of Parties

Parties and partisanship can wax and wane as the tides. No matter in which political subdivision a party in question participates, it is often possible that either the individual parties or the party system in which they operate will vary widely in strength and influence. And as parties are amalgams of multiple different entities, it is possible for one segment of the party to be strong while others are relatively weaker. Therefore, we must determine what it means for a party to be strong or weak.

Many measures of party strength are available, and each must be considered. From the broadest sense, polities have shared political cultures that can embrace parties or hold them at bay. While some states such as Germany are more to accepting a partisan political culture, the United States has always been ambivalent about parties, even during the time of party importance in the machine era.[86] Each nation's political culture helps determine how strong each polity will allow parties to become. But parties that become strong in a weak-party culture may find that reformist reactions, such as the direct primary, are easier to impose upon them than in other more pro-party nations. Furthermore, challenges to party strength in weak-party states will often have more significant and sustained impacts on those parties.[87]

Within government, a similar pattern of partisan decline is evident.[88] The end of Speaker dominance ushered in a new era where partisanship mattered significantly less compared with seniority. Regional divisions created a bipartisan consensus of sorts that ran the House under the nickname the conservative coalition, so called because northern and midwestern Republicans allied with their conservative southern Democratic colleagues to hold sway over most operations in Congress during the twentieth century.[89]

Among voters, the lack of party loyalty beyond material incentives such as employment has been exposed by the direct primary era. Unable to provide tangible benefits, voters were denied the party's essential linkage role as an information shortcut to determine the ideological leanings of candidates for nomination.[90] Voters either retrenched within an ideologically extreme cadre or lost loyalty to their parties entirely. The healthy balance of material and ideological forces—combined with a reasonable sense of group solidarity—that exemplified the earlier party system has broken down. We simultaneously have intensely loyal political tribes under the sway of an "official" ideology and a huge sea of citizens who don't vote or feel much connection to the parties or, indeed, the political process.

In sum, the American political party has come to mean less to the voters. In marketing parlance, parties can be said to have lost their essential brand identity.[91] The direct primary was intended to activate a public yearning to participate without the interference of party organizations. Instead, the Progressives assumed a natural orientation to participate in politics that did not exist in voters. Rather than bolstering reforms to enhance participation, the Progressives imposed direct democratic principles on a public neither ready nor willing to accept the added commitments and burdens of direct and unaided participation.

Chapter 8

The Problem with Primaries

Figure 8.1. Hans Noel Tweet, 2016.

The above tweet, by political scientist Hans Noel, was written during the approach to the 2020 Democratic presidential primaries, where no fewer than twenty-five candidates had declared themselves for the race. The notion of twenty-five people competing for the highest political office in the United States is daunting. The twenty-five people were just somewhat more than the seventeen competitors who sought the Republican nomination only four years prior. Noel's point was to show that there should still be a place for party organizations in the candidate nomination process, and that the plethora of candidates is a sign of need for those organizations to be stronger.

The abundance of candidates presents numerous examples of the complicated role of parties in American politics. Viewed one way, the presence of so many candidates seeking an office is an example of a robust and well-functioning politics. Numerous candidates with ambition seek an office, giving voters many choices and an opportunity to articulate a clear policy direction for the eventually successful candidate going into the general election. The multitude of candidates also could mean to the primary apologist that there are many coalitions actively trying to become the controlling interest in a political party, suggesting that the party label has ample value to make it worth pursuit.

Other interpretations exist, however, that run counter to these rosy explanations. Primaries have, over time, changed the political landscape for the worse in a variety of ways. The most direct and immediate impacts are cataloged in chapter 6, but the effects of the primaries are not limited to that list. The direct primary severely limited the parties in all elements of their existence, which was certainly part of the Progressives' intent. Had the Progressive will been explicitly stated to eliminate political parties entirely, the result would not be particularly surprising. But the long-term effects of weakening the parties were unknown to the Progressives, so the extent of the damage not only to parties but to American democracy is worthy of discussion.[1]

Primaries have had a significant impact not only on the parties, as discussed in chapter 6, but also on the general American electoral system. The weakness of parties as linkage institutions becomes evident when we examine the health of a political system. Often, we think of the parties in isolation, and winning is frequently interpreted to mean that at least one party is doing well. But that can be quite misleading—after all, someone has to win an election. (Although obviously, in our complex system the different branches of government and federalism create all sorts of winners and losers.) However, to get a good sense of the health of our democracy we need to understand the system as a whole and to think of how the party system as a whole is operating. Three significant areas of long-term effect of party weakness have emerged from the immediate-term damage to the parties noted in chapter 6: ideological polarization, turnout, and campaign spending. All results are unintended consequences of the institutional weakening of political parties brought on by the direct democratic impulses of the Progressive move to direct primaries.

The Joe Lieberman Conundrum

Direct primaries present a conundrum for partisans, pundits, and politicos alike. Former Connecticut Senator Joe Lieberman provides one of the best examples of this confounding environment because of his career straddling the line between the two major American political parties. Lieberman won his seat in the Senate as a Democrat in 1988, defeating Republican Lowell Weicker. Weicker himself was a symbol of the divisions into which primaries force parties, since he was politically more liberal than the typical Republican.

Lieberman's victory in 1988 would have only been possible in a primary era. Connecticut was fairly Republican at the time, and Weicker was reasonably popular with his constituents. But Lieberman's narrow 10,000-vote victory would not have been possible without open dissension within the Republican ranks. Weicker's more liberal record became an issue in the campaign when famed conservative commentator William F. Buckley crossed over and threw his support behind Lieberman's candidacy, having been unable to find and support a more conservative Republican to challenge Weicker in the primary.[2]

Over the coming eighteen years, Lieberman would benefit from a gradual realignment in Connecticut away from a Republican majority and toward a Democratic one. Lieberman handily won reelection in 1994 and 2000. He even attempted to leverage his lack of alignment with his own party into an unsuccessful presidential nomination bid in 2004. Lieberman's hawkish stance, particularly on foreign policy and security issues, which he admitted to being a contributing factor to his lack of success in the Democratic presidential primaries, would return to further distance him from his party two years later.[3]

By the time of his 2006 reelection bid, Connecticut had become strongly Democratic. But Lieberman had always made concerted attempts to appeal to Republicans, knowing that he owed his initial election to GOP crossover support. That centrism, which worked particularly well during the state's realignment, would cost him his party and its nomination. A challenge from the left in liberal Ned Lamont was successful, using a platform of opposing the ongoing wars in Afghanistan and Iraq, which Lieberman had supported in his presidential bid.[4] It appeared that Lieberman would leave the Senate after three terms.

Connecticut was unusual in that it lacked "sore loser" laws, ones that prevent candidates who have lost primary elections from contesting the general as an independent. Lieberman knew that the primary electorate who gave the nomination to Lamont was not representative of the general election voting pool, and that he had a chance to win reelection but without the label of the Democratic Party. Thus, Lieberman entered the general election as a third candidate, facing both Lamont and Republican nominee Alan Schlesinger.[5] Despite not having the official backing of his own party,

Lieberman won, thanks to scandals that Schlesinger faced. Having contested his primary as a Democrat, Lieberman functionally ran in the general election as a Republican. As they had during his initial pursuit of the seat, conservative Republicans rallied around Lieberman, including notable leaders such as New York mayor Rudolf Giuliani and former GOP vice presidential nominee Jack Kemp, and he even campaigned at Republican rallies with sitting GOP members of Congress.[6]

Lieberman won the general election with 50 percent of the state vote, ten points ahead of Lamont.[7] Immediately after winning with a Republican-backed coalition, Lieberman returned to Congress and caucused with the majority Democrats. He leveraged both political parties without ever committing to a firm declaration of support to either. Even though he caucused with Democrats, he still behaved very much like a Republican at times. Lieberman was a prime mover behind the post-9/11 creation of the Department of Homeland Security, and while caucusing with Democrats after 2006 he endorsed Republican John McCain for president in 2008.[8] He was the only Democrat to break ranks and refuse to endorse Barack Obama's candidacy, going so far as to speak at the Republican National Convention in favor of McCain.

The Lieberman example is viewed in two different ways, but one of those perspectives is important to our analysis. In the first view, Lieberman is a wise politico who represents his state more so than his party. The second view presents Lieberman as an opportunist, one who would not succeed or survive in a partisan regime where the party could control nominations and keep the rational self-seeker from undermining the party through the convenient mechanism of the primary.

Lieberman likely would have never won nomination to the Senate within his party had leadership held the power to select nominees. Party systems are predicated on the ability of a party to select nominees who align with the party's platform and strategic goals. Lieberman was always to the right of his own party's positions, whether they be the War on Terror, trade policy, or health care.[9]

The direct primary allowed Lieberman to stake out positions outside partisan orthodoxy and insulate himself from any loss of prestige or power that would come from bucking one's own party. Nomination-by-primary also allowed Lieberman to abandon his party fully when he saw fit, exemplified by the McCain nomination. In what way, other than for his own power and political career, was Lieberman even a Democrat? In his legislative alliances, policy positions, and public declarations Lieberman was far outside the Democratic mainstream except when it suited his purposes. When he won his general election campaign in 2006, he had the option to caucus with the same Republicans who had powered his efforts. However, Lieberman knew that with 49 Democrats, 49 Republicans, and one other Independent in the Senate who would caucus with the Democrats (Vermont's Bernie Sanders), he had a difficult choice. Had he caucused with Republicans, he would have caused a 50–50 split, with tiebreaks decided by a Republican vice president. But that VP, Dick Cheney, would be term-limited out with his president by 2009, and with that came the possibility of a Democrat taking the White House and leaving Lieberman with limited power. Lieberman decided to caucus with Democrats, putting him in a 51–49 majority, which he brokered to maintain a powerful committee chair position.[10]

Lieberman's example shows that parties in a nomination-by-primary regime are little more than leverage points that can be effectively used by rational politicians. But what do his mercurial partisan and policy positions mean for the voters of Connecticut who repeatedly sent him to Washington? What sense could voters make of Lieberman's position, and how did they respond to the cognitive dissonance provided by his lack of alignment with his party? Lieberman used the cueing mechanism of partisanship but did not repay that support with partisan loyalty. Primaries allow candidates to use parties without being part of them.

Primaries and Polarization

Understanding the connection between primary elections and political polarization is a difficult task. Polarization as a political phenomenon has many contributing factors, though the impact of the direct primary are one of the most significant components. Polarization in the electorate is a relatively recent phenomenon and one that, on review of the events of the twentieth century, may seem counterintuitive.

Weak parties should result in a continuation of the process we saw through much of the twentieth century and described in chapter 6: a gradual retreat of voters from partisanship toward independence or sporadic loyalty to one party or the other. If parties cannot provide a stable home for the public, they should be of declining marginal utility to the general public. And indeed such was the case through much of the twentieth century. Not only did partisan identification among the electorate decline, but so did partisan intensity among elected officials. Governing coalitions regularly crossed party lines in Congress and state legislatures, the frequency of party-line voting decreased, and party ties became ever less important to leadership within legislative chambers.

Polarization presents itself as the opposite, supposing a strong partisan attachment or organization as the reason people would connect with parties and in extreme ways. However, polarization can be explained as a byproduct of the system driven by the direct primary. In short, the unaligned centrists have disengaged not only from parties but from government itself. The partisan intensity appears because those who have still maintained party ties see no incentive to embrace the middle. So while the actual number of people who have moved to the political fringes has not changed, their percentage of the overall electorate has increased, since many people have selected themselves out of political activity entirely. So-called moderates, usually measured by the percentage of the electorate self-identifying as independent or an independent leaner, have withdrawn from political engagement, leaving the more extreme partisans as the most active.[11] With the partisan extremes making up the largest portion of the active electorate, candidates and parties will gravitate to where they are. As the electorate has moved toward the extremes, so have the party organizations and elected representatives who make up the party in government.

A significant and sizable literature exists attempting to explain the root causes of political polarization. Most of the models capture polarization well, in a single direction. However, we argue that when the models are considered together, a more complete picture emerges that helps explain the root causes of the polarization of parties in twenty-first-century American politics. The particularized models see polarization as products of either the electorate, the party in government, or the news media. We propose a new model that brings all of the particular models together into one larger-scale explanatory framework driven by the direct primary election.

A Polarized Public

The polarized electorate of today has its roots in the ideological realignment, particularly of conservative southern Democrats, dating back to the 1980s, though most notable in the 1990s.[12] Since the first noticeable signs came during the Reagan presidency, some attribute the shift to Reagan's electoral success in the South. However, the true precedent force behind the realignment can be traced to the Southern Strategy devised by Barry Goldwater in 1964 and implemented by Richard Nixon four years later.[13]

Some argue that partisan politics may not even be the primary source of increased polarization: for those, the root cause of polarization lies more in changing social mores and habitation patterns. Putnam pointed out that social capital, the sense of belonging to a larger community and the trust that accompanied it, was on the decline.[14] As social capital declined, people would self-select into more homogenous communities. Those groups, often called echo chambers, can manifest in the groups with whom one interacts politically.[15] Even housing patterns have come to reflect a greater amount of ideological sorting, leading to a reinforcing social stratum that encourages political polarization.[16] As the journalist Bill Bishop writes,

> Beginning nearly thirty years ago, the people of this country unwittingly began a social experiment. Finding cultural comfort in "people like us," we have migrated into ever-narrower communities and churches and political groups. We have created, and are creating, new institutions distinguished by their isolation and single-mindedness.[17]

Of course, Bishop is reporting about geographical sorting; we argue these stark divisions are partially rooted in prior political reforms that restructured party processes.

In all of its forms, self-sorting into semi-homogenous groups contributes to the same eventual effect. When social, living, and work environments are semi-conscious litmus tests for ideological homogeneity, the effect is the reduction of belief that there are other people with lives and viewpoints different from one's own.[18] The lack of ideological and partisan diversity in peoples' lives leads them to believe that their way of thinking is the only reasonable and legitimate view of politics. Thus, others who disagree are alien and unworthy of deliberative consideration. Polarization is the manifestation of this belief that an individual's own viewpoint is sacrosanct and not subject to challenge or moderation.

Regardless of its origins, today the American electorate appears to be highly polarized. For many, when the polarization began is less important than with whom the polarization began. Some models present the polarization as beginning within the electorate, and the electoral polarization subsequently causing the party in government to become polarized as well, as shown in figure 8.2.

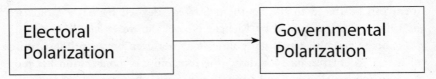

Figure 8.2. Electoral Polarization Driving Governmental Polarization.

Brewer points to issue-based decisions as having increased electoral polarization. Using American National Elections Study (ANES) data from 1952 to 2000, we can see a number of important trends developing indicating a widening divide between members of the electorate. The percentage of respondents seeing important differences between the parties increased, from just over 50 percent in the 1960s to roughly 80 percent by 2000.[19] Burden points to primary elections in Congress as a significant driver of the issue-based electoral polarization noted later by Brewer.[20] As parties lost their nomination power, interest groups with specific and usually single-issue focus emerged as a powerful force in primary elections. Where parties need to worry about coalition-building and consensus, interest groups allow for an extreme and unbending set of policy preferences that rational candidates will pursue for their electoral gains. Thus, the compensatory rise of interest groups in the primary era serves to explain the electoral polarization at issue here.

Measuring polarization as beginning during the 1968 election of Richard Nixon, Jacobson points to a president's growing inability to assemble bipartisan coalitions in government as driven by the public's expanding ideological and partisan distance. In Jacobson's model, electoral polarization is measured through ideological self-identification and presidential voting patterns in congressional constituencies. As voters moved further out to the left and right, so did the candidates they elected to serve. As governmental polarization increased in Congress, the incentives to agree to bipartisan policies decreased.[21] Interest groups may, consistent with Burden's findings, be an important driver of that gradual creep to the ideological poles.

Layman and Carsey believe that the electorate has polarized as a reaction to party elites, based on issue positions taken by candidates and party organizational leaders. ANES data from 1972 to 2000 in their study concentrates on three core issue areas: race, culture, and social welfare. In Layman and Carsey's model, the disengagement of moderates and weak party adherents leaves a smaller cadre of highly engaged party loyalists who take their ideological cues from those party elites. While the general public had not fully polarized in the scope of the study, those hard-core party loyalists did polarize on all three issue dimensions over the thirty-year scope of the data.[22]

Some suggest that partisans have simply become more closely aligned with their party under a realignment of southern conservatives to the Republican Party. However, other research clearly shows that there are differences between the strength of partisan attachment one holds and the tendency one has to polarize one's views. Carmines, Ensley, and Wagner find that polarization tends to occur mostly to those with already strong partisan attachments.[23] Citizens with consistently liberal or conservative preferences in both economic and social issues tended to respond to elite polarization with mass polarization. However, they also found that the sizable number of citizens who hold preferences on economic and social issues that do not align perfectly to elite Republican and Democratic cues did not respond to elite polarization. These marginally party faithful citizens were more likely to shift their partisan allegiance in the short term and less likely to strengthen their party identification in the long term. Strong parties would inspire polarization across the board, but the electoral polarization literature appears to be eliciting a two-tier division within the parties. That two-tiered division, which can be operationalized into two different electorates, suggests that the direct primary has midwifed the birth of a new sub-electorate: the primary electorate. And this kind of electorate poses tremendous challenges to the underlying theory that justified primaries—that primaries were the ideal structures to allow the citizenry to become involved directly in politics. The formation of a sub-electorate is hardly the democratic ideal of wide participation. Indeed, it is problematic because, although it does create a wider level of participation, that participation is still very limited. Yet, it creates an illusion of robust democratic participation that hides from us the reality: an unrepresentative group imposing its choices on the wider society.

American-style direct primary elections, with differences between party registration requirements for ballot access (open, closed, and hybrid systems) and types of primary (ballot elections and caucuses), tend to draw only a small portion of the electorate out to the polls. That small group tends to be ideologically more extreme than the electorate in the general election, meaning that the two groups are distinct. Strong party adherents are the only portion of the electorate with enough of an incentive to vote in primaries, which makes the results of primary elections unrepresentative of the electorate as a whole.[24]

Furthermore, the primary electorate diverges from the general electorate in every House district and even from supporters of the party in the general election in almost every district, which is consistent with a centrifugal influence on primary voters.[25]

One of the arguments in favor of primaries is that they are closer to the spirit of representative democracy than allowing nominations to be decided by party leaders, because the nominating electorate is more representative. But are primaries more representative of the electorate as a whole? Do primaries actually increase representation? Some promising findings suggested that primary electorates were indeed more representative of the electorate as a whole.[26]

Negative Partisanship

A closer look at the changing attitudes of voters adds to our knowledge of how the weakened state of political parties has contributed to increasing polarization. Negative partisanship is a recently discussed phenomenon that seems on its face to reject the notion of weak parties when in reality it is a symptom of them. The attitudes displayed by partisans in a negative environment are polarized not in favor of their own party, but against the one they oppose.

Few elected officials embody the concept of negative partisanship as well as Donald Trump. While fiery rhetoric is expected on the campaign trail, open advocacy for the incarceration of one's opponent, as Trump encouraged with chants of "Lock Her Up" in reference to Hillary Clinton on the campaign trail in 2016, is extreme. Even when in office, when presidents would be expected to temper their rhetoric to strategically achieve policy objectives, Trump used Twitter to personally attack Democrats and their entire party. Following that cue, Republican partisans (and Democrats in response) chose to coarsen their language and begin referring to the other party as an "enemy" of American interests. Using such terms regularly suggests that disagreements between parties moved into a virulent place where the simple legitimacy of another party was not accepted by many partisans. This hearkens back to some of the earliest criticisms of parties themselves. Many eighteenth-century critics of party, most notably George Washington in his Farewell Address, worried that parties by their very nature called into question the fundamental loyalties of partisans. For much of the next 200 years a functioning, and mostly healthy, two-party system put that worry to rest. But today we have a variation on that fear—except, in some ways, worse: partisans harshly question the loyalties of the opposite party and its supporters.

For the last half of the twentieth century, most partisans remained positive in their attitudes toward their own party but were not far from neutral in those evaluations of the other party.[27] Regarding the other major party, most partisans were avowedly neutral. But as the late twentieth century approached, under a post-McGovern-Fraser nationalized primary election regime, attitudes began to intensify on both sides of the partisan divide. Republicans and Democrats both became slightly more positive toward their own party, but Republican attitudes towards Democrats and Democratic attitudes toward Republicans became much more negative over the same span of time as the electorate and politicians became more partisan.[28]

The relentless push toward the poles is a product of primary elections, and negative partisanship is a symptom of that push. As moderates neither run nor turn out to vote, and as partisans share polarized views more commonly, the perceived gap between the two main parties has grown. Accompanying that sense of difference is a belief that the other party is a significantly worse option than the one to which one is loyal.

Again, negative partisanship appears on its face to suggest a resurgence of political parties. A partisan with strong feelings toward her own party may understandably view the other party negatively, especially when one's partisanship is an extension of a social or group identity.[29] Strong sentiments toward the parties suggest loyalty to one's own party, not just a negative attitude toward the other party; however, loyalty to one's own party is not strong, which suggests a different explanation.

American National Elections Study data from 1978 to 2016 shows a strong and consistent trend of a worsening of attitudes toward both parties. Out-party sentiments on a 100-point feeling thermometer have decreased, especially since the mid-1990s. But positive evaluations toward one's own party have not increased concomitantly. Republicans and Democrats look only marginally favorably at their own party, but strongly oppose the other. To make the case stronger, the average feeling thermometer scores toward parties in general have decreased fifteen points, indicating that the public has become opposed to partisanship in general.[30] In retrospect, the general neutrality expressed toward the parties was not the sign of overall party weakness interpreted at the time, but instead part of a gradual decline of party faith over time. The sign of party weakness is the general negativity seen today, not the ambivalent neutrality of the mid-1900s.

Open Versus Closed Primaries

Primaries also polarize the electorate by subdividing them into cadres based on whether a state uses the open or closed system of primary elections. Primaries are very different types of elections from their general counterparts, because there are many ways they can be conducted. General elections must be conducted on ballots and at set times. But there is more potential variability involved with primaries. Primary elections can be conducted via caucuses without any ballots. When primaries are on ballots, there are multiple available formats for voter eligibility that complicate the process and provide different possibilities of influence.

Most importantly, states are allowed to determine voter eligibility in their primaries. While southern states mostly used this freedom to perversely restrict the franchise of African American citizens in the late nineteenth to mid-twentieth centuries, there are many states that set non-racial ballot access rules for their primaries. Mostly those access rules focus on whether or not a voter must register as a member of one of the parties on the ballot prior to casting their vote. States that require some statement of positive partisan allegiance are "closed" primary states, while those that allow party choice at the ballot box are termed "open" primary states. Variations exist even with the closed and open states, with some allowing partially open ballots where voters register with a party but can change their minds and switch parties at the polling place. A partially closed option exists as well, where voters who do not affiliate formally with a political party can vote in selected parties' primaries. Finally, some strong one-party states as well as the nation's sole non-partisan legislature in Nebraska have a top-two primary where all voters can choose among candidates from both parties on one ballot. Thus, a party is not guaranteed a spot on the general election ballot, since the top two candidates that go on to the general election may emerge from the same party.[31]

With different methods of implementation, there comes the possibility of different effects. Since primaries were not uniformly binding across all states and elections until the McGovern-Fraser reforms were implemented prior to the 1972 campaign, only data in elections since 1972 is reliable enough to inform the effects of the different types of primary administration.

Take for example the state of Kansas, with a century-old political tradition of strong voter adherence to the Republican Party. Often, the winner of the GOP primary becomes the de facto winner of the general election because of the base strength the Republicans hold. When Democrats win, it is often because the GOP nominee is a more extreme conservative while the Democratic nominee appeals to more centrist voters.[32] In such a circumstance, there is a built-in incentive for Kansas Democrats, who often have uncontested primaries, to cross over and vote in Republican elections to attempt to put enough votes behind the most extreme or unelectable candidate so that their nominee is better positioned to win the general election.

Philosophically, why should someone with no allegiance to a political party be allowed to vote in its primary? Kansas limits that practice by requiring prior registration with a political party, barring late changes in party registrations, and only providing registered Republicans with access to the GOP primary ballot. But Kansas is an exception to the general rule in other states, where voters with either no party loyalty or the desire to negatively influence their nomination can participate in any party primary.

One of the most significant concerns regarding open primaries is the possibility that individuals with no allegiance to a political party are given the opportunity to influence that party's nominee. According to the logic critical of open primaries, why should a voter with no partisan allegiance, or one whose allegiance lies with Republicans, be allowed to determine the Democratic Party's nominee (and vice versa) for any office? The criticism of open primaries leads to two general hypotheses: 1) nominees are less representative of their party's rank-and-file views, and 2) opposing party adherents can cross over and "sabotage" the nomination process of a party.

Initial research showed that little opposite-party or strategic voting (often called sabotage voting) occurred from 1972 into the 1980s. Much more likely was unaffiliated independent voters taking advantage of the opportunity to vote in whichever party's contest was more interesting to them.[33] In Wisconsin, then a strong Republican state, little evidence emerged of Democrats participating in the GOP primary, but independents did tend to cast ballots in Republican primary elections more than they did Democratic ones. Furthermore, evidence did emerge showing that the high participation of non-Republican voters impacted partisan nominations, because the few Democrats and many independents who participated exhibited different candidate preferences and vote choices than those loyal to the GOP.

Strategic cross-party voting, however, has been shown to be much more limited in scope than is often speculated in media stories of primary voting. For instance, the only occurrences where significant amounts of party-to-party (as opposed to unaffiliated-to-party) crossover voting can be ascertained from data are when one party has uncontested or lightly contested primary elections.[34] Should a party have a strong and unchallenged incumbent (as Republicans did in 1984 or Democrats did in 2012), sabotage voting becomes more common. However, even that rate of crossover voting rarely exceeds 10 percent of one party's primary vote. Sabotage voting is thus much rarer and less impactful than usually described.

Chen and Yang further the work on sabotage voting by identifying the circumstances in which such strategic activity occurs and its impact. The effect of strategic voting behavior on the result of a primary depends on the size of the party, the turnout rate of non-party members, the positions of the candidates, and the proportion of voters who vote strategically.[35]

Though strategic crossover voting is uncommon and has limited effects on the outcomes of elections, altering the eligible electorate for a given race can have significant effects. Research is largely divided on the electoral composition effects of different types of primaries, but King finds that purely open primaries significantly change the primary electorate and actually produce more extreme candidates and issue positions than in closed primaries. While the results might seem counterintuitive, King's point is that closed primaries tend to bring out strategically minded party loyalists whose preferences tend toward pragmatic electability in the general election for party nominees; thus closed primaries tend toward centrism. Open primaries attract not necessarily moderates, but fringe voters who push issue positions and campaigns out to the extremes.[36]

Closed primary systems have intuitive advantages, since the electoral pool is limited to party loyalists, but also some systemic advantages. For instance, one study found that states with semi-closed primaries (ones where at least one party requires registration with that party to vote in the primary) are more representative of the electorate and the district's estimated median voter position, hence more moderate.[37]

Still, others find that closed primaries have the effect of pushing campaigns to the extremes themselves. Kanthak and Morton suggest that closed primaries feature more ideological polarization of candidates, issue positions, and voters.[38] Kanthak and Morton differ from King in modeling the effects of primaries, but both share a common finding that primary electorates are substantially at variance with their general election counterparts. Studies of the presidential electorate after 1972 suggests that ideological polarization has been increasing regardless of the type of primary rules used.

Even though strategic crossover voting is uncommon, its very existence calls the intent of primary elections into question. Parties are organizations that exist to win elections, and to do that they make every effort to best represent the ideologies, goals, and identities of their loyal voters. To wrest control over the nomination process, one of the core methods by which parties establish their electoral brand is to take away the very power of a party to determine its own destiny. That challenge, in combination with the electoral polarization that follows all primaries, points to significant and deleterious effects on the American political system imposed by primaries.

Caucuses are another form of primary election, but an area little studied in the political science literature. This is all the more interesting because there is some evidence that the Democratic Party reformers in the early '70s tended to envision caucuses being very common and even the preferred method of nominating candidates. The public and highly participatory nature of caucuses, not necessarily in the sense of numbers but in the quality of political interaction, made caucuses in a sense the logical method for selecting delegates. Caucuses fit with the democratic theory that animated the reformers—open, representative, participatory, and deliberative. Common citizens coming together to bring their concerns forward, debate the issues, and select delegates appeared to be quite compelling. That was, anyway, the ideal method that would make the underlying democratic theory make sense.

A caucus, as a formal procedure, is much more difficult to analyze. Caucuses are public meetings, with spotty to no record-keeping of votes. Data collection is much more difficult than in primary elections conducted on ballots. Furthermore, multiple ballots make discerning voter intent difficult. What research is available shows that caucus participants are highly differentiated from their ballot primary counterparts. Campaign spending, name recognition, and sociodemographic influences such as candidates with similar racial and social class characteristics are more influential with primary voters, who tend to focus on economic issue positions. Ballot primary electorates thus bear more resemblance to their general election counterparts than do caucus participants.[39]

Finally, the top-two primary administration system impacts elections and electorates differently than either caucuses or traditional party ballot primaries. California began an experiment with the top-two primary in 2012. Since California has very stable partisan preferences in a small number of districts, reformers believed that in areas with strong Democratic preferences it made little sense for a Republican with no chance to win in a general election to go forward with a nomination when the preponderance of voters preferred different Democrats, and vice versa. The top-two primary combines all candidates regardless of party into one pool from which voters choose. The new system is thus less a traditional party primary than a qualifying or knockout round: the top two vote-getters win a primary, regardless of party affiliation, meaning that two candidates from the same party may be on the general election ballot. Findings from experiments over the 2012 pilot of the top-two primary suggest, though, that voters could not identify issue positions of the different candidates well and were prone to conflate issue positions. The confusion led to voters choosing more ideologically disparate candidates and further exacerbating polarization. Moderate candidates, who were touted as potential beneficiaries of the top-two primary, were actually hindered more in their efforts.[40]

Regardless of format, the direct primary has, especially since the inception of binding presidential primaries beginning in 1972, accelerated polarization in the electorate regardless of what format the primary took. Since no form of primary appears immune from polarization, evidence strongly suggests that ipso facto primaries are a significant contributor to the political polarization experienced in modern-day American politics.

Turnout

Another significant area of study regarding the health of any representative polity is its voter turnout. The United States, like many countries, has seen a steady decline in voter turnout throughout the last century, though it has been more acute in America than in most other western industrialized republics. A significant contributor to that declining turnout is the lack of voter mobilization, which immediately refers back to the weakness of parties as linkage institutions. Under a weak regime, the parties lack the personnel, brand identity, or other resources to reach out to voters, and without effective and aggressive group mobilization efforts the general public will not turn out to vote.[41]

General election voter turnout in American presidential elections has hovered just around 50 percent for the last four decades, generally in a state of decline since the 1950s. Midterm general elections have lower turnout, averaging to roughly the mid-30-percent range. (Although turnout in the 2018 midterms spiked to close to 50 percent, this is probably tied to the controversial nature of the Trump presidency rather than any long-term factors encouraging higher participation. And turnout did increase in the 2020 general election.) Primary elections are lower still, and highly volatile. Early primaries such as New Hampshire feature turnout over 50 percent, but overall the turnout rate in primaries has been under one-quarter of all eligible voters throughout the McGovern-Fraser era. Caucuses, because of their greater time commitment, see turnout of under 10 percent, save the all-important ones in Iowa.[42]

Primary elections add a second (and, where runoff elections occur, a third) layer of expected voter participation to the American context. In polities without primaries, voters must only concern themselves with becoming informed and casting a ballot in a single election. The additional time and complexity involved in primaries have been shown to have a suppressive effect on voter turnout. At the very least, the way primaries often include more than two candidates means that the level of research necessary to make an informed choice increases dramatically. The more elections to which voters must devote attention dilutes and distracts them, not only producing a lower primary turnout but reducing general election turnout by roughly 5 percent.[43]

Beyond the parties' reduced linkage capacity, primaries are a direct contributor to lower voter turnout as well. Neither party's loyalists turned out better over time, suggesting the inability to increase turnout is not endemic to any one party but systemic.[44] When parties do engage in mobilization drives, they can induce an increase in voter turnout, but those increases are small and must be sustained for occasional voters. Chronic nonvoters, despite having the opportunity to participate in the decision of which candidates will be represented on a general election ballot, are immune from partisan mobilization efforts.[45]

The low turnout function of primaries is not limited to the presidential campaign level, though. In the states, gubernatorial elections provide an experimental laboratory to determine if primaries generally have a suppressive effect on turnout or if those effects are limited to the presidential level. In state-level executive elections, the type of primary administration, strongly contested primaries between competitive candidates, midterm versus presidential election years, and open-seat contests all significantly affect voter turnout. Most importantly, when gubernatorial primaries are held concurrently with their presidential counterparts, voter turnout is 6 percent higher than if they are held either on different days within the same year or during an off-year election. In other words, sub-presidential primary turnout hovers at roughly 10 percent. While electorates in primaries may seem representative, their small numbers suggest otherwise.[46]

Overall, the literature on primaries and voter turnout clearly indicates that regardless of format or calendar placement, primaries have a significant depressive effect on voter turnout. Neither is that suppression of turnout limited to primary elections themselves; in fact, it bleeds over into general election turnout. This not only calls into question the democratic value of primaries as methods for nominating candidates, it suggests that primaries are detrimental to the entire democratic process itself.

Since primaries are suppressive of turnout, we should return to the Progressives' notion that the American public was yearning to participate more in democracy and simply needed to be relieved of the burden of partisanship to do so. Throughout this work we have stressed that the Progressives made a crucial error in their efforts to reform the parties. The massive weakening of the parties imposed by the direct primary did not empower a public yearning to take more of its linkage to politics into its own hands. Had such been the case, voter turnout in primaries would at least measure up to their general election counterparts. However, primary turnout has steadily decreased from substandard levels in their very beginning. The direct primary did not energize an electorate, but instead removed its very lifeline to politics.

Legislative Polarization

Primary elections drive legislative polarization as well, especially noted at the federal level. In scholarship following this model, elected officials make policy choices and public pronouncements, which in turn exacerbate partisan differences in the electorate, driving polarization among voters. Figure 8.3 shows the causal chain begun by legislative polarization.

Legislative polarization means that the two parties in a given legislature vote increasingly more as unified blocs and those two blocs are increasingly differentiated from each other's voting patterns.[47] Polarization in Congress does follow a similar temporal path to electoral polarization, in that the phenomenon appears to have significantly accelerated starting in the 1990s.[48] To scholars subscribing to the theory that legislative polarization drives other nodes of polarization, the realignment of southern conservatives was a product of members of Congress realigning first.

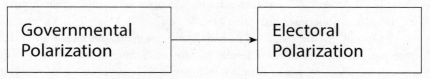

Figure 8.3. Governmental Polarization Driving Electoral Polarization.

There is an inexorable connection between the electoral forces behind polarization and those of its legislative counterpart. For instance, the same open primaries discussed above tend not only to feature a less representative electorate but also to elect more extreme candidates in a directly opposite result to what they intend.[49]

Regardless of primary type, region of the country, interparty competition, or other factors, primary elections have most certainly pushed candidates for office out to the extreme poles of partisanship over the last two decades. Those polarized and extreme candidates thus bring their campaign rhetoric and promises into elected office and attempt to act on them.[50]

As parties have weakened, other external forces have come to have great effect. Repeatedly throughout this book we have shown how organized interests have supplanted many of the linkage duties formerly provided by the parties, and the deleterious effects this has had on modern-day American politics. The rise of interests has also contributed to the legislative polarization seen today. Organized interests can and do coordinate with donors to target specific candidates in primary elections to bring them out toward a polarized state.[51]

Ideological moderates also see no point in entering contests that naturally push them out to the extremes. Moderate voices tend to opt against running in partisan races specifically because they know that they will not be competitive in primary elections that intrinsically favor extreme candidates and viewpoints.[52] Primaries push candidates out toward the poles by encouraging those with more centrist views not merely to alter them, but to reduce those views from the campaign environment entirely.

Certainly, there are other causes to polarization within legislatures. Gerrymanders, income inequality, career incentives for strategically minded candidates, and geographic self-sorting by ideologically driven voters, are all additional contributors to the increasing polarization seen in American legislatures over the last two decades and more.[53] But many of the forces pushing elected officials out to the extremes are rooted in the processes that drag them to the extremes while running for office. The advent of the direct primary certainly is a contributing factor to the polarization phenomenon.

The model that posits the root cause of polarization as legislative behavior is as limited as the party-in-the-electorate model discussed above. The polarization process affecting both the electorate and legislators appears to be happening simultaneously and in a recursive pattern. As neither the electorate nor legislators appear to be driving polarization on their own, primaries become a better explanation of both polarization processes together.

Mediated Polarization

Another explanation offered for increasing political polarization related to the era of primary elections is media coverage. As noted by Iyengar, the mass media can be seen as the post-primary inheritor of the linkage role taken from political parties.[54] Iyengar's case is a strong one, but the media do not provide the same quality of political linkage to the electorate that parties provided. First and foremost, mass media are not inherently political entities. While the stories they cover focus on politics and they are a vital source of information for a polity, they are (at least in the United States) private businesses whose core goals have nothing to do with public policy. American media entities are profit driven, meaning their successes are measured not by election of a certain party's candidates, nor of an ideologically driven policy initiative through the lawmaking process. Media are successful when they make a profit, determined by advertising and/or subscription revenue. Parties, and even to a lesser extent interest groups, have inherently political goals: electing candidates to office and/or passing a policy agenda into law. But since the media are profit driven, they have an incentive structure that does not include political linkage in any way. In other words, even if the media contribute to the failure of a civic society, they will not be concerned as long as they are making money. In an era where ideologically driven cable and online news entities can profit based on catering to that self-same ideological extremity, the media will act as an accelerator for that polarization driven by the primaries. This means the media are not well-suited linkage institutions even though the primary-driven weakness of parties has unwittingly thrust the media into such a role.[55]

As such, figure 8.4 shows the model where the media, as an unmotivated linkage institution, provides voters with skewed views of politics because ratings and revenue indicate that is what people want. The polarized views shown through the media then drive polarization within the electorate, ending with a polarized government through the electoral process.

Findings of media-driven polarization are mixed. As media outlets have become more partisan over the last twenty years, political attitudes of most

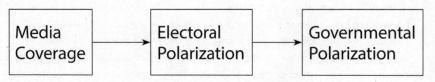

Figure 8.4. Media Coverage Driving Polarization.

Americans have remained fairly moderate. However, the division between the highly engaged partisan and the disengaged moderate emerges even more. Evidence points to some polarization among the politically involved while expanding news source choices decreased the number of less interested, less partisan voters casting ballots, making elections more partisan. But evidence in at least one study for a causal link between more partisan messages and changing attitudes or behaviors is mixed at best. Measurement problems hold back research on partisan selective exposure and its consequences. Ideologically one-sided news exposure may be largely confined to a small, but highly involved and influential, segment of the population. There is no firm evidence that partisan media are making ordinary Americans more partisan, but the politically active class has become significantly more so from their media consumption choices.[56]

One significant mechanism by which media content consumption translates into political polarization is through selective exposure. With a myriad of ideologically aligned content provider options (such as FOX News on the right and MSNBC on the left) available to the general public, politically interested individuals can tailor their news choices to conform with their own belief systems. That selective exposure to reinforcing media eliminates the individuals' belief that there are other views worthy of understanding or converting into public policy. One study, using National Annenberg Election Survey data, provided statistically significant evidence that partisan selective media exposure created or exacerbated individual-level political polarization.[57]

Consistent with the model, media coverage of polarization itself tends to increase polarization. In one study, media coverage of polarization increases citizens' perceptions that the electorate was polarized. Furthermore, the picture of that polarized electorate caused voters to increase their dislike of the opposing party. Journalistic coverage can then be seen as "anti-cues" to media consumers.[58]

As with the prior evidence of polarization, mediated polarization appears to occur simultaneously with its legislative and electoral counterparts. Other factors are driving all of the different forms of polarization, suggesting an even deeper root cause.

Campaign Spending

Election campaigns need money to operate. Even the most amateur-driven local election campaign will need some form of seed money to pay filing fees, print a few T-shirts or yard signs, and mail postcards to voters. So, the presence of a second layer of election campaigning in the direct primary will obviously add more spending to the totals needed to fund American political campaigns. But the amount of money spent on primary elections is a significant amount when one considers that every partisan race in the country now has a direct primary to which it is attached.

Consider the 2016 presidential election, a good race to measure campaign spending in primaries because the term limitation of President Barack Obama created an automatic open primary on both sides of the partisan divide. Democrats spent nearly a half-billion dollars in the quest to replace Obama.[59] Out of any other context, the number is staggeringly large. Hillary Clinton and Bernie Sanders spent nearly equal amounts, or roughly a quarter of a billion dollars each. Outside groups added another $20 million to the Democratic primary outlay, meaning a full $500 million went into one party's primary alone. The Republicans spent less, despite there being seventeen candidates in the field.[60] The presidential primary alone accounted for roughly one billion dollars in campaign spending in 2016, a massive amount.

When all campaigns at all levels are combined, the aggregate price tag for 2016's elections was about $6.5 billion, meaning the presidential primaries accounted for one-sixth of all campaign spending.[61] Separating the primary elections for all races out from the general election and spending on nominations alone accounts for $2.6 billion in 2016.[62] Primary spending thus adds two-thirds of the total general election campaign spending onto the tab for presidential campaign years. Primaries do not quite double American campaign spending, but they do significantly increase the cost of campaigning. Campaigning is expensive, and campaigning on a nationwide level is particularly expensive. When we calculate the amount each candidate in 2016 spent per vote earned, the picture becomes more favorable but still massive. Unsuccessful candidates like Chris Christie and Carly Fiorina spent more than $100 per vote, but the nominees spent amounts that seem frugal by comparison: Trump at $5.19 per vote and Clinton with $13.97 per vote.[63]

The added spending on campaigns has created more need for campaign funds, which further empowers and involves organized interests in campaigns.[64] Primaries lengthen the election calendar, produce unrepresentative elected officials, and exacerbate the inherent incumbency advantage already present in American elections.[65]

Perhaps most importantly, though, is the threat to the legitimacy of American elections that the added fundraising and spending needs have had on the political system. With parties weaker in their linkage roles to moderate campaign rhetoric and facilitate fundraising, outside groups have taken much larger roles, and candidates devote significant amounts of time to fundraising. The fundraising imperative is so dominant that the public has begun to believe that the candidates' fundraising needs have supplanted their desire to do the work of their elected positions. In a Pew public opinion poll, more than half of all respondents indicated frustration with the amount of money in politics. Two-thirds of respondents said they believed that many quality potential candidates decide not to run for office because of the high cost of campaigning. Further, three-quarters of respondents to the same poll believed that money has a greater and undue influence on political decision-making than in prior eras.[66]

Even when accounting for the per-vote spending noted above, the public believes that the imperative to fundraise comes at the expense of constituent connection. Political professionals will point to the disengaged public as a need for the high fundraising and spending on campaigns, but such explanations do little to quell public concerns about influence over elected officials.[67] Again, we see where the direct primary has negatively influenced American politics. Parties have become minor fundraising players in today's campaign environment and thus cannot intervene against the narrative that campaigns are "too expensive" or that the public's voice is ignored when campaign money is introduced. In the absence of a political linkage, the public is left without help interpreting the amounts of money and what funders receive in return for their contributions. The direct primary creates a spiral of difficulty for parties: an entire second campaign environment makes a more expensive political season; parties are marginalized in the fundraising process and demonized by the outside groups that supplant them, and are unable to salve the public's concerns about outside influence.

A New Model of Campaign-Driven Polarization

All of the models we have used to explain the deleterious effects of primary elections on American politics today have two common threads and limitations. First, they are narrowly focused on single elements of causation. In actuality all of the different models provide a portion of the explanation for how primaries have weakened parties and, by extension, weakened politics. Second, they all provide evidence of a change that is happening concurrently, suggesting a common causation from an as-yet-undefined source. The models

172 | Primary Elections and American Politics

are not wrong; they just need to be included in a larger model that encompasses all of the causes of partisan weakness into a single explanatory path.

Figure 8.5 presents our theoretical model to explain the effect primaries have had on politics in twenty-first-century America. The core of our model is the understanding that, as parties have been weakened in their linkage role, they have simultaneously driven multiple interacting changes that combine to provide significant threats to the political system.

We begin with the root cause of the current challenges to politics being primary elections. As we have documented throughout this work, primaries have been the single most significant threat to the parties in American history, and parties are certainly weaker as linkage institutions in a primary regime. The weakened state of parties is not the only effect of primaries, however, because weakened linkage institutions lead to weaker republics.

As parties have been weakened progressively over the last century, other forces have entered into the political realm to serve as the public's linkage. Organized interests have taken over a portion of the funding role that parties played, but the information and mobilization roles have been taken on more by the media. A more present and dominant role for the mass media has been the main compensation for party withdrawal from the linkage role. Where the parties' weakness has truly emerged and drives our model is the advent of candidate-driven rational electioneering, which in turn has polarized the parties and led to a simultaneous process of polarization within the electorate and government.

What is rational electioneering? Put simply, it is the professional campaign milieu that has supplanted parties as the organizing force behind electioneering efforts. Parties used to conduct all of the work behind a campaign for office. But the introduction of primaries reduced the role those parties could play, by eliminating their core role in deciding candidates for office. Other Progressive reforms contributed to the weakening of parties by eliminating the spoils system, simultaneously taking away the parties' abilities to fundraise and offer substantive incentives to participate. Together, those changes took the parties out of campaigns.

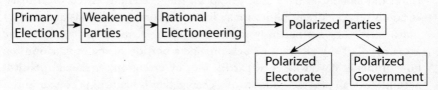

Figure 8.5. Primary as Polarization Driver.

Almost immediately after the parties began to suffer the effects of the primaries, professionals who could substitute for party involvement became part of the campaign environment. Members of the California assembly felt compelled to hire Hollywood public relations professionals to wage an information campaign against Pacific Gas & Electric as far back as the 1920s. As stronger media took the parties further out of the center of the campaign process, new forms of media to which the parties could not adapt required more specialized knowledge and skills that would develop into the world of professional campaign consultants.[68]

Those professional consultants were both necessary to fill the gap left by the shrinking party organization and a cause of their further diminution as a linkage institution. Parties did not have the resources to devote to campaign management teams provided to candidates; they were limited in their fundraising capacities, which in turn brought outside money sources into politics; and their inability to hold primary-winning nominees accountable and aligned with the party primary led to the decay of their public value as an information shortcut to the voting public.[69]

Rational electioneering is the style of campaigning dominant in the American context for the last forty years, brought on as a necessary response by campaigns to losing their core provider of support, the party. In the absence of party as an organizing force, campaigning became more technological, more strategic, more expensive, and more divisive.[70]

The parties experienced a false dawn during the soft-money era, when parties were allowed to partially replicate their linkage role. The era of the party as the central coordinating hub of an electioneering network, though, was short-lived.[71] Parties could provide informal connections between candidates, funding sources, and professional campaign staff, but even that role was limited, and professionals began to see diminishing returns on party involvement even before the soft-money era ended under the McCain-Feingold BCRA reforms.[72]

Parties campaign as a unit, but the focus of campaigns in the primary era has shifted to the candidates and their campaigns. The parties cannot consolidate their candidates at the national, state, or even local level behind a common platform. As issues specific to particular constituencies emerge, what it means to be a partisan at one level is not necessarily consistent with that same party's candidates and views at other levels. The compartmentalization of races and campaigns has further stretched what a party means to people, lessening its value to the public and further distancing the public from its politics.[73]

Professional electioneering has embraced many of the trends that hallmarked the decline of parties: extreme issue-position taking, alignment with organized interests, reduction in party allegiance in campaigning, and sophisticated micro-targeting over mass mobilization, as well as compartmentalization.[74]

As parties have been minor players for an extended period of time, the money sources and extreme views necessary to become competitive have forced campaigns to polarize in their views and issues. The further apart the parties have become, the more a concurrent polarization has occurred among the public and elected officials. Partisans, at least those who are left, use the campaign rhetoric from their candidates as cues for their issue preferences, stretching them out to the extremes. Professional campaigning means that elected officials know that unkept campaign promises will put their future reelection in jeopardy, thus making policy agendas and votes more polarized at the same time. The common source of polarization, therefore, is the primary-driven campaign environment in which professional campaigns operate. And, on the other end, we have an electorate who either are driven from politics or are individual political consumers of ideological extremism. In either case, the ancient ideal of citizen, as one devoted to seeing their role as full of responsibility in fostering the greater good, is lost or diminished.

Chapter 9

Conclusion

I don't care who does the electing, so long as I get to do the nominating.[1]

—William Magear "Boss" Tweed

The reality is that it [a primary] scrambles power among faction chiefs and their bands, while the people are despoiled and oppressed. The fact that the thing is done in the name of the people, and with the pretense that it is done for the people, ought not to obscure the patent facts of the situation.[2]

—Henry Jones Ford

As 2019 ended, there was a flurry of commentary, from scholars and journalists, sharply attacking the nomination process. This is not surprising. The 2016 primaries had produced arguably the two most unpopular general election candidates in US history. Hillary Clinton and Donald Trump did have devoted followers, but overall a strong majority of voters were deeply unsatisfied with the choices. Certainly, it occurred to many to ask, "Couldn't we do better?"

The campaign for president, as it unfolded in 2019 into early 2020, appeared just as unsettling. The Republicans were busy canceling primaries clearing the path for Trump's easy renomination. Although a number of Republicans did announce they would seek the party's nomination, none of these candidates were prominent in the party. Presidential incumbents rarely attract serious challengers; nonetheless, given his controversial administration and an approval rating that was rather low in a good economy, Trump's total command of the party is worthy of comment. Furthermore, Trump's control of the Republican Party worried many as they contemplated the long-term health of the GOP.

On the Democratic side, the number of candidates rose to over twenty and the fall of 2019 included several back-to-back days of debates to handle the scores of contenders. As the campaigned progressed, the field narrowed. But by year's end, the field included a mayor of a mid-sized city who had never polled more than 10,991 votes (Pete Buttigieg), an entrepreneur and social activist who had held no elected office (Andrew Yang), and a hedge-fund billionaire with no political experience (Tom Steyer), yet it no longer included a respected US senator (Cory Booker; another US senator, Michael Bennet of Colorado, was polling poorly). By this time, as well, successful Democratic governors from Washington, Montana, and Colorado had already dropped out (Jay Inslee, Steve Bullock, and John Hickenlooper). Another important Democratic senator qualified for the final debate of the year, but dropped out of the race instead (Kamala Harris); however, a sometime Democratic, former Republican, former independent mayor of New York City had entered the race (Michael Bloomberg).

Complaints about the primaries are hardly new. Indeed, they are quite common and nearly every election cycle will feature some important criticisms of the process from candidates, pundits, and academics alike. Earlier criticisms had often been about what caused certain candidates not to enter the race or that the process needed fine-tuning to produce better candidates. Why did the very popular and nationally appealing governor of New York, Mario Cuomo, not run in 1992? In 1988, would Gary Hart have made a better Democratic candidate than Michael Dukakis, if he had not been beset by scandals (was the media ruining the process by its intrusive reporting of private lives or finally waking up to the need to cover the candidates thoroughly)? How did a journalist and media-driven personality like Pat Buchanan do so much damage to a sitting president in 1992? Was it fair and right for the Republican governors, and other members of that party's establishment, to so forcefully back George W. Bush in 2000 and short-circuit what should have been a more open nomination process after eight years out of power for that party? The working assumption for several decades was that primaries were a given, they were fundamentally good, and whatever problems they created were eminently fixable. The Democrats, in particular, seemed devoted to making a quadrennial effort at tinkering with the process—changing the threshold for winning delegates and adding superdelegates to the nomination process. But, overall, the basic assumption was that the primaries simply are a "given" almost natural process. They were, in some sense, like the weather, just something with which you dealt.

Somewhat new, though, were the strong cases being made against the entire process itself. Primaries were not some fixed system to be accepted as is. These new arguments alleged that primaries didn't simply need a few tweaks to make them better: they needed to be overhauled completely, and there was more than a hint, from some commentators, that the entire process was suspect. One of the strongest arguments came from Jonathan Rauch and Ray La Raja, writing in *The Atlantic*. Their argument was careful and nuanced, but the title of their article—"Too Much Democracy Is Bad for Democracy"—neatly summarized their conclusions. Rauch and La Raja pointed out the odd nature of many of the 2020 Democratic candidates and the triumph of Trump himself as signs of trouble. They also pointed out that the old system, with much less democracy, had produced Lincoln, both Roosevelts, Wilson, and Truman. Rauch and La Raja also cited polls showing that voters themselves—the supposed recipients and wielders of this direct political power—were skeptical of the process. Though research showed heighten interest in politics, only a distinct minority of voters thought the system was producing good nominees.

Of course, that older pre-binding-primary system also produced less-than-ideal results, such as the nomination of Warren G. Harding and Richard Nixon's first nomination for president. The era of nomination by convention also gave us largely forgettable presidents such as Benjamin Harrison, Grover Cleveland, William Howard Taft, and Calvin Coolidge. Still, that system with its abhorred "establishment" kept people like Henry Ford or Huey Long from getting anywhere near the nomination. And, as Levitsky and Ziblatt remind us, in their comparative study of democracies, efforts to slowly weaken the parties' traditional powers have led to all sorts of problems. And, in a global perspective, American reforms can be seen as having weakened essential institutions and practices and threatening democracy itself.[3] The recent scholarship on the crisis in democracy is alarming. Levitsky and Ziblatt's *How Democracies Die* shows how the transformation of parties contributed to the state we are in. Healthy democratic norms are under assault and the institutions, such as parties, that taught "egalitarianism, civility, sense of freedom, and shared purpose" are weaker than ever.[4] No one is seriously suggesting that we try to resurrect the nineteenth- and early-twentieth-century practice of powerful conventions with corrupt party bosses. Even if that were desirable, how would it be done? That world is dead. American politics has moved on and the culture has changed.

However, something is amiss in our political world. We live in a world that is highly polarized and prone to political paralysis, and with a system unable to deal with chronic problems or plan for long-term challenges. Certainly, the causes of our predicament are many. However, the state of the political parties is clearly one of the causes, and primaries have exacerbated the parties' weaknesses, making matters even worse. To better our situation, at least in part, the objective must be to significantly improve the way parties nominate candidates. And to do that, we need to think clearly about just what parties are.

Political parties are more than just ideological homes for citizens. We have a plethora of good words—liberal, conservative, progressive, socialist, nationalist, to name a few—that people can use to identify their policy beliefs and any philosophical frameworks they employ. But, though the Republicans are clearly the conservative party, the party is more than that. The same can be said of the Democratic Party—it is the left-wing party but it is not the same thing as being liberal or progressive. The Democratic and Republican parties are institutions that provide linkages between elected officials and between different branches of government. They also provide, as an institution, links between citizens and those officials. They also include a mass element to the party system. But this mass element exists within a larger society that includes a very complex governmental structure. For over two centuries parties have been central to making that government work. Not only do they serve to staff government and make the branches of government function well (at times), they also have been vital forces in providing democratic legitimacy to the United States. This has been done by bringing the voter into the party system. People do identify as Democrats or Republicans. However, while voter input into how parties function is a good thing, we should not embrace it as the only thing.

The past fifty years have thrown the carefully calibrated political world of American party politics out of balance. By weakening the additional functions of parties with regard to nominating candidates, we have embraced a pseudo-democracy. We have sought to graft direct democracy onto a large representative constitutional republic. The authors of this book are emphatically not anti-democratic. Rather, we seek to understand how to make democracy work in such a complex system. And instead of seeing parties as obstacles to be worn down or thrown aside, as we argue the Progressives did, we instead want to be clear-headed about what they do—and can do well. Direct democratic efforts have failed because they were not participatory democratic efforts. These recent experiments at giving citizens such a direct role in selecting nominees have not achieved the promised goals of the reformers—the highly participatory world of deliberative citizens engaged in collective rule. Instead, we have weakened the system by enhancing polarization and bolstering the power of the largely unaccountable media, the very wealthy and others who have access to great amounts of cash. Thus, it is not surprising that no other democratic country approaches nominations our way and why, before the 1970s, neither did the US.

We are not suggesting that the old system was perfect. Nor do we suggest that the primary system produced nothing but failures. Reagan and Obama, in particular, both have their champions among citizens and scholars. But it seems obvious that the while the primary system can produce successful politicians and good presidents, the system is doing that despite itself. Furthermore, this system is too prone to produce unpopular candidates and presidents without the skills necessary to succeed in office. We are apt, in the future, to see more Trump-like candidates and presidents. And this will not be confined to the Republican Party. The Democrats will have their celebrity media candidates with little government experience—just with the requisite leftist policy positions. Especially now that Democrats have eliminated the role of superdelegates in the first round of nomination votes at their conventions, Democrats are as prone to a Trump-like takeover as the Republicans have been shown to be.

In short, we live in a representative democracy and, on the face of it, it is odd to think that established party leaders lack a greater explicit role in the process of nominating candidates. This is not to say that party leaders play no role; however, it is patent that they play a diminished role compared to fifty years ago. These leaders are the ones who know what is required of winning and serving in office (even if no one can ever be fully prepared to sit in the Oval Office). And they have the capacity, in ways the average person simply does not, to know which candidates are more likely to be successful—both in a general election and in office. Through personal experience and a lifetime devoted to politics, they have what must be accepted as political expertise.

Whatever else a party is, and it is many things, its job must be to present good candidates to the office. At the beginning, Madison warned that "enlightened statesmen will not always be at the helm," but he also expected that good men would plentifully fill many offices.[5] He also thought that most of the time, politicians would generally be those "whose wisdom may best discern the true interest of their country, and whose patriotism and love of justice, will be least likely to sacrifice it to temporary or partial considerations." Madison's patriarchal assumptions and language should not hide from us that we need good, talented politicians at the helm. And the first step in that regard is to make sure the parties are nominating good people.

The Purposes of the Nomination Process

To think clearly about how to improve the nomination process we need to step back and ask what the main purpose of a nomination process should be. Obviously it is to find a party candidate for the general election. But to say just that says little beyond a political platitude. There are any number of ways to do that—voting, drawing straws, appointment by party elders. Beyond the obvious, the nomination process actually has a number of important purposes, and some methods are better able to achieve these goals than others. The goals of a well-functioning nomination process appear, to us, to have four main features.

1. A Good Candidate

Parties must choose a candidate that can unite the party and appeal to a broad enough coalition of voters to win the general election. Simply put, winning elections is what parties do. Ideologies do matter and the parties have always stood for something. But parties in democracies have to include a very significant commitment to winning. American parties are emphatically not Marxist-Leninist parties that seek to impose an agreed-upon ideology above all other considerations. While it is certainly true that the parties have, from time to time, badly miscalculated about this, their goal is always to seek the strongest candidate to win the general election. Yes, it is true that Goldwater and McGovern both represented parties that failed to sufficiently account for the need to appeal to a large enough set of voters. (To be fair, in both cases the incumbent would almost certainly have won. But we can make a strong case that different candidates would have performed better against Johnson in 1964 or Nixon in 1972.) And, in each case, the parties quickly returned to offering candidates who could and did win—Nixon in 1968 and Carter in 1976.

2. Democratic Legitimacy

The process needs to confer democratic legitimacy upon the nominee. On the surface, this is an appealing part of the primaries and one of the justifications for its adoption in the first place. Americans have a strong inclination, one could almost say instinct, to decide things democratically. Tocqueville noticed this in his visit as he wrote, "circumstances combine to render the power of the majority in America not only preponderant, but irresistible."[6] Tocqueville, while hopeful that a better America would prevail, feared that this majoritarianism would tyrannize American politics. Many others have commented on the numerous elections that occur in the US. We seek elections on all sorts of offices—high to low. So, why not have an election, within the party, to decide who should represent the party in the general election?

Yet, as we have pointed out, turnout is usually quite low in primaries and caucuses. Tocqueville's fears about democracy evolved into a more devious system—one where the arguments for the system shield the way the very few control politics in the name of this Potemkin democracy. The power of the unelected media and big-money donors in the current system is painfully clear. Indeed, how democratic is a system in which one extraordinary wealthy man can keep his favorite candidate, almost pet-like, alive for a long stretch through the primaries? That is what happened in 2012, when Sheldon Adelson bankrolled the extremely weak candidacy of Newt Gingrich.

Furthermore, the US is almost alone, among contemporary democracies, in providing voters with this much theoretical power in deciding party nominees. We need to think differently about what democratic legitimacy must mean. After all, as hard as it is to believe, conventions once conferred a real kind of democracy legitimacy. This suggests that democratic legitimacy is real, but not tied to any one nomination process. What a nomination process should do is, as Rauch and La Raja write, "bring information to the nominating process . . . test candidates' ability to excite voters and campaign effectively . . . provide points of entry for up-and-comers and neglected constituencies . . . force candidates to refine their message and prove their stamina."[7] Indeed, one can imagine many different methods to achieve these goals. None of these qualities demand that we hold a long series of low-turnout primaries for months where the vagaries of primary order or the length of time between state primaries looms so large over the undertaking. Ordering and front-loading skew the process and favor certain groups over others. The primacy of the Iowa caucuses and New Hampshire primary are problematic for both parties. However, one can definitely make the case that it is particularly troubling for Democrats. Iowa and New Hampshire are two racially homogenous states, largely rural, carrying disproportionate weight in nominating the candidate. For all the Norman Rockwell–like appeal of the pictures of voters talking directly with candidates in living rooms, the voters of only two states receive such lavish benefits and neither state is representative of the nation as a whole. Even Republicans might be leery, given the southern base of that party, of acquiescing to two northern states influencing matters so greatly.

3. A Good President

As Nelson Polsby reminded us at the dawn of the new primary system in the 1970s, the goal is to elect a president. We cannot lose sight of this basic fact. What makes for a good president in a system like ours? There are a great number of good answers offered to this question, but Polsby's list is worthy of serious consideration. The job of president requires "intelligence, sobriety of judgment, intellectual flexibility, ability to work well with others, willingness to learn from experience, detailed personal knowledge of government, and other personal characteristics which can best be revealed through personal acquaintance."[8] The qualities that Polsby suggests a president needs remind us of the need for political experience, adaptability, and the ability to work well in a complex system with lots of political players and power centers. Too many people believe in what the political scientist Brendan Nyhan has identified as the "Green Lantern" theory of the presidency.[9] Through sheer willpower and the overwhelming legitimacy conferred by the voters themselves, a president will impose his ideas upon the world. This is an adolescent view of politics and shows a remarkable misunderstanding of the system of checks and balances and separation of powers the framers created in the first place. As Rauch and La Raja observe, "In reality, political influence in our system comes primarily from the soft power of relationships and political debate. Professionals judge the strength of those relationships."

4. Peer Review

Flowing from this last point, the nomination process needs some kind of peer review. Elaine Kamarck, of the Brookings Institution, has argued strenuously for this idea. She rightly points out, "We accept peer review in most aspects of life—except politics."[10] This just echoes what the political scientist Henry Jones Ford observed over 100 years ago: voters will look to others to provide information to voters, evaluate candidates, and offer support. As Ford wrote, "Politics has been, is and always will be carried on by politicians, just as art is carried on by artists, engineering by engineers, business by business men."¹¹ The current system is largely abdicating much of the decision-making in the political world to journalists and wealthy donors. But these groups are not actually adept at governing. In fact, their priorities are often aligned quite sharply against the goals of parties or the public whom the elected officials are eventually meant to serve and be accountable to. Even as many journalists bemoaned the process in 2016, they found Trump such good copy that he got media coverage that some have valued as high as $5 billion. As Leslie Moonves, chairman and CEO of CBS in 2016, famously said, the Trump campaign "may not be good for America, but it's damn good for CBS."¹²

Other elected officials, along with people who work for the national or state party committees, have the ability to get to know the candidates and discover those "personal characteristics which can best be revealed through personal acquaintance," as Polsby suggested.¹³ Furthermore, elected officials are the very people a future president is going to have to work with. Politics, in a representative democracy, is going to have to create a place for experts—political experts. In a small community, parties and such experts are not necessary. We can know, directly, the political actors without such a great need for an intermediary institution such as a political party. Transport me back to ancient Athens, as a citizen devoting much of my time to politics, and I don't need a political expert to tell me what Pericles was like. I might very well interact with Pericles from time to time. Certainly, I have close friends who do. There are very personal ways an individual could make informed decisions by the personal gathering of information. Primaries, in an unsettling way, confused the kind of democracy possible in ancient Greece (or any relatively small community) with the practice of politics in a large nation-state. This kind of grafting of a particular form of deliberative, direct democracy onto the nomination process is ill suited to making contemporary politics function well. Defenders of the current system think they are creating a more democratic system but this is illusory. They are, as Ford suggests, just changing the unique smaller subset of people who have real power.

What Is to Be Done?

Something must be done. There are, of course, any number of changes that could be adopted. But we would like to explore three changes that offer quite distinct ways to remedy some of the problems associated with the current system.

1. Strengthening the Parties

To strengthen parties and the peer review process, one idea would be to give party leaders the explicit power to shape the field. For instance, leaders could meet in an earlier nominating convention. However, instead of nominating the candidate, they would select a field of candidates, three or four, who have the approval of the party to proceed to the primary stage. This would have a number of advantages. First, it would give party leaders the explicit power to endorse a number of possible candidates. Candidates could still declare early. They could compete in sponsored debates well prior to the first caucuses and primaries. However, at some point between candidates announcing their run and those inputs of voters, a brief meeting/convention of party elites could vet those candidates. Candidates could still fight to get on the ballot even if they were not an endorsed candidate, but they would need to gather significant signatures to do so.

At the same time, citizens would still have a great deal of input. They would continue to vote in primaries—democratic practices would be preserved. However, it would be a constrained process. This would, of course, likely result in many candidates being excluded or forced to overcome hurdles to get "back in the game." But it would guarantee that party-approved candidates would be there in those winter-to-spring elections. By early 2020 the very diverse Democratic Party had lost most of its candidates of color. Harris, Booker, and Castro had dropped out before the first contest. An earlier convention might very well guarantee that at least one prominent non-white candidate would enter the primaries with a legitimate shot at getting the final nod. On the Republican side, although we can't know for sure, such a system might have excluded Trump in 2016. It almost certainly would have helped consolidate support behind fewer establishment figures instead of dispersing the vote so broadly—a phenomenon that greatly helped Trump win the nomination. Furthermore, for those who feared too much concentration of power in the party establishment, one could create a process to allow party activists and other non-elected people to be part of the early convention. There are endless ways to imagine how this convention might be populated.

There are also ways in which one could run this convention system the other way. The primaries could exist as they currently do; however, they would serve as forwarding names to a national convention of elected officials, state and national committee members, and former elected officials. In some ways this is what Utah does at the state level. In this case, the people would have a great deal of say, but not complete say. There could be a rotating series of regional primaries where any number of candidates could

Conclusion | 185

enter and campaign as they always have. However, instead of accumulating delegates, they would simply be winning votes. At the end of the process, one to three names would be advanced to the convention. There would, of course, be some minimum threshold—winning X percentage overall of the overall primary vote throughout the nation. (We would still probably have endless debates, particularly among Democrats, about how low or high to set the threshold.) The advantage of this system could be that all the candidates have been "endorsed" by the voters in some sense. This could confer democratic legitimacy on a number of candidates. It would also certainly signal to party leaders what kinds of candidates and messages are important to voters. However, in this arrangement, the experts could properly vet the candidates and consider a wide range of characteristics, skills, and appeals of the individuals. We believe that a candidate winning a clear majority of the votes in the primaries would have an extremely strong case to the convention. And, given the power of the democratic ideal, party leaders would be scared to reject such an appealing candidate. However, in the years when, say, three candidates showed strong appeal but failed to get a majority of the votes, the convention would serve as a place to collectively deliberate about who best represents the party and its needs.

Some might suggest that this is what superdelegates were supposed to do. But in practice their influence was limited. Conventions in this era have always served to ritualistically ratify the choice of the primaries. However, in this scenario, delegates would not be tied to candidates selected by the outcome of a primary, but rather would be tied first and foremost to the party.

The advantages of this suggestion, in light of the arguments of this book, are that it strengthens parties and gives party leaders powers they once had. Their expertise would be of value in a more systematic way than it is today. Yet, in some ways, by giving final say to the voters, the spirit of the Progressives would be maintained. The people would have a decisive role in selecting nominees. As different as this model is, in some ways it is a moderate proposal that would recover some of the old functions of the parties while recognizing we cannot go back to that old world. In effect, the fundamental role of parties is revived, but revived in light of the values, if not the specifics, the Progressives championed.

2. Helping Voters

A different approach would be to push for ranked-choice voting in primaries. Ranked-choice voting is a method by which voters can rank the candidates in order of preference. When the votes are counted, the least-supported candidate is eliminated and votes are redistributed to second choices. This continues until a clear winner emerges. This can be done quickly, and this method is sometimes called instant runoff voting. This idea is strongly defended by many students of elections and democracy when there are more than two candidates. The somewhat crude measure of just voting for one candidate can create suboptimal outcomes in multi-candidate elections. In traditional voting there are many hypothetical cases (in which historical analogs could easily be found) where a strongly favored second choice of all voters loses to a candidate who is strongly favored by a plurality.

Ranked-choice voting (RCV) eliminates this possibility. A fair number of countries use this method and it is being adopted by the state of Maine. At the local level, sixteen US cities use some form of RCV—Cambridge, Massachusetts, adopted theirs in 1941. In 2020, Andrew Yang supported such an idea, arguing that it would lead to higher turnout, reflect preferences better, lead to moderate candidates, and lessen negative campaigning. All elections call on us to make tradeoffs between desirable outcomes. Arrow's paradox reminds us that ranked-choice voting is not a cure-all to create a perfect election system. Still, there are apparent advantages to the ranked-choice method. If primaries are predicated on the concept of maximizing public choice, then RCV is a natural extension of that premise. Rank ordering provides an opportunity to share nuanced personal evaluations of multiple candidates in a quantifiable fashion. If RCV were implemented with one of the previously mentioned hybrid primary-convention models, the public would have an opportunity for richer input, and party elites would have a superior sense of the public's temperament toward their candidates.

Pushing for this alternative has a number of appeals. It would not require extensive changes to the process. Everything would be the same except this method of voting. If it worked, there is a possibility that extremist candidates, or weaknesses that most voters see in some individual but a plurality ignores, would not get nominated. In effect, it would likely eliminate the very worst possible candidates. Also, since most things would stay the same and ranking candidates does not remove the voters' control over the nomination process, it would maintain the democratic legitimacy of the current system. Of course, such a proposal is unlikely to solve more foundational problems that go deeper than a few bad candidates. It does little to change the power of the media or the wealthy. It does nothing to strengthen the peer review process, foster party unity, and empower the collective wisdom found in party organizations—though, to critics of parties, such collective wisdom is a myth that needs to be exposed and rejected.

There are also arguments that giving voters more choices might solve one of the main criticisms of the current system: its notorious low turnout. The claim is also made that we need it to get more moderate candidates—the nation hungers for the sensible middle that lacks the ability to organize effectively in the current system. However, all this remains to be seen, as it has not been widely adopted yet. Preliminary data does show, though, that voters appear to like it.

This reform would be the easiest to adopt. It could be phased in and adopted incrementally. Of course, this method does not substantially revive a strong role for parties in shaping the election. It would also accept that systematic deliberative democracy is just not feasible. This model fundamentally accepts the world wrought by the Progressive Movement, but seeks to reform it—to tweak it to lessen the worse outcomes possible in the current system.

3. Ending the Party Duopoly

One of the common arguments advanced against the current system is the stranglehold the main two parties have. The problem for critics is not political parties, but these two parties. Indeed, congresswoman Alexandria Ocasio-Cortez, a very progressive Democrat, said as much in early 2020 when she bemoaned having to be in the same party with Joe Biden. The "big tent" nature of the two parties is very frustrating to many members—particularly to those on either ideological extreme, since they frequently view themselves as shut out by the demands of the centrist tug to which both parties often give in. (This criticism actually is the opposite from the concerns of those pushing for ranked-choice voting, who often tout the moderating effects of their suggested reform.)

There is merit to this criticism. After all, most other democracies have some form of a functioning multiparty system. Even if two parties often dominate the political world, such as in Germany, there are a number of significant parties that play a very active role in most other nations. The United States is nearly unique in having such an all-powerful duopoly. Libertarians and Greens may attract voters, but they win only a handful of local offices. This is made even more remarkable, at least to some, by the diversity of this country. At its harshest, some critics even argue that for all the polarization, the two parties are not that far apart. The intense party fights are just intense battles between establishment tribes who don't disagree that much—at least not on fundamental issues. In the recent past, some have suggested that the two parties are really the same except divided on the question of abortion. Decades ago, segregationist George Wallace, in his 1968 run for president, said there was "not a dime's worth of difference between the Democrat and Republican parties"—a sentiment echoed years later by Ralph Nader in the 2000 campaign. To others, like Alexandria Ocasio-Cortez or Senator Bernie Sanders, the Democrats are clearly different from Republicans. Fear, however, or the corrupting power of the moneyed elites, is always pulling the party back to the center. The 2020 campaign saw many progressives arguing that Biden was far too compromising to be a real agent of change—only somewhat better than Trump. A similar phenomenon is seen on the right. Trump's triumph in 2016 could be explained by the desire, by many, to attack the Republican establishment.

If the two-party system is at fault, though, the question becomes how to end this duopoly. Leaving aside the merits of any desired party system, what creates a two-party system? From one perspective the American two-party system reflects the basis of the constitutional system—the existence of the single-office presidency as opposed to shared governance in a cabinet government encourages the formation of two parties. This is reinforced by the method of choosing the president—the Electoral College, which, with its winner-take-all approach, also makes the two-party system logical. This is furthered bolstered by the first-past-the-post, plurality-based nature of American elections. Simply put, in the United States there is no value in coming in second. The winner-take-all nature of elections encourages the formation of two parties, as out-groups have a strong incentive to unite, if possible.

These logical reasons lend themselves to the formation of two dominant parties. This is then reinforced by American history and political practice. The two US parties are very old, and they have dominated politics for so long it is hard to imagine breaking free of them. Whatever you may think of the Democrats and Republicans, they have been doing this for a long time.

However, there are those who argue that in reality the two parties are simply propped up, not by constitutional law, but by a complex set of lesser statutes and customs. These critics believe the Democrats and Republicans got into office and then entrenched themselves in power. For instance, the Democrats and Republicans have given themselves automatic ballot access—once someone wins the nomination of either party they are automatically placed on the ballot in November. For anyone else, the first hurdle is just getting on the ballot in the first place. Enormous resources, relatively speaking, must be expended gathering signatures to simply earn the right to compete as a non-major-party candidate. (This may be why people such as Ross Perot are appealing as candidates—they can fund such efforts and, indeed, generally fund a great many party-building activities.) The difficulty of doing so varies by state, with some states creating extremely hard barriers for third parties. In general, though, all states make it more difficult for third parties to get on the ballot. Given this head start that the two major parties have, it is simply too difficult to make any headway against them. People either become apolitical, waste time quixotically trying to build a third party, or throw up their hands and join whichever party is least offensive to them.

Whether the two-party system reflects a deeply entrenched constitutional logic or is largely fostered by state laws, proponents for change have argued for efforts to weaken the two major parties and open up the system for more parties. There is a belief that in such a system there would be a flowering of interest as people had more political options. The hope would be that citizens would become much more engaged in the process. They would find a party that more closely reflects their views. We would have a truer, more meaningful democracy. Of course, this line of argument is often advanced by those on the political extreme. Suppose we had a Congress with members from four or five or six parties? How would that work? Would it be more productive? Possibly it would be—the shifting alliances might be able to get things done. Or maybe it would just engender more gridlock. And that still leaves the tricky question of how we elect a president. Nonetheless, for those who see the problem as the Democrats and Republicans, the solution is not to work on the nomination process but to radically transform the entire political system.

From our perspective, weakening the party duopoly might create more engagement from the populace—as citizens finally see a party option that more closely aligns with their ideological views. Also, it is conceivable that more parties, and consequently more party activists, might bolster turnout and engagement.

The problem with ideas about breaking the party duopoly is that to be realistic it would probably take the most extensive reforms and is, thus, the most challenging to make work. We also have to wonder if more parties might lead to even more divisions in the country. The two parties, at their best, served to unify various groups and foster compromise among those groups. Indeed, the two parties have become institutions that teach the importance of compromise among supporters. Of course, in a deeply polarized world, maybe the intense fights between Republicans and Democrats make the stakes too high and a multi-party system could lower the political temperature some. In some sense, this is the most Progressive of reforms. One of the problems Progressives had with parties were the very intense, often irrational, attachments people had to them. Progressives might find their ultimate solution in the creation of lots of parties—parties that, for most people, only inspire weaker loyalties.

These possibilities are just three noteworthy ones. One can imagine many more, and variations on the three explored here. The first envisions strengthening the two parties themselves and attempting to adapt those parties with the best of the old ways of doing things while recognizing the new realities. The second places its hopes in enhanced voter power and is aligned with notions of power to the people and has the appeal of being fairly straightforward. The final suggestion is the most radical—an untried effort that, given the unknowns, is very appealing to those who see the current system as hopelessly corrupt or possibly foolhardy for those who still see real value in American politics and its history.

Dysfunctional polarization and fanatic partisanship are hardly worthy of praise. But to see political parties through that lens distorts their value. Parties are simply essential to making democracies work. We need to realize that they are not just for aggregating the unfiltered expression of mass opinion. They have an essential role in managing the political system. The nomination process, in particular, is where the democratic impulse must be channeled and regulated. Yes, the voice of the people must be heard, but it does not sing alone. Parties simplify a chaotic political world and give citizens meaningful choices. This sounds elitist, but that is because there is a role for politicians who are experts at the task of politics. Evidence of the public eschewing their ability to expand their participation through the primary system simply reinforces the need for intermediary institutions as helpers for a disengaged public. Parties can gather information more readily and judge candidates in ways the average voter cannot. And, as we have seen, to remove or weaken parties in this regard creates only an illusion of more democracy while empowering other elites with a less tangible concern for the greater good. At its best, an active role for parties in the nomination process offers respect to the democratic concerns of voters while drawing on the expertise of those who devote their lives to politics. Our constitutional system has always been about balancing competing forces. It is time, once again, to recognize that assertive parties have a central role in achieving that balance. The direct primary, with its intent to undermine party power, has taken the political system out of its proper balance.

Notes

Chapter 1

1. Thomas Jefferson, "Letter from Thomas Jefferson to Francis Hopkinson, 13 March 1789," *Founders Online*, accessed April 12, 2022, founders.archives.gov/documents/Jefferson/01-14-02-0402.

2. Michael A. Memoli, "Eric Cantor Upset: How Dave Brat Pulled Off a Historic Political Coup," *Los Angeles Times*, June 11, 2014.

3. Russ Choma, "Dave Versus Goliath, by the Numbers," *Open Secrets*, June 11, 2014, opensecrets.org/news/2014/06/dave-versus-goliath-by-the-numbers/.

4. Steven Levitsky and Daniel Ziblatt, *How Democracies Die* (New York: Broadway Books, 2018), 41.

5. James Lindley Wilson, *Democratic Equality* (Princeton, NJ: Princeton University Press, 2019), 170.

6. Wilson, *Democratic Equality*, 5.

7. Aristotle, *The Politics*, trans. Carnes Lord (Chicago: University of Chicago Press, 1984), book 3, chapter 4. Philip Ethington, in his essay on progressivism and democracy, defines democracy as "a condition in which all segments of the people of a sovereign polity take a role in the exercise of power over themselves." See Ethington, "The Metropolis and Multicultural Ethics," in *Progressivism and the New Democracy*, ed. Sidney Milkis and Jerome Mileur (Amherst: University of Massachusetts Press, 1999), 196.

8. The literature on democracy is extensive and varied. A good place to start is David Held, *Models of Democracy* (Stanford, CA: Stanford University Press, 1996), and Carol Pateman, *Participation and Democratic Theory* (Cambridge: Cambridge University Press, 1990). More recent works include James Lindley Wilson, *Democratic Equality* (Princeton, NJ: Princeton University Press, 2019), James T. Kloppenberg, *Toward Democracy* (Oxford: Oxford University Press, 2016), Christopher H. Achen and Larry M. Bartels, *Democracy for Realists* (Princeton, NJ: Princeton University Press, 2017), and Levitsky and Ziblatt, *How Democracies Die*.

9. Wilson, *Democratic Equality*, 143. See chapter 6 for a detailed discussion of democratic deliberation.

10. However, contemporary demands for equality, most forcefully articulated by Wilson, were lacking in ancient Greece, given that culture's views on slavery and gender.

11. Robert Dahl, *Democracy and Its Critics* (New Haven, CT: Yale University Press, 1989), 30.

12. Achen and Bartels, *Democracy for Realists*, 1.

13. Achen and Bartels, *Democracy for Realists*, 61.

14. Roosevelt himself authored the plank in the 1912 Progressive Party platform that was vague but called "a more easy and expeditious method of Amending the federal constitution." See Sidney M. Milkis, *Theodore Roosevelt, the Progressive Party, and the Transformation of American Democracy* (Lawrence: University Press of Kansas, 2009), 157.

15. Robert Talisee, *Overdoing Democracy: Why We Must Put Politics in its Place* (Oxford: Oxford University Press, 2019), 11.

16. Giulia Sandri, Antonella Seddone, and Fulvio Venturino, eds., *Party Primaries in Comparative Perspective* (Farnham, UK: Ashgate, 2015).

17. Morris P. Fiorina, Samuel J. Abrams, and Jeremy C. Pope, *Culture War? The Myth of a Polarized America* (New York: Pearson Longman, 2005); Willam G. Mayer and Andrew E. Busch, *The Front-Loading Problem: The Making of the Presidential Candidate* (Lanham, MD: Rowman and Littlefield, 2004), 83–132; Sean M. Theriault, "Party Polarization in the US Congress: Member Replacement and Member Adaptation," *Party Politics* 12, no. 4 (2006): 483–503.

18. James Morone, *The Democratic Wish* (New York: Basic Books, 1990).

19. John H. Aldrich, *Why Parties? The Origin and Transformation of Political Parties in America* (Chicago: University of Chicago Press, 1995).

20. James Reichley, *The Life of the Parties: A History of American Political Parties* (Lanham, MD: Rowman and Littlefield, 2000).

21. David M. Farrell and Paul Webb, "Political Parties as Campaign Organizations," in *Parties without Partisans: Political Change in Advanced Industrial Democracies*, ed. Russell J. Dalton and Martin P. Wattenberg (Oxford: Oxford University Press, 2002), 102–128.

22. There is an implicit reference to parties in the 24th Amendment, but no explicit discussion anywhere in the Constitution.

23. James Madison, *Federalist* no. 10, in *The Debate on the Constitution*, ed. Bernard Bailyn (New York: Library of America, 1993), 404–412.

24. Madison, *Federalist* no. 10, 406.

25. James Ceaser, *Presidential Selection: Theory and Development* (Princeton, NJ: Princeton University Press, 1979), 90–91: "The paradox of Jefferson's election in 1800 was that while he was chosen for partisan reasons, he did not intend to institute a system of permanent party competition. . . . Once a regime has been established on a sound basis there can be no further need for parties, unless as a temporary instrument to rescue the regime from subversion."

26. Marjorie Randon Hershey, *Party Politics in America* (New York: Routledge, 2017).

27. Michael Kammen, *A Machine that Would Go of Itself* (New York: St. Martin's Press, 1986).

28. For both a historical and a rational choice explanation for the development of parties see Aldrich, *Why Parties?*, chapter 1.

29. Noble E. Cunningham, *The Jeffersonian Republicans: The Formation of Party Organization, 1789–1801*, vol. 2 (Chapel Hill: University of North Carolina Press, 1957).

30. Reichley, *The Life of the Parties*, chapter 5.

Chapter 2

1. J. A. North, "Democratic Politics in Republican Rome," *Past & Present*, no. 126 (February 1990): 3–21.

2. Caroline M. Hibbard, *Charles I and the Popish Plot* (Chapel Hill: UNC Press Books, 2017).

3. David Ogg, *England in the Reign of Charles II* (Westport, CT: Greenwood Press, 1979).

4. Robert Willman, "The Origins of 'Whig' and 'Tory' in English Political Language," *Historical Journal* 17, no. 2 (June 1974): 247–264.

5. Robert M. Calhoon, *The Loyalists in Revolutionary America, 1760–1781* (New York: Harcourt, 1973).

6. Frederick B. Tolles, "The American Revolution Considered as a Social Movement: A Re-Evaluation," *American Historical Review* 60, no. 1 (October 1954): 1–12.

7. Alan I. Abramowitz and Kyle L. Saunders, "Exploring the Bases of Partisanship in the American Electorate: Social Identity vs. Ideology," *Political Research Quarterly* 59, no. 2 (June 2006): 175–187.

8. Ronald P. Formisano, "Federalists and Republicans: Parties, Yes—System, No," in *The Evolution of American Electoral Systems*, ed. Paul Kleppner (Westport, CT: Greenwood Press, 1981), 33–76.

9. Herbert J. Storing, "Introduction," in *The Complete Anti-Federalist*, ed. Herbert J. Storing (Chicago: University of Chicago Press, 1981), vol. 1, 6.

10. Forrest McDonald, *The Presidency of George Washington* (Lawrence: University Press of Kansas, 1974), chapter 2.

11. Darren Staloff, *Hamilton, Adams, Jefferson: The Politics of Enlightenment and the American Founding* (New York: Macmillan, 2005).

12. There were of course other people notable in the creation of the first two parties. Madison was quite important in helping Jefferson form the Republican (or Democrat-Republican) party. See John E. Ferling, *The Ascent of George Wash-*

ington: The Hidden Political Genius of an American Icon (New York: Bloomsbury, 2010).

13. George Washington, *George Washington's Farewell Address* (Krill Press via PublishDrive, 2015).

14. David P. Currie, *The Constitution in Congress: The Federalist Period, 1789–1801* (Chicago: University of Chicago Press, 1997).

15. E. E. Schattschneider, *Party Government* (New York: Rinehart, 1942), 1.

16. Russell J. Dalton, David M. Farrell, and Ian McAllister, *Political Parties and Democratic Linkage: How Parties Organize Democracy* (Oxford: Oxford University Press, 2011).

17. Sarah A. Binder, *Minority Rights, Majority Rule: Partisanship and the Development of Congress* (Cambridge: Cambridge University Press, 1997).

18. Herbert Kitschelt and Steven I. Wilkinson, "Citizen-Politician Linkages: An Introduction," in *Patrons, Clients, and Policies: Patterns of Democratic Accountability and Political Competition*, ed. Herbert Kitschelt and Steven I. Wilkinson (Cambridge: Cambridge University Press, 2007), 1–49.

19. See Aldrich, *Why Parties?*, 4. Our basic argument is that the major party is the creature of the politicians, the ambitious office seeker and officeholder.

20. James L. Sundquist, *Dynamics of the Party System: Alignment and Realignment of Political Parties in the United States* (Washington, DC: Brookings Institution, 1983), chapter 4.

21. Reichley, *The Life of the Parties*, 80.

22. V. O. Key Jr., *Politics, Parties, and Pressure Groups* (New York: Crowell, 1955).

23. Robert J. Dinkin, *Campaigning in America: A History of Election Practices* (Westport, CT: Praeger, 1989).

24. See Reichley, *The Life of the Parties*, chapter 5.

25. Aldrich, *Why Parties?*, chapter 3.

26. Schattschneider, *Party Government*.

27. Maurice Duverger, "Duverger's Law: Forty Years Later," in *Electoral Laws and Their Political Consequences*, ed. Bernard Grofman and Arend Lijphart (New York: Agathon Press, 2003), 69–84.

28. Cunningham, *The Jeffersonian Republicans*.

29. Paul Starr, *The Creation of the Media: Political Origins of Mass Communications* (Princeton: Princeton University Press, 2004), 92–94.

30. Robert V. Remini, *The Life of Andrew Jackson* (New York: Harper & Row, 1988).

31. James F. Hopkins, "Election of 1824," in *History of American Presidential Elections, 1789–1968*, ed. Arthur M. Schlesinger (London: Chelsea House, 1971), 4.

32. Reichley, *The Life of the Parties*, 88–89.

33. Marquis James, *Andrew Jackson: Portrait of a President* (New York: Grosset & Dunlap, 1937).

34. Jon Meacham, *American Lion: Andrew Jackson in the White House* (New York: Random House, 2009), chapter 16.

35. Lynn Hudson Parsons, *The Birth of Modern Politics: Andrew Jackson, John Quincy Adams, and the Election of 1828* (Oxford: Oxford University Press, 2009).

36. Reichley, *The Life of the Parties*, chapter 5.

37. Joseph Ellis, *American Sphinx: The Character of Thomas Jefferson* (New York: Knopf, 1997), 197–201.

38. Daniel Walker, *What Hath God Wrought: The Transformation of America 1815–1848* (Oxford: Oxford University Press, 2007), 246–247. Crawford, though, turned down the offer.

39. R. R. John, "Affairs of Office: The Executive Departments, the Election of 1828, and the Making of the Democratic Party," in *The Democratic Experiment: New Directions in American Political History*, ed. Meg Jacobs, William Novack, and Julian Zelizer (Princeton, NJ: Princeton University Press, 2003), 50–84.

40. David A. Schultz and Robert Maranto, *The Politics of Civil Service Reform* (New York: Peter Lang, 1998).

41. Dinkin, *Campaigning in America*.

42. Reichley, *The Life of the Parties*, 90–92.

43. Ceaser, *Presidential Selection*, chapter 3, "Martin Van Buren and the Case for Electoral Restraint."

44. Frank R. Kent, *The Democratic Party: A History* (Whitefish, MT: Kessinger Publishing, 2005).

45. Reichley, *The Life of the Parties*, chapter 5.

46. Andrew Jackson, "First Annual Message," *The American Presidency Project*, ed. Gerhard Peters and John T. Woolley, accessed November 30, 2021, www.presidency.ucsb.edu/ws/index.php?pid=29471.

47. Nathan Glazer and Daniel P. Moynihan, *Beyond the Melting Pot: The Negroes, Puerto Ricans, Jews, Italians, and Irish of New York City* (Cambridge, MA: MIT Press, 1970).

48. Richard J. Neuhaus, *The Naked Public Square: Religion and Democracy in America* (Grand Rapids, MI: Wm. B. Eerdmans Publishing, 1986).

49. Willam L. Riordan, *Plunkitt of Tammany Hall: A Series of Very Plain Talks on Very Practical Politics* (New York: Penguin, 1995).

50. Jerome Mushkat, *Tammany: The Evolution of a Political Machine, 1789–1865* (Syracuse, NY: Syracuse University Press, 1971).

51. James C. Scott, "Corruption, Machine Politics, and Political Change," *American Political Science Review* 63, no. 4 (December 1969): 1142–1158.

52. A. DiGaetano, "The Rise and Development of Urban Political Machines: An Alternative to Merton's Functional Analysis," *Urban Affairs Quarterly* 24, no. 2 (December 1988): 242–267.

53. Kenneth D. Ackerman, *Boss Tweed: The Rise and Fall of the Corrupt Pol Who Conceived the Soul of Modern New York* (New York: Carroll & Graf Pub, 2005).

54. Tracy Campbell, *Deliver the Vote: A History of Election Fraud, an American Political Tradition, 1742–2004* (New York: Basic Books, 2005).

55. Riordan, *Plunkitt of Tammany Hall*, 3–7.

56. Mike Royko, *Boss: Richard J. Daley of Chicago* (New York: Penguin, 1988), 12–14.

57. Jessica Trounstine, "Representation and Accountability in Cities," *Annual Review of Political Science* 13 (February 2010): 407–423.

58. Lyle W. Dorsett, *The Pendergast Machine* (Oxford: Oxford University Press, 1968).

59. For the Crump machine see "The Crump Era," The Benjamin L. Hooks Institute for Social Change, University of Memphis, accessed February 16, 2022, www.memphis.edu/benhooks/mapping-civil-rights/crump-era.php, and David Tucker, "Edward Hull 'Boss' Crump," *Tennessee Encyclopedia*, March 1, 2018, tennesseeencyclopedia.net/entries/edward-hull-and-crump/.

60. Thomas C. Reeves, "Chester A. Arthur and Campaign Assessments in the Election of 1880," *Historian* 31, no. 4 (December 1969): 573–582.

61. Reichly, *The Life of the Parties*, 156.

62. Ari Hoogenboom, "The Pendleton Act and the Civil Service," *American Historical Review* 64, no. 2 (January 1959): 301–318.

Chapter 3

1. "People's Party Platform," *Omaha Morning World-Herald*, July 5, 1892, available at wwnorton.com/college/history/eamerica/media/ch22/resources/documents/populist.htm. Walter Nugent makes the case that populist ideas were in the air and frequently adopted by later Progressives. See Nugent, *Progressivism: A Very Short Introduction* (Oxford: Oxford University Press, 2010), chapter 2.

2. Peter F. Galderisi, and Marni Ezra, "Congressional Primaries in Historical and Theoretical Context," in *Congressional Primaries and the Politics of Representation*, ed. Peter F. Galderisi, Marni Ezra, and Michael Lyons, 11–28 (Lanham, MD: Rowman and Littlefield, 2001).

3. David W. Noble, *The Paradox of Progressive Thought* (Minneapolis: University of Minnesota Press, 1958).

4. Wilson Carey McWilliams, "Standing at Armageddon," in *Progressivism and the New Democracy*, edited by Sidney Milkis and Jerome Mileur (Amherst: University of Massachusetts Press, 1999), 104.

5. Joyce E. Williams and Vicky M. MacLean, "In Search of the Kingdom: The Social Gospel, Settlement Sociology, and the Science of Reform in America's Progressive Era," *Journal of the History of the Behavioral Sciences* 48, no. 4 (2012): 339–362.

6. Kevin Mattson, *Creating a Democratic Public: The Struggle for Urban Participatory Democracy during the Progressive Era* (University Park: Penn State Press, 2010).
7. Nugent, *Progressivism*, 2.
8. Robert Wiebe, *The Search for Order, 1877–1920* (New York: Hill and Wang, 1983), 44.
9. Nell Irvin Painter, *Standing at Armageddon: A Grassroots History of the Progressive Era* (New York: Norton, 2008), xv.
10. Quoted in Painter, *Standing at Armageddon*, 99.
11. Herbert Croly, *The Promise of American Life* (Indianapolis: Bobbs-Merrill, 1965), 116.
12. There are a host of reasons to explain the persistence of a two-party system. Without going into all the causes, we could cite Duverger's law about single-member districts and plurality winning of congressional seats, the existence of the presidency itself as an undivided prize (as opposed to cabinet governments), and the historical traditions that built up, over time, in creating party loyalty in one of the two major parties. Finally, the two major parties often were quite accommodating and flexible enough in their ideologies that new movements were often absorbed by one of the major parties. This was what happened to the People's Party as it was absorbed into the Democratic Party with the nomination of Bryan in 1896.
13. Joseph Leon Blau, ed. *Social Theories of Jacksonian Democracy: Representative Writings of the Period 1825–1850* (Indianapolis: Hackett, 2003).
14. Alexander Keyssar, *The Right to Vote* (New York: Basic Books, 2000), 160.
15. Theodore Roosevelt, *An Autobiography* (New York: Library of America, 2004), 404.
16. For the militaristic metaphors about machines, see Walter Dean Burnham, *Critical Elections and the Mainsprings of American Politics* (New York: Norton, 1970), 72–73.
17. Ackerman, *Boss Tweed*, 54.
18. Richard White, *The Republic for which It Stands* (Oxford: Oxford University Press, 2017), 198.
19. White, *The Republic for which It Stands*, 535.
20. Riordan, *Plunkitt of Tammany Hall*, chapter 3.
21. Mary K. Simkhovitch, "Friendship and Politics," *Political Science Quarterly* 17, no. 2 (June, 1902): 191.
22. For a discussion of the number of jobs available to parties at a later time (1950s), see James Q. Wilson, *Political Organizations* (Princeton, NJ: Princeton University Press, 1995), 98–99.
23. Adam Cohen and Elizabeth Taylor, *American Pharaoh: Mayor Richard J. Daley* (Boston: Little, Brown and Co., 2000), 160. In many ways this formula is deceptive. If patronage workers could be constantly counted on in producing ten votes in each election, a fairly reasonable assumption in a well-functioning machine,

that meant that in lower-level city elections with lower participation rates those ten votes went even farther than they did for the big race for governor or president. This meant the races for city council or alderman could be very much in the grip of the machine. Control of these offices enabled the machine to persist for decades.

24. Daniel D. Stid, *The President as Statesman: Woodrow Wilson and the Constitution* (Lawrence: University Press of Kansas, 1998), 98–99.

25. Theodore Roosevelt, "The New Nationalism," in *Theodore Roosevelt: Letters and Speeches* (New York: Library of America, 2004), 811.

26. Ackerman, *Boss Tweed*, 358.

27. Painter, *Standing at Armageddon*, 10.

28. Painter, *Standing at Armageddon*, 390.

29. Painter, *Standing at Armageddon*, 405. See also Jane Addams, "Ethical Survivals in Municipal Corruption," *International Journal of Ethics* 8, no. 3 (April 1898): 273–291. She writes, "The alderman, therefore, bails out his constituents when they are arrested, or says a good word to the police justice when they appear before him for trial; uses his 'pull' with the magistrate when they are likely to be fined for a civil misdemeanor, or sees what he can do to 'fix up matters' with the State's attorney, when the charge is really a serious one."

30. Cohen and Taylor, *American Pharaoh*, 132.

31. Simkhovitch, "Friendship and Politics," 195.

32. Cohen and Taylor, *American Pharaoh*, 150. The only thing that changed was Daley's dress—he wore hand-tailored suits. Otherwise, he maintained the same lifestyle he had before winning the mayorship.

33. Simkhovitch, "Friendship and Politics," 198–199. See also Richard Hofstadter, *The Age of Reform* (New York: Vintage, 1955), 284.

34. Simkhovitch, "Friendship and Politics," 197.

35. Kevin Baker, "The Soul of the Machine," *New Republic*, August 17, 2016.

36. Selwyn Raab, *Five Families: The Rise, Decline, and Resurgence of America's Most Powerful Mafia Empires* (New York: Thomas Dunne Books, 2005), 45.

37. Keyssar, *The Right to Vote*, 160.

38. Keyssar, *The Right to Vote*, 159–160.

39. Quoted in Painter, *Standing at Armageddon*, 282.

40. Sheldon Wolin, *Democracy Incorporated: Managed Democracy and the Specter of Inverted Totalitarianism* (Princeton, NJ: Princeton University Press, 2008).

41. Roosevelt, "The New Nationalism," 813.

42. Austin Ranney, *Curing the Mischiefs of Faction: Party Reform in America* (Berkeley: University of California Press, 1976), 122.

43. Woodrow Wilson, *The New Freedom* (New York: Doubleday, Page and Company, 1913), 108. And the problem he sees comes in the form of special interest and machines: "We have seen many of our governments under these influences cease to be governments representative of the people, and become governments

representative of special interests, controlled by machines, which in their turn are not controlled by the people" (50).

44. For his views on race, see John Milton Cooper, Jr., *Woodrow Wilson: A Biography* (New York: Knopf, 2009), 79–80; 87–88; 205–206; 407–411.

45. Keyssar, *The Right to Vote*, 121.

46. Keyssar, *The Right to Vote*, 151–159.

47. Keyssar, *The Right to Vote*, 159.

48. Milkis, *Theodore Roosevelt, the Progressive Party, and the Transformation of American Democracy*, 69–70.

49. Cooper, *Woodrow Wilson*, 309.

50. Stid, *The Presidential as Statesman*, 32.

51. Anthony Downs, *An Economic Theory of Democracy* (New York: HarperCollins, 1957).

52. Stephen Ansolabehere, Shigeo Hirano, John Mark Hansen, and James M. Snyder Jr., "Primary Elections and Partisan Polarization in the US Congress," *Quarterly Journal of Political Science* 5, no. 2 (2010): 169–191.

53. David W. Brady, Hahrie Han, and Jeremy C. Pope, "Primary Elections and Candidate Ideology: Out of Step with the Primary Electorate?" *Legislative Studies Quarterly* 32, no. 1 (January 2011): 79–105.

54. Jeffrey M. Berry and Clyde Wilcox, *The Interest Group Society* (New York: Routledge, 2018), chapter 4.

55. Eric McGhee, Seth Masket, Boris Shor, Steven Rogers, and Nolan McCarty. "A Primary Cause of Partisanship? Nomination Systems and Legislator Ideology." *American Journal of Political Science* 58, no. 2 (October 2013): 337–351.

56. Morris P. Fiorina and Matthew S. Levendusky, "Disconnected: The Political Class versus the People," *Red and Blue Nation* 1 (2006): 49–71.

57. Drew DeSilver, "Turnout Was High in the 2016 Primary Season, but Just Short of 2008 Record," *Pew Research Center*, June 10, 2016, www.pewresearch.org/fact-tank/2016/06/10/turnout-was-high-in-the-2016-primary-season-but-just-short-of-2008-record/.

58. See Ian Sue Wing and Joan L. Walker, "The Geographic Dimensions of Electoral Polarization in the 2004 US Presidential Vote," in *Progress in Spatial Analysis*, ed. Antonio Páez, Julie Gallo, Ron N.Buliung, and Sandy Dall'erba (New York: Springer, 2010), 253–285; G. C. Jacobson, "Partisan Polarization in Presidential Support: The Electoral Connection," *Congress & the Presidency: A Journal of Capital Studies* 30, no. 1 (March 2003): 1–36; Mark D. Brewer, "The Rise of Partisanship and the Expansion of Partisan Conflict within the American Electorate," *Political Research Quarterly* 58, no. 2 (June 2005): 219–229; and Fiorina, Abrams, and Pope, *Culture War?*

59. See Aaron M. McCright, Chenyang Xiao, and Riley E. Dunlap, "Political Polarization on Support for Government Spending on Environmental Protection

in the USA, 1974–2012," *Social Science Research* 48 (July 2014): 251–260; Jamie L. Carson, Michael H. Crespin, Charles J. Finocchiaro, and David W. Rohde, "Redistricting and Party Polarization in the US House of Representatives," *American Politics Research* 35, no. 6 (November 2007): 878–904; John H. Aldrich and James S. Coleman Battista, "Conditional Party Government in the States," *American Journal of Political Science* 46, no. 1 (January 2002): 164–172.

Chapter 4

1. Elaine Kamarck, "Why Is the Presidential Nominating System Such a Mess?" *Center for Effective Public Management at Brookings*, January 2016, www.brookings.edu/wp-content/uploads/2016/07/primaries.pdf.

2. Theodore Roosevelt, "Who Is a Progressive," in *American Progressivism: A Reader* (Lanham, MD: Lexington Books, 2008), 40.

3. Michael McGerr, *A Fierce Discontent: The Rise and Fall of the Progressive Movement in America, 1870–1920* (New York: Free Press, 2003), 42.

4. For a discussion of the prohibition movement, see McGerr, *A Fierce Discontent*, 81–88.

5. Wyoming enfranchised women in 1869. Kevin B. Smith and Alan Greenblatt, *Governing States and Localities*, 6th ed. (Los Angeles: Sage, 2018), 66.

6. For a discussion of scientific management and the famous Frederick Winslow Taylor, see McGeer, *A Fierce Discontent*, 128–129. For Taylor's influence on public administration, see Brian Fry and Jos C. N. Raddschelders, *Mastering Public Administration from Max Weber to Dwight Waldo* (Washington: CQ Press, 2008).

7. Woodrow Wilson, "The Study of Administration," *Political Science Quarterly* 2, no. 2 (June 1887): 197–222. For a discussion of Wilson's groundbreaking article, see Jay Shafritz, E. W. Russell, and Christopher Borick, *Introduction to Public Administration*, 8th ed. (New York: Pearson, 2013), 26–27.

8. Daniel T. Rodgers, *Atlantic Crossings: Social Politics in a Progressive Age* (Cambridge, MA: Harvard University Press, 1998), 125.

9. Rodgers, *Atlantic Crossings*, p. 154.

10. Wilson, "The Study of Administration," 201.

11. Quoted in Edward Stettner, *Shaping Modern Liberalism: Herbert Croly and Progressive Thought* (Lawrence: University Press of Kansas, 1993), 64.

12. Herbert Croly, "Progressive Democracy," in *American Progressivism: A Reader*, ed. Ronald Pestritto and William Atto (Lanham, MD: Lexington Books, 2008), 240.

13. Croly, "Progressive Democracy," 241.

14. Croly, "Progressive Democracy," 249.

15. Frank Johnson Goodnow, "The American Conception of Liberty," in *American Progressivism: A Reader*, 63.

16. J. Birchall, *The International Co-operative Movement* (Manchester: Manchester University Press, 1997).

17. For a discussion of the concept of citizenship see Dennis Hale, "The Natural History of Citizenship," in *Friends and Citizens: Essays in Honor of Wilson Carey McWilliams*, ed. Peter Dennis Bathory and Nancy L. Schwartz (Lanham, MD: Rowman & Littlefield, 2001).

18. L. L. Gould, *America in the Progressive Era, 1890–1914* (New York: Routledge, 2014).

19. M. Shefter, "Regional Receptivity to Reform: The Legacy of the Progressive Era," *Political Science Quarterly* 98, no. 3 (Autumn 1983): 459–483.

20. P. G. Filene, "An Obituary for the Progressive Movement," *American Quarterly* 22, no. 1 (Spring 1970): 20–34.

21. Hofstadter, *The Age of Reform*, chapter 6.

22. Mushkat, *Tammany*.

23. S. E. Scarrow, "The Nineteenth-Century Origins of Modern Political Parties: The Unwanted Emergence of Party-Based Politics," in *Handbook of Party Politics*, ed. Richard Katz and William Crotty (Thousand Oaks, CA: Sage, 2006), 6–24.

24. Hofstadter, *The Age of Reform*, 166.

25. Ranney, *Curing the Mischiefs of Faction*, 79.

26. Peter Brent, "The Australian Ballot: Not the Secret Ballot," *Australian Journal of Political Science* 41, no. 1 (August 2006): 39–50.

27. Alan Ware, "Anti-partism and Party Control of Political Reform in the United States: The Case of the Australian Ballot," *British Journal of Political Science* 30, no. 1 (January 2000): 1–29.

28. Alan Ware, *The American Direct Primary: Party Institutionalization and Transformation in the North* (Cambridge: Cambridge University Press, 2002).

29. Richard P. McCormick, *The Presidential Game* (Oxford: Oxford University Press, 1982), 119–123.

30. G. Ecelbarger, *The Great Comeback: How Abraham Lincoln Beat the Odds to Win the 1860 Republican Nomination* (New York: Macmillan, 2008).

31. Aldrich, *Why Parties?*, chapter 2.

32. S. Wilentz, *Chants Democratic: New York City and the Rise of the American Working Class, 1788–1850* (Oxford: Oxford University Press, 2004).

33. Robert Keith Murray, *The 103rd Ballot: The Legendary 1924 Democratic Convention that Forever Changed Politics* (New York: HarperCollins, 2016).

34. *National Conference on Practical Reform of Primary Elections* (New York: W. C. Hollister & Bro., 1898), accessed on Google Books.

35. Toni McClory, *Understanding the Arizona Constitution* (Tucson: The University of Arizona Press, 2010), chapter 4.

36. Hofstadter, *The Age of Reform*, 257–270.
37. Nathaniel A. Persily, "The Peculiar Geography of Direct Democracy: Why the Initiative, Referendum and Recall Developed in the American West," *Michigan Law and Policy Review* 2 (January, 1997): 11–41.
38. Shigeo Hirano and James M. Snyder Jr., *Primary Elections in the United States* (Cambridge: Cambridge University Press, 2019).
39. Clarence J. Hein, "The Adoption of Minnesota's Direct Primary Law," *Minnesota History* 35, no. 8 (December 1957): 341–351.
40. Ware, *The American Direct Primary*, chapter 4.
41. Hein, "The Adoption of Minnesota's Direct Primary Law," 345–346.
42. Cortez A. M. Ewing, *Primary Elections in the South: A Study in Uniparty Politics* (Norman: University of Oklahoma Press, 1953).
43. Henry Jones Ford, *The Rise and Growth of American Politics: A Sketch of Constitutional Development* (New York: The Macmillan Company, 1898), 270.
44. Frank R. Baumgartner, Bryen D. Jones, and Peter B. Mortensen, "Punctuated Equilibrium Theory: Explaining Stability and Change in Public Policymaking," in *Theories of the Policy Process*, ed. Paul Sabateir and Christopher Weible (Boulder, CO: Westview Press, 2014), 59–103.
45. See Barbara Sinclair, "Senate Styles and Senate Decision Making, 1955–1980," *Journal of Politics*, 48, no. 4 (November 1986): 877–908; David W. Rohde, "Studying Congressional Norms: Concepts and Evidence," *Congress & the Presidency: A Journal of Capital Studies* 15, no. 2 (September 1988): 139–145; and Morris P. Fiorina and David W. Rohde, eds., *Home Style and Washington Work: Studies of Congressional Politics* (Ann Arbor: University of Michigan Press, 1991).
46. Don S. Kirschner, "The Ambiguous Legacy: Social Justice and Social Control in the Progressive Era. *Historical Reflections/Réflexions Historiques* 2, no. 1 (Summer 1975): 69–88.
47. Wilson, "The Study of Administration," 200.
48. Robert M. Crunden, *Ministers of Reform: The Progressives' Achievement in American Civilization, 1889–1920* (Champaign: University of Illinois Press, 1984).
49. Wilson, "The Study of Administration," 201.
50. Julius Turner, "Primary Elections as the Alternative to Party Competition in 'Safe' Districts," *Journal of Politics* 15, no. 2 (May 1953): 197–210.
51. Leo Alilunas, "The Rise of the 'White Primary' Movement as a Means of Barring the Negro from the Polls," *Journal of Negro History* 25, no. 2 (April 1940): 161–172.
52. V. O. Key Jr., *Southern Politics in State and Nation: A New Edition* (Knoxville: The University of Tennessee Press, 1984), chapter 19.
53. Darlene Clark Hine, Steven F. Lawson, and Merline Pitre, *Black Victory: The Rise and Fall of the White Primary in Texas* (Columbia: University of Missouri Press, 2003).
54. Nixon v. Herndon, 273 U.S. 536 (1927).

55. Nixon v. Condon, 286 U.S. 73 (1932).
56. Smith v. Allwright, 321 U.S. 649 (1944).
57. Ware, *The American Direct Primary*, chapter 5.
58. Ranney, *Curing the Mischiefs of Faction*, 79.
59. Stephen Ansolabehere, John Mark Hansen, Shigeo Hirano, and James M. Snyder Jr., "The Decline of Competition in US Primary Elections, 1908–2004," *The Marketplace of Democracy: Electoral Competition and American Politics* 74 (2006): 82–96.
60. Austin Ranney, "Turnout and Representation in Presidential Primary Elections," *American Political Science Review* 66, no. 1 (March 1972): 21–37; Richard W. Boyd, "The Effects of Primaries and Statewide Races on Voter Turnout," *Journal of Politics* 51, no. 3 (August 1989): 730–739.
61. See, for example, Peverill Squire, "Competition and Uncontested Seats in US House Elections," *Legislative Studies Quarterly* 14, no. 2 (May 1989): 281–295; R. Morris Coats and Thomas R. Dalton, "Entry Barriers in Politics and Uncontested Elections," *Journal of Public Economics* 49, no. 1 (October 1992): 75–90; Peverill Squire, "Uncontested Seats in State Legislative Elections," *Legislative Studies Quarterly* 25, no. 1 (February, 2000): 131–146.
62. Ansolabehere, Hansen, Hirano, and Snyder, "More Democracy."
63. James W. Davis, *US Presidential Primaries and the Caucus-Convention System: A Sourcebook* (Westport, CT: Greenwood, 1997).

Chapter 5

1. Quoted in Lewis Gould, *Four Hats in the Ring: The 1912 Election and the Birth of Modern American Politics* (Lawrence: University Press of Kansas, 2008), 23.
2. The counterpoint to Truman's praise of conventions is his observation that "primaries are just eyewash." Quoted in John Greene, *I Like Ike: The Presidential Election of 1952* (Lawrence: University Press of Kansas, 2017), 72.
3. This is the argument of Plato, most notably though not exclusively, in *The Republic*.
4. These include amending the Constitution to allow the direct election of senators, giving African Americans the right to vote (in theory at first), and extending the franchise to women and to younger people. There have been state-level actions (eliminating property requirements) to expand the voting population. But at this point these state-level actions are now backed by Supreme Court decisions to equalize voting. This is most powerfully expressed in the court ruling in Baker v. Carr (1962) and its ringing endorsement of the principle of "one man, one vote."
5. For a discussion of this topic, see Robert Dahl, *How Democratic Is the American Constitution?* (New Haven, CT: Yale University Press, 2001).

6. Elaine Kamarck, "Qualifying for the Debate: The Lost Role of Peer Review," *Brookings Institution*, September 11, 2019, www.brookings.edu/blog/fixgov/2019/09/11/qualifying-for-the-debate-the-lost-role-of-peer-review/.

7. For a fine, brief, summary of the evolution of the nomination process from the founding period to 1968, see Rhodes Cook, *The Presidential Nominating Process: A Place for Us?* (Lanham, MD: Rowman and Littlefield, 204), chapter 2.

8. Betrand de Jouvenel, "The Chairman's Problem," *American Political Science Review* 55, no. 2 (June 1961). Collected in *The Nature of Politics: Selected Essays of Bertrand de Jouvenel*, edited by Dennis Hale and Marc Landy (New York: Shocken Books, 1987).

9. Jouvenel, *The Nature of Politics*, 51.

10. Obviously, this is where questions of race, gender, and class (to name a few) come into play most forcefully.

11. Of course, we are not taking Jouvenel's discussion literally—it deals with actual meetings, but he meant to use it to illustrate challenges to democratic practice.

12. Morton Keller, *America's Three Regimes: A New Political History* (Oxford: Oxford University Press, 2007), 71.

13. M. Margaret Conway, *Political Participation in the United States*, 2nd ed. (Washington, DC: CQ Press, 1991), 99.

14. See Michael P. McDonald, "National General Election VEP Turnout Rates, 1789–Present," *United States Elections Project*, 2018, www.electproject.org/national-1789-present. Voter turnout in presidential elections before 1828 ranged from a low of 6.3 percent (1792) to a high of 40.4 percent (1812). Even the highly partisan, contentious election of 1800 between John Adams and Thomas Jefferson only had a participation rate of 32.3 percent. 1828 saw the first time that over 50 percent of the eligible voters cast a ballot.

15. We don't mean to suggest he thought up the idea of the convention. But he was open to the idea when it was presented to him.

16. Joel Silbey, *The American Political Nation, 1838–1893* (Stanford, CA: Stanford University Press, 1991), 59–60.

17. Michael Schudson, *The Good Citizen: A History of American Civil Life* (New York: The Free Press, 1998), 156.

18. Silbey, *The American Political Nation*, 60, 63.

19. Silbey, *The American Political Nation*, 62.

20. Silbey, *The American Political Nation*, 93.

21. Silbey, *The American Political Nation*, 71.

22. Reichley, *The Life of the Parties*, 206.

23. Of course, we should note Aristotle's gendered assumption about what it means to be a citizen. And, to be sure, conventions were almost exclusively male-dominated affairs in the nineteenth and early twentieth centuries. The first woman to become a delegate to a national convention was Francis Warren of Wyoming, who was a delegate to the Republican National Convention of 1900. That same year

Elizabeth Cohen, of Utah, was selected as an alternate delegate for the Democratic convention. When that delegate became ill, Cohen became a delegate to that convention. See Center for American Women and Politics, "Milestones for Women in American Politics," *CAWP*, 2021, cawp.rutgers.edu/facts/milestones-for-women.

24. Ranney, *Curing the Mischiefs of Faction*, 108.

25. With the rise of radio in the 1920s the public was more aware than ever about what was happening at these conventions. This almost certainly changed the nature of conventions as well.

26. Ware, *The American Direct Primary*, 57.

27. Ware, *The American Direct Primary*, 63.

28. All quotes taken from Robert La Follette's speech at the University of Chicago, February 22, 1897, as reported in "Peril in the Machine," *Chicago Times-Herald*, February 23, 1897; see *Wisconsin Historical Society*, www.wisconsinhistory.org/Records/Newspaper/BA1995.

29. On corruption and the rise of progressivism, see Richard Levis McCormick, "The Discovery that Business Corrupts Politics: A Reappraisal of the Origins of Progressivism," in *The Party Period and Public Policy* (Oxford: Oxford University Press, 1986), 311–356.

30. From a newspaper article (*American Review*, 1848), quoted by Joel Silbey, in *The American Political Nation*, 67.

31. This is from the end of his speech, "The Menace of the Machine." For good measure, La Follette follows this observation about enslavement with a quote from Lincoln's Gettysburg Address and concludes his oration linking his ideas with the savior of the Republic.

32. For a detailed discussion of La Follette and the adoption of the primary in Wisconsin see, Allen Fraser Lovejoy, *La Follette and the Establishment of the Direct Primary in Wisconsin, 1890–1904* (New Haven, CT: Yale University Press, 1941).

33. See Robert La Follette, "The Danger Threatening Representative Government" (1897), *U.S. History Primary Source Reader | HIS 20 BCC CUNY*, bcc-cuny.digication.com/ushistoryreader/Robert_La_Follette_The_Threat_to_Representative_Go.

34. Ranney, *Curing the Mischiefs of Factions*, 125.

35. Ranney, *Curing the Mischiefs of Factions*, 125.

36. La Follette claims in his *Autobiography* that he had never heard of the Crawford system until 1896 and that it was a stunning revelation to him that such an idea even existed. *La Follette's Autobiography: A Personal Narrative of Political Experiences* (Madison, WI: Robert M. La Follette Co., 1913), 196.

37. Ware, *The American Direct Primary*, chapter 3.

38. James Morone, *The Democratic Wish: Popular Participation and the Limits of American Government* (New York: Basic Books, 1990), 1.

39. Morone, *The Democratic Wish*, 126.

40. This is not to suggest that all Progressives were reading *The Social Contract*. We merely suggest the ideals that moved them were Rousseauian in nature. For a

more recent take on parties from an avowed follower of Rousseau, see Benjamin Barber, "The Undemocratic Party System: Citizenship in an Elite/Mass Society," in *A Passion for Democracy* (Princeton, NJ: Princeton University Press, 1998). Barber writes that parties are "deeply inimical to real democracy."

41. Louise Overacker, *Presidential Primary* (New York: Arno Press, 1974), 167.

42. See the section "The Rule of the People" in "Minor/Third Party Platforms: Progressive Party Platform of 1912," *The American Presidency Project*, ed. Gerhard Peters and John T. Woolley, www.presidency.ucsb.edu/documents/progressive-party-platform-1912.

43. Woodrow Wilson, "First Annual Message," December 2, 1913, *The American Presidency Project*, ed. Gerhard Peters and John T. Woolley, accessed January 10, 2019, www.presidency.ucsb.edu/documents/first-annual-message-18.

44. For a recent discussion of a national primary, see Cook, *The Presidential Nominating Process*, 137–139.

45. John Preimesberger, *Presidential Elections: 1789–1992* (Washington, DC: CQ Press, 1995), 149–150.

46. For a discussion of Taft's politically brutal, but hardly uncommon, approach in the South see James Chance, *1912: Wilson, Roosevelt, Taft and Debs—The Election that Changed the Country* (New York: Simon and Schuster, 2004), 110. Republicans in the South were emphatically told they would lose their jobs if they didn't support Taft.

47. Cooper, *Woodrow Wilson*, 151–153.

48. Chance, *1912*, 140–141.

49. Overacker, *Presidential Primary*, 175.

50. Quoted in David Pietrusza, *1920: The Year of the Six Presidents* (New York: Basic Books, 2007), 177. He was also considered at the 1928 Republican convention but Hoover won easily on the first ballot.

51. Quoted in Overacker, *Presidential Primary*, 105.

52. Overacker, *Presidential Primary*, 125–126.

53. Overacker, *Presidential Primary*, 134.

54. For the role of money in Wilson's 1912 presidential bid, see Gould, *Four Hats in the Ring*, 80 and 86–87. See also Cooper, *Woodrow Wilson*, 154.

55. L. Sabato, *The Rise of Political Consultants: New Ways of Winning Elections* (New York: Basic Books, 1981).

56. Overacker, *Presidential Primary*, 121.

57. On the Wood campaign, see Pietrusza, *1920*, 167–175, and Overacker, *Presidential Primary*, 121. Internal conflicts in campaigns have always existed. However, these matters spilling over into public and even affecting public opinion is much more likely in the primary process.

58. For turnout in 1912 primaries as compared to turnout in the general election, see Cook, *The Presidential Nominating Process*, 24.

59. Overacker, *Presidential Primary*, 249–251.

60. One thing that would have shocked a scholar such as Overacker is the role of money in the primary process today. Writing in the 1920s, Overacker sees no great problem with expenses and how the money is spent. She writes "The presidential primary may cost the candidate more or it may cost him less, but most of what is spent is spent openly and the voter may act accordingly" (159). However, even then she saw whatever problems that emerged could be handled "by regulating contributions rather than expenditures" because clearly "there seems little doubt that large contributors often expect to influence the policy of the administration if their candidate is successful" (160).

61. Donald Ritchie, *Electing FDR: The New Deal Campaign of 1932* (Lawrence: University Press of Kansas, 2007), 85–87. See Jean Edward Smith, *FDR* (New York: Random House, 2007), 259–261.

62. For a detailed account of the 1944 Republican primary in Wisconsin, see David M. Jordan, *FDR, Dewey, and the Election of 1944* (Bloomington: Indiana University Press, 2011), 85–91.

63. Cook, *The Presidential Nominating Process*, 31–33.

64. John S. Jackson III and William Crotty, *The Politics of Presidential Selection* (New York: HarperCollins, 1996), 34.

65. Nelson Polsby, Aaron Wildavsky, Steen Schier, and David Hopkins, *Presidential Elections: Strategies and Structures of American Politics* (Lanham, MD: Rowman and Littlefield, 2012), 97.

66. See Ceaser, *Presidential Selection*, 228–229. Our examples are not comprehensive, but rather illustrative.

67. Of course Truman never wavered in his outward confidence in being renominated. In July of 1948 he remarked, "Tell those amateurs at the ADA [Americans for Democratic Action, a Progressive group opposed to Truman's renomination] that any shit-head behind this desk can get re-nominated." In David Pietrusza, *1948: Harry Truman's Improbable Victory and the Year that Transformed America* (New York: Union Square Press, 2011), 210.

68. Gerald Pomper, *Nominating the President: The Politics of Convention Choice* (New York: Norton, 1966), 108–113, argues that Truman benefited from the primaries.

69. Pomper, *Nominating the President*, 291–292. Wilkie's defeat in the Wisconsin primary in April of 1944 crushed his hopes and signaled the end for him. See Lewis Gould, *Grand Old Party: A History of the Republican Party* (New York: Random House, 2003), 294.

70. John W. Jeffries, *A Third Term for FDR: The Election of 1940* (Lawrence: University Press of Kansas, 2017), 74.

71. Our account of the 1940 nomination process is drawn from Jeffries, *A Third Term for FDR*, and Charles Peters, *Five Days in Philadelphia* (New York: Public Affairs, 2005).

72. Greene, *I like Ike*, 6–15.

73. Greene, *I like Ike*, 18–22.
74. Greene, *I like Ike*, 18–22.
75. Nancy Beck Young, *Two Suns of the Southwest: Lyndon Johnson, Barry Goldwater and the 1964 Battle between Liberalism and Conservatism* (Lawrence: University Press of Kansas, 2019), 52.
76. For a sketch of White, see Theodore White, *The Making of the President, 1964* (New York: Harper Perennial, 1965), 94–101.
77. Young, *Two Suns of the Southwest*, 55–68.
78. Quoted in Young, *Two Suns of the Southwest*, 96.
79. Pomper, *Nominating the President*, 215.

Chapter 6

1. David Hume, *Essays: Moral, Political and Literary* (Indianapolis: Liberty Classics, 1987), 60.
2. James Wilson, *Collected Works of James Wilson*, vol. 1, ed. Kermit L. Hall and Mark David Hall (Indianapolis: Liberty Fund, 2007), 162.
3. Mark Kurlansky, *1968: The Year that Rocked the World* (New York: Random House, 2004), 276.
4. Peter Augustine Lawler and Robert Martin Schaefer, eds., *American political rhetoric: A reader* (Lanham, MD: Rowman & Littlefield, 2005).
5. Pomper, *Nominating the President*, 43.
6. Actually, none of the major party conventions went past the first ballot in the 1960s. The last convention to take more than one ballot was the 1952 Democratic convention. However, there were a number of conventions that came close. The last convention that might have gone multiple ballots was the 1976 Republican convention.
7. For an account of the Democratic primaries and convention in 1960 see Theodore White, *The Making of the President, 1960* (New York: Atheneum, 1961) chapters 2, 4–6.
8. The last sitting president to be denied nomination by his party was Chester Arthur in 1884. Today it is virtually inconceivable.
9. For a discussion of the 1964 Democratic Convention and the signs of future troubles see Ronald Radosh, *Divided They Fell: The Demise of the Democratic Party, 1964–1996* (New York: Free Press, 1966), chapter 1. See also Philip Klinkner, *The Losing Parties: Out Party National Committees, 1956–1993* (New Haven: Yale University Press, 1994), 89–90.
10. James Ceaser makes the case that the Republican nominating fight in 1964 was actually revealing in the weaknesses of the system at that time. The rise of "amateurs" over party regulars was a central part of the story of Goldwater's nomination. See Ceaser, *Presidential Selection*, 4, 240.

11. James Q. Wilson, *The Amateur Democrat: Club Politics in Three Cities* (Chicago: University of Chicago Press, 1966), 18–19. See also Wilson's *Political Organizations*, 106–110.

12. Ceaser, *Presidential Selection*, 266. He adds, following Wilson's lead, that professionals are motivated by "material interests, traditional allegiances, and friendship."

13. James Reston, "Humphrey Staff Sure of Nomination," *New York Times*, June 25, 1968.

14. See Ceaser, *Presidential Selection*, 226.

15. White, *The Making of the President, 1960*, 79.

16. Elaine Kamarck, *Primary Politics: Everything You Need to Know about How America Nominates Its Presidential Candidates* (Washington, DC: Brookings Institution, 2016), 10–11.

17. See Robert Caro, *The Years of Lyndon Johnson: The Passage of Power* (New York: Knopf, 2012), 88–102. This, of course, shows that primaries were not irrelevant. Kennedy's striking win in the West Virginia primary was key.

18. Kamarck, *Primary Politics*, 8–9.

19. Caro, *The Years of Lyndon Johnson*, 84.

20. Tom Hayden, *The Port Huron Statement: The Visionary Call of the 1960s Revolution* (New York: Thunder's Mouth Press, 2005), 4.

21. Hayden, *The Port Huron Statement*, 4.

22. We should note that in writing *The Port Huron Statement* Tom Hayden consulted John Dewey's *The Public and Its Problems*. See also James Miller, *Democracy Is in the Streets: From Port Huron to the Siege of Chicago* (Cambridge, MA: Harvard University Press, 1994), 148–149. For Hayden's own account see chapter 1, "The Way We Were and the Future of the Port Huron Statement," in Tom Hayden's *The Port Huron Statement*.

23. "Port Huron Statement," in Isaac Kramnick and Theodore Lowi, *American Political Thought: A Norton Anthology* (New York: Norton, 2009), 1292 and 1295.

24. "Port Huron Statement," 1290, 1295.

25. Hayden, *The Port Huron Statement*, 9.

26. For a discussion of the importance of *The Port Huron Statement*, see Miller, *Democracy Is in the Streets*. For a thoughtful and fair-minded critique of the statement, see Garry Wills, *Nixon Agonistes: The Crisis of the Self-Made Man* (New York: Penguin Books, 1979), 327–338.

27. Miller, *Democracy Is in the Streets*, 320.

28. Sol Stern, "The Battle of Chicago, 1968," *Tablet Magazine*, August 26, 2018, www.tabletmag.com/sections/news/articles/the-battle-of-chicago-1968.

29. James MacGregor Burns, *The Deadlock of Democracy* (Engel Cliffs, NJ: Prentice Hall, 1963), 1.

30. Burns, *The Deadlock of Democracy*, 266.

31. V. O. Key, *The Responsible Electorate: Rationality in Presidential Voting, 1936–1960* (New York: Vintage Books, 1966), 7–8.

32. The literature on critical elections and realignment theory is quite extensive and complex. V. O. Key, "A Theory of Critical Elections," *Journal of Politics* 17, no. 1 (February, 1955): 3–15, and Burnham, *Critical Elections and the Mainsprings of American Politics*. For a historical analysis, see James L. Sundquist, *Dynamics of the Party System: Alignment and Realignment of Political Parties in the United States* (Washington, DC: Brookings Institution, 1983). For criticisms of the concept see David R. Mayhew, *Electoral Realignments: A Critique of an American Genre* (New Haven, CT: Yale University Press, 2002).

33. Data is from National Election Studies and can be found in Norman Luttbeg and Michael Gant, *American Electoral Behavior, 1952–1992* (Itasca, IL: F. E. Peacock Publishers, 1995), 40.

34. John F. Bibby, "Party Organizations 1946–1996," in *Partisan Approaches to Postwar American Politics*, ed. Byron E. Shafer (New York: Chatham House, 1998), 154.

35. See chapter 5 of H. W. Brands, *The Strange Death of American Liberalism* (New Haven, CT: Yale University Press, 2001).

36. Robert Kennedy's opposition to the war was hesitant in the making. See chapter 13, "Cautious Critic," in Ronald Steel, *In Love with Night: The American Romance with Robert Kennedy* (New York: Simon and Schuster, 2000).

37. See Steel, *In Love with Night*, 179.

38. Robert Dallek, *Flawed Giant: Lyndon Johnson and His Times, 1961–1973* (Oxford: Oxford University Press, 1998), 571.

39. Michael Nelson, *Resilient America: Electing Nixon in 1968, Channeling Dissent, and Dividing Government* (Lawrence: University Press of Kansas, 2014), 93–94.

40. Norman Mailer, "The Siege of Chicago," in *Reporting Vietnam, Part One: American Journalism 1959–1969*, compiled by Milton J. Bates, Lawrence Lichty, Paul Miles, Ronald H. Spector, and Marilyn Young (New York: The Library of America, 1998), 632.

41. Mike Royko's famous biography of Daley is simply titled *Boss: Richard J. Daley of Chicago*. For an account of Daley and the 1968 Democratic convention see Cohen and Taylor, *American Pharaoh*, chapter 13.

42. Jules Witcover, *Party of the People: A History of the Democrats* (New York: Random House, 2003), 562.

43. Alan Brinkley, *Liberalism and Its Discontents* (Cambridge, MA: Harvard University Press, 1998), 259.

44. Cohen and Taylor, *American Pharaoh*, 460.

45. See Witcover, *Party of the People*, 563–564.

46. This was the *Walker Report* to the US National Commission on the Causes and Prevention of Violence. Radosh, in *Divided They Fell*, counters that view somewhat by highlighting the calls to violence by many of the protestors; see 115–126.

47. Brinkley, *Liberalism and Its Discontents*, 258.

48. Nelson, *Resilient America*, 153–176.

49. Nelson, *Resilient America*, 169.

50. The exclusion of the Mississippi delegation was the first time a delegation had been so punished for racial discrimination. See, Nelson, *Resilient America*, 169.

51. Theodore H. White, *The Making of the President 1968* (New York: Pocket Books, 1970), 376.

52. Rick Perlstein, *Nixonland: The Rise of a President and the Fracturing of America* (New York: Scribner, 2008), 327.

53. Hayden, *The Port Huron Statement*, 23.

54. Kamarck, *Primary Politics*, 14.

55. For discussion of the creation of the Hughes Commission and its influence on 1968 Democratic Convention see Byron E. Shafer, *Quiet Revolution: The Struggle for the Democratic Party and the Shaping of Post-Reform Politics* (New York: Russell Sage Foundation, 1983), chapter 1.

56. Shafer, *Quiet Revolution*, 116.

57. Douglas Martin, "Anne Wexler, an Influential Political Operative and Lobbyist, Is Dead at 79." *New York Times*, August 8, 2009.

58. Cook, *The Presidential Nominating Process*, 42–43. For an account of the various maneuvering concerning the proposals for delegate reforms see Radosh, *Divided They Fell*, 109–114.

59. Jackson and Crotty, *The Politics of Presidential Selection*, 59.

60. Randall Adkins, *The Evolution of Political Parties, Campaigns, and Elections: Landmark Documents, 1787–2007* (Washington, DC: CQ Press, 2008), 267.

61. Klinkner, *The Losing Parties*, 102–103.

62. Quoted in Shafer, *Quiet Revolution*, 166.

63. Shafer, *Quiet Revolution*, 347.

64. Schattschneider, *Party Government*, 60.

65. Quoted in Radosh, *Divided They Fell*, 137.

66. For a good summary of the various methods used to nominate presidential candidates see Steven S. Smith and Melanie J. Springer, "Choosing Presidential Candidates," in *Reforming the Presidential Nomination Process*, ed. Steven S. Smith and Melanie J. Springer (Washington, DC: Brookings Institution, 2009), 1–22.

67. Shafer, *Quiet Revolution*, covers the reformist bent of the staff. See chapter 4 in particular.

68. For an alternative perspective, one that does not see such striking changes, see Marty Cohen, David Karol, Hans Noel, and John Zaller, *The Party Decides: Presidential Nominations Before and After Reform* (Chicago: The University of Chicago Press, 2008), 13, and chapters 4 and 5.

69. For the story of why the unions declined to attend the meetings, see Shafer, *Quiet Revolution*, 92–96. For the power of unions before and after the reforms see Taylor E. Dark, "Organized Labor and Party Reform: A Reassessment," *Polity* 28, no. 4 (Summer 1996): 497–520.

70. Shafer, *Quiet Revolution*, 184.

71. See also Candice J. Nelson, "The Nominating Conventions," in *Grant Park: The Democratization of Presidential Elections, 1968–2008* (Washington, DC: Brookings Institution, 2011), chapters 4 and 5.

72. For a good analysis of the competing notions of the roles of parties and the various nomination procedures in democratic theory see Dennis F. Thompson, "The Primary Purpose of Presidential Primaries," *Political Science Quarterly* 125, no. 2 (Summer 2010): 205–232.

73. For a brief summary of the McGovern-Fraser reforms see John S. Jackson, "The Era of Party Reform," in *The American Political Party System: Continuity and Change Over Ten Presidential Elections* (Washington, DC: Brookings Institution Press, 2015), 47–61.

74. For union reactions see Shafer, *Quiet Revolution*, 361.

75. Christopher Achen and Larry Bartels, *Democracy for Realists* (Princeton, NJ: Princeton University Press, 2017), 325. Achen and Bartels talk only briefly about the McGovern-Fraser commission, 63–65.

76. Shafer, *Quiet Revolution*, chapter 17.

77. See Nelson W. Polsby, "The Reform of Presidential Selection and Democratic Theory," *PS* 16, no. 4 (Autumn 1983): 695–698.

78. Ceaser, *Presidential Selection*, 274.

79. Shafer, *Quiet Revolution*, 118.

80. Cook, *The Presidential Nominating Process*, 44.

81. Jáime Sanchez, Jr., "Revisiting McGovern-Fraser: Party Nationalization and the Rhetoric of Reform," *Journal of Political History* 32, no. 1 (January 2020): 1–24.

82. Cousins v. Wigoda, S. Ct. 541 (1975), at 549.

83. For a sharp criticism of the reformers' view of democracy, see Jeffrey Becker, *Ambition in America: Political Power and the Collapse of Citizenship* (Lexington: University Press of Kentucky, 2014), chapter 5.

84. Shafer, *Quiet Revolution*, 148.

85. James Q. Wilson, *Political Organizations*, 107. For the classic account of the "iron law of oligarchy," see Robert Michels, *Political Parties* (New York: Free Press, 1958). For a general account of party leaders taking precedence over the democratic wishes of elected officials see Maurice Duverger, *Political Parties* (New York: John Wiley and Sons, 1962).

86. James Q. Wilson, *The Amateur Democrat*, 128.

87. For a strong criticism of the state of the Democratic Party, in part due to the reforms, see William G. Mayer, *The Divided Democrats: Ideology Unity, Party Reform and Presidential Elections* (Boulder, CO: Westview Press, 1996).

88. Shafer, *Quiet Revolution*, 202.

89. Shafer, *Quiet Revolution*, 345.

90. Shafer, *Quiet Revolution*, 518–519.

91. Sundquist, *Dynamics of the Party System*, 330.

92. Hayden, *The Port Huron Statement*, 14.
93. Everett Ladd, *Transformation of the American Political System* (New York: Norton, 1975), 317.
94. Sanchez, "Revisting McGovern-Fraser." Sanchez's article emphasizes the role of the commissioners, whereas Bryon Shafer's work focuses more on the idea and actions of the staff.
95. Shafer, *Quiet Revolution*, 312.
96. Shafer, *Quiet Revolution*, 311 and 424.
97. See Paul R. Wieck, "Defying the Bosses in Illinois and Texas," *New Republic*, March 1, 1971, and Andrew J. Glass and Jonathan Cottin, "Democratic Reform Drive Falters as Spotlight Shifts to Presidential Race," *National Journal*, June 19, 1971.
98. Shafer, *Quiet Revolution*, 112.
99. Klinkner, *The Losing Parties*, 90.
100. Klinkner, *The Losing Parties*, 92–95.
101. John W. Ellwood and Robert J. Spitzer, "The Democratic National Telethons: Their Successes and Failures," *Journal of Politics* 41, no. 3 (August 1979): 828–864.
102. Shafer, *Quiet Revolution*, 275–290.
103. Klinkner, *The Losing Parties*, 99.
104. Shafer, *Quiet Revolution*, chapter 11.
105. R. W. Apple Jr., "The Democrats Reform Rules on Convention Delegates," *New York Times*, February 20, 1971.
106. Joseph California, *A Presidential Nation* (New York: Norton, 1975), 147–148.
107. Sanchez insightfully analyzes the role of nationalizing power by enhancing the DNC at the expense of state parties. Sanchez appears to see weakening the state parties as the main goal and that it was all for the good. We see the democratic ideals that provide the justification for reforms as far more deleterious to a well-functioning party system that enhances effective representative democracy.

Chapter 7

1. J. David Goodman, "Crowley's Loss Heralds an 'End of an Era,'" *New York Times*, June 28, 2018.
2. Andy Newman and Tyler Pager, "How a Political Machine Works: Candidates Running for 21 Seats, All Unaware," *New York Times*, August 24, 2018.
3. Chapman Rackaway, "Weak Parties and Strong Partisans," *American Political Parties Under Pressure*, ed. Chapman Rackaway and Laurie L. Rice (Cham, Switzerland: Palgrave Macmillan, 2017), 169–187.

4. Harry Enten, "Why Donald Trump Isn't a Real Candidate, in One Chart," *FiveThirtyEight*, June 16, 2015, fivethirtyeight.com/features/why-donald-trump-isnt-a-real-candidate-in-one-chart/.

5. Erwin Chemerinsky, "Challenging Direct Democracy," *Michigan State Law Review* (2007): 293–306.

6. Christopher Achen and Larry Bartels even show how the hallowed theory of retrospective voting as rational is not beyond question. See *Democracy for Realists*, chapter 4.

7. Bernard Bailyn, ed., *The Debate on the Constitution* (New York: Library of America, 1993), 314.

8. *The Economist*, "The Perils of Extreme Democracy," *Economist*, April 23, 2011, www.economist.com/leaders/2011/04/20/the-perils-of-extreme-democracy.

9. Hofstader, *The Age of Reform*, 257.

10. Scarrow, "The Nineteenth-Century Origins of Modern Political Parties" *Handbook of Party Politics*, 16–24.

11. Kevin P. Murphy, *Political Manhood: Red Bloods, Mollycoddles, and the Politics of Progressive Era Reform* (New York: Columbia University Press, 2008).

12. Robert D. Johnston, "Re-Democratizing the Progressive Era: The Politics of Progressive Era Political Historiography," *Journal of the Gilded Age and Progressive Era* 1, no. 1 (January 2002): 68–92.

13. Louis Hartz, *The Liberal Tradition in America: An Interpretation of American Political Thought Since the Revolution* (New York: Houghton Mifflin Harcourt, 1955); James Weinstein, *The Corporate Ideal in the Liberal State: 1900–1918* (Westport, CT: Praeger, 1969).

14. Paul Allen Beck, "The Electoral Cycle and Patterns of American Politics," *British Journal of Political Science* 9, no. 2 (April 1979): 129–156; Jeffrey L. Pasley, Andrew W. Robertson, and David Waldstreicher, eds., *Beyond the Founders: New Approaches to the Political History of the Early American Republic* (Chapel Hill: University of North Carolina Press, 2009); Andrew J. Polsky, "Partisan Regimes in American Politics," *Polity* 44, no. 1 (January 2012): 51–80; Joel H. Silbey and Allan G. Bogue, eds., *The History of American Electoral Behavior* (Princeton, NJ: Princeton University Press, 2015).

15. Martin Van Buren, *Inquiry into the Origin and Course of Political Parties in the United States* (New York: Augustus M. Kelly, 1967), 4.

16. Burnham, *Critical Elections and the Mainsprings of American Politics*.

17. Jonathan Knuckey, "Classification of Presidential Elections: An Update," *Polity* 31, no. 4 (Summer 1999): 639–653; Bruce A. Campbell and Richard J. Trilling, eds., *Realignment in American Politics: Toward a Theory* (Austin: University of Texas Press, 2012); Willam G. Mayer, "Changes in Elections and the Party System: 1992 in Historical Perspective," in *The New American Politics* (New York: Routledge, 2018), 19–50.

18. Russell J. Dalton, Ian McAllister, and Martin P. Wattenberg, "The Consequences of Partisan Dealignment," in *Parties without Partisans: Political Change in Advanced Industrial Democracies*, ed. Russell J. Dalton and Martin P. Wattenberg (Oxford: Oxford University Press, 2002), 37–63; James L. Sundquist, *Dynamics of the Party System: Alignment and Realignment of Political Parties in the United States* (Washington, DC: Brookings Institution, 1983).

19. Bruce E. Keith, David B. Magleby, Candice J. Nelson, Elizabeth A. Orr, Mark C. Westlye, and Raymond E. Wolfinger, *The Myth of the Independent Voter* (Berkeley: University of California Press, 1992).

20. David B. Magleby, Candice J. Nelson, and Mark C. Westlye, "The Myth of the Independent Voter Revisited," in *Facing the Challenge of Democracy: Explorations in the Analysis of Public Opinion and Political Participation*, ed. Paul M. Sniderman and Benjamin Highton (Princeton, NJ: Princeton University Press, 2012), 238–263.

21. Angus Campbell and Warren E. Miller, "The Motivational Basis of Straight and Split Ticket Voting," *American Political Science Review* 51, no. 2 (June 1957): 293–312; Paul Allen Beck, Lawrence Baum, Aage R. Clausen, and Charles E. Smith Jr., "Patterns and Sources of Ticket Splitting in Subpresidential Voting," *American Political Science Review* 86, no. 4 (December 1992): 916–928; Ian McAllister and Robert Darcy, "Sources of Split-Ticket Voting in the 1988 American Elections," *Political Studies* 40, no. 4 (December 1992): 695–712; Richard Born, "Congressional Incumbency and the Rise of Split-Ticket Voting," *Legislative Studies Quarterly* 25, no. 3 (August 2000): 365–387.

22. Sundquist, *Dynamics of the Party System*, 171–177.

23. Nelson W. Polsby, "The Institutionalization of the US House of Representatives," *American Political Science Review* 62, no. 1 (March 1968): 144–168.

24. David T. Canon, "The Institutionalization of Leadership in the US Congress," *Legislative Studies Quarterly* 14, no. 3 (August 1989): 415–443.

25. Samuel C. Patterson, "Party Opposition in the Legislature: The Ecology of Legislative Institutionalization," *Polity* 4, no. 3 (Spring 1972): 344–366.

26. Keith Krehbiel, Kenneth A. Shepsle, and Barry R. Weingast, "Why Are Congressional Committees Powerful?" *American Political Science Review* 81, no. 3 (September 1987): 929–945.

27. David W. Rohde, *Parties and Leaders in the Postreform House* (Chicago: University of Chicago Press, 2010).

28. James T. Patterson, "A Conservative Coalition forms in Congress, 1933–1939," *Journal of American History* 52, no. 4 (March 1966): 757–772; Keith T. Poole and Howard Rosenthal, "Analysis of Congressional Coalition Patterns: A Unidimensional Spatial Model," *Legislative Studies Quarterly* 12, no. 1 (February 1987): 55–75; Samuel C. Patterson and Gregory A. Caldeira, "Party Voting in the United States Congress," *British Journal of Political Science* 18, no. 1 (January 1988): 111–131.

29. John H. Aldrich and David W. Rohde, *The Logic of Conditional Party Government: Revisiting the Electoral Connection* (Chapel Hill, NC: Political Institutions and Public Choice, 2000).

30. W. T. Bianco and I. Sened, "Uncovering Evidence of Conditional Party Government: Reassessing Majority Party Influence in Congress and State Legislatures," *American Political Science Review* 99, no. 3 (September 2005): 361–371.

31. Raymond E. Wolfinger and Joan Heifetz, "Safe Seats, Seniority, and Power in Congress," *American Political Science Review* 59, no. 2 (June 1965): 337–349; Kenneth A. Shepsle and Barry R. Weingast, "The Institutional Foundations of Committee Power," *American Political Science Review* 81, no. 1 (March 1987): 85–104; Barry R. Weingast, "Floor Behavior in the US Congress: Committee Power under the Open Rule," *American Political Science Review* 83, no. 3 (September 1989): 795–815.

32. Dean McSweeney and John E. Owens, eds., *The Republican Takeover of Congress* (Cham, Switzerland: Palgrave Macmillan, 1998).

33. William Corkery, "Newt Gingrich and GOPAC: Training the Farm Team that Helped Win the Republican Revolution of 1994," undergraduate honors thesis, College of William & Mary, 2011.

34. Burrel Vann, "Persuasive Action and Ideological Polarization in Congress," *Social Problems* 68, no. 4 (November 2021): 809–830.

35. Shiro Kuriwaki, "The Swing Voter Paradox: Electoral Politics in a Nationalized Era," PhD diss., Harvard University, 2021.

36. Christopher A. Martínez, Mariana Llanos, and Raymond Tatalovich, "Impeaching the President: Mapping the Political Landscape in the House of Representatives," *Congress & the Presidency*, July 8, 2021, doi.org/10.1080/07343469.2021.1934186.

37. Brian Alexander, *A Social Theory of Congress: Legislative Norms in the Twenty-First Century* (Lanham, MD: Lexington Books, 2021).

38. Francesco Bianchi, Howard Kung, and Roberto Gomez Cram, *Using Social Media to Identify the Effects of Congressional Partisanship on Asset Prices*, No. w28749, National Bureau of Economic Research, 2021.

39. Jessica Buffamonti, "Identity Politics in America: The Role of Catholicism and Its Implications," presentation, SUNY Geneso, 2021, knightscholar.geneseo.edu/cgi/viewcontent.cgi?article=1126&context=great-day-symposium.

40. Bryan W. Marshall, and Patrick J. Haney, "The Impact of Party Conflict on Executive Ascendancy and Congressional Abdication in US Foreign Policy," *International Politics*, July 13, 2021, doi.org/10.1057/s41311-021-00326-z.

41. For development of party-in-government, see Aldrich, *Why Parties?* chapter 7. For the party in the electorate, see Reichley, *The Life of the Parties*, 10–12.

42. Richard S. Katz and Robin Kolodny, "Party Organization as an Empty Vessel: Parties in American Politics," in *How Parties Organize: Change and Adaptation in Party Organizations in Western Democracies*, ed. Richard S. Katz and Peter Mair (Thousand Oak, CA: Sage, 1995), 23, 24–29.

43. Leon D. Epstein, *Political Parties in Western Democracies* (Piscataway, NJ: Transaction, 1980); Peter Mair, "Party Organizations: From Civil Society to the State," in *How Parties Organize*, 1–22.

44. Reichley, *The Life of the Parties*, chapter 5.

45. Hopkins, "Election of 1824."

46. Everett S. Brown, "The Presidential Election of 1824–1825," *Political Science Quarterly* 40, no. 3 (September 1925): 384–403.

47. For a detailed discussion of the "corrupt bargain" see Robert Remini, *Henry Clay: Statesman for the Union* (New York: Norton, 1991), 251–272.

48. S. P. Adams, ed., *A Companion to the Era of Andrew Jackson* (Hoboken, NJ: Wiley-Blackwell, 2013).

49. Parsons, *The Birth of Modern Politics*.

50. Donald B. Cole, *Vindicating Andrew Jackson: The 1828 Election and the Rise of the Two-Party System* (Lawrence: University Press of Kansas, 2009).

51. Glyndon G. Van Deusen, *Jacksonian Era, 1828–1848* (New York: Harper & Row, 1959).

52. Cornelius P. Cotter, James L. Gibson, John F. Bibby, and Robert J. Huckshorn, *Party Organizations in American Politics* (Pittsburgh: University of Pittsburgh Press, 1989).

53. Martin Saiz and Hans Geser, eds., *Local Parties in Political and Organizational Perspective* (Boulder, CO: Westview, 1999).

54. Martin Shefter, *Political Parties and the State: The American Historical Experience* (Princeton, NJ: Princeton University Press, 1993), 66–71.

55. Frank J. Sorauf, "State Patronage in a Rural County," *American Political Science Review* 50, no. 4 (December 1956): 1046–1056; Phillip Althoff and Samuel C. Patterson, "Political Activism in a Rural County," *Midwest Journal of Political Science* 10, no. 1 (1966), 39–51.

56. Cornelius P. Cotter and Bernard C. Hennessy, *Politics without Power: The National Party Committees* (Piscataway, NJ: Transaction, 2009).

57. Cotter and Hennessy, *Politics without Power*, chapter 2.

58. Robin Kolodny, *Pursuing Majorities: Congressional Campaign Committees in American Politics* (Norman: University of Oklahoma Press, 1998).

59. Daniel M. Shea, *Transforming Democracy: Legislative Campaign Committees and Political Parties* (Albany: State Uniersity of New York Press, 1995), chapter 3.

60. Katz and Kolodny, "Party Organization as an Empty Vessel," 23, 24–29.

61. J. A. Schlesinger, *Political Parties and the Winning of Office* (Ann Arbor: University of Michigan Press, 1994).

62. Michael J. Malbin, ed., *The Election after Reform: Money, Politics, and the Bipartisan Campaign Reform Act* (Lanham, MD: Rowman & Littlefield, 2006).

63. Conor M. Dowling and Michael G. Miller, *Super PAC!: Money, Elections, and Voters after Citizens United* (New York: Routledge, 2014), chapter 2.

64. Raymond J. La Raja and Brian F. Schaffner, *Campaign Finance and Political Polarization: When Purists Prevail* (Ann Arbor: University of Michigan Press, 2015).
65. Scarrow, "The Nineteenth-Century Origins of Modern Political Parties," 16–24.
66. Dinkin, *Campaigning in America*.
67. Riordan, *Plunkitt of Tammany Hall*.
68. David C. Barker, Adam B. Lawrence, and Margit Tavits, "Partisanship and the Dynamics of 'Candidate Centered Politics' in American Presidential Nominations," *Electoral Studies* 25, no. 3 (2006): 599–610.
69. John F. Bibby and L. Sandy Maisel, "State Party Organizations: Strengthened and Adapting to Candidate-Centered Politics and Nationalization," in *The Parties Respond: Changes in American Parties and Campaigns*, ed. Mark D. Brewer and L. Sandy Meisel (Boulder, CO: Westview Press, 2002), 19–46.
70. Angus Campbell, Philip E. Converse, Warren E. Miller, and Donald E. Stokes, *The American Voter* (Chicago: University of Chicago Press, 1980).
71. Warren E. Miller and J. Merrill Shanks, *The New American Voter* (Cambridge, MA: Harvard University Press, 1996), 182–185.
72. Martin P. Wattenberg, *The Decline of American Political Parties, 1952–1996* (Cambridge: Harvard University Press, 2009).
73. American National Election Studies, "Party Identification 7-Point Scale 1952–2020," *ANES*, accessed November 22, 2021, electionstudies.org/resources/anes-guide/top-tables/?id=21.
74. See Campbell and Miller, "The Motivational Basis of Straight and Split Ticket Voting"; J. G. Rusk, "The Effect of the Australian Ballot Reform on Split Ticket Voting: 1876–1908," *American Political Science Review* 64, no. 4 (December 1970): 1220–1238; and Franco Mattei and John S. Howes, "Competing Explanations of Split-Ticket Voting in American National Elections," *American Politics Quarterly* 28, no. 3 (July 2000): 379–407.
75. McAllister and Darcy, "Sources of Split-Ticket Voting in the 1988 American Elections."
76. David P. Redlawsk, "What Voters Do: Information Search During Election Campaigns," *Political Psychology* 25, no. 4 (August 2004): 595–610; Shigeo Hirano, Gabriel S. Lenz, Maksim Pinkovskiy, and James M. Snyder Jr., "Voter Learning in State Primary Elections," *American Journal of Political Science* 59, no. 1 (March 2015): 91–108.
77. Peter H. Argersinger, "New Perspectives on Election Fraud in the Gilded Age," *Political Science Quarterly* 100, no. 4 (Winter 1985): 669–687; Kerstin Zimmer, "The Comparative Failure of Machine Politics, Administrative Resources and Fraud," *Canadian Slavonic Papers* 47, no. 3–4 (September–December 2005): 361–384; Jordan Gans-Morse, Sebastián Mazzuca, and Simeon Nichter, "Varieties of Clientelism: Machine Politics During Elections," *American Journal of Political Science* 58, no. 2 (April 2014): 415–432.

78. Stephen Ansolabehere and David M. Konisky, "The Introduction of Voter Registration and Its Effect on Turnout," *Political Analysis* 14, no. 1 (Winter 2006): 83–100.

79. Richard W. Boyd, "Decline of US Voter Turnout: Structural Explanations," *American Politics Quarterly* 9, no. 2 (April 1981): 133–159.

80. Mark Gray and Miki Caul, "Declining Voter Turnout in Advanced Industrial Democracies, 1950 to 1997: The Effects of Declining Group Mobilization," *Comparative Political Studies* 33, no. 9 (November 2000): 1091–1122.

81. *ANES*, "Party Identification 7-Point Scale 1952–2020."

82. Michael P. McDonald, "Voter Turnout," *United States Elections Project*, 2020, www.electproject.org/home/voter-turnout/voter-turnout-data.

83. Patrick J. Kenney, "Explaining Primary Turnout: The Senatorial Case," *Legislative Studies Quarterly* 11, no. 1 (February 1986): 65–73.

84. Barry C. Burden, "The Polarizing Effects of Congressional Primaries," in *Congressional Primaries and the Politics of Representation*, ed. Peter Gadlerisis, Marni Ezra, and Michael Lyons (Lanham, MD: Rowman and Littlefield, 2001), 95–115.

85. Boyd, "The Effects of Primaries and Statewide Races on Voter Turnout," 730–739.

86. Shaun Bowler, David J. Lanoue, and Paul Savoie, "Electoral Systems, Party Competition, and Strength of Partisan Attachment: Evidence from Three Countries," *Journal of Politics* 56, no. 4 (November 1994): 991–1007.

87. Scott C. Flanagan and Russell J. Dalton, "Parties under Stress: Realignment and Dealignment in Advanced Industrial Societies." *West European Politics* 7, no. 1 (December 2007): 7–23.

88. Eric M. Uslaner, "Partisanship and Coalition Formation in Congress." *Political Methodology* 2 (Fall 1975): 381–414.

89. Patterson, "A Conservative Coalition Forms in Congress, 1933–1939"; David W. Brady and Charles S. Bullock III, "Is There a Conservative Coalition in the House?" *Journal of Politics* 42, no. 2 (May 1980): 549–559; Poole and Rosenthal, "Analysis of Congressional Coalition Patterns."

90. Samuel L. Popkin, *The Reasoning Voter: Communication and Persuasion in Presidential Campaigns* (Chicago: University of Chicago Press, 1994).

91. Helmut Schneider, "Branding in Politics—Manifestations, Relevance and Identity-Oriented Management," *Journal of Political Marketing* 3, no. 3 (December 2002): 41–67.

Chapter 8

1. For an argument about the health of American democracy, written from a comparative perspective, see Levitsky and Ziblatt, *How Democracies Die*. They focus on polarization and the decline of democratic norms. Their focus is not exclusively

on the state of the parties, but they do see the changing nature of parties as central in their disturbing interpretation of our current political state. See particularly chapter 3, "The Great Republican Abdication."

2. Clifford D. May, "Buckleys Are Backing a Democrat?" *New York Times*, August 16, 1988.

3. Elizabeth Hamilton, "Lieberman Reflects on Candidacy," *Hartford Courant*, April 15, 2004.

4. Adam Nagourney, "A Referendum on Iraq Policy," *New York Times*, August 9, 2006.

5. Ellen Barry, "Lieberman Is Defeated in Primary," *Los Angeles Times*, August 9, 2006.

6. Jennifer Medina and Patrick Healy, "As Outsider, Lieberman Walks a Tricky Path," *New York Times*, September 9, 2006.

7. CNN, "American Votes 2006," *CNN.com*, accessed May 6, 2010, www.cnn.com/ELECTION/2006/.

8. Josh Rogers, "McCain Wins Lieberman Endorsement," *Reuters*, December 16, 2007, www.reuters.com/article/us-usa-politics-lieberman/mccain-wins-lieberman-endorsement-idUSN1634401920071217.

9. See Charles Arthur, "WikiLeaks Cables Visualization Pulled after Pressure from Joe Lieberman," *The Guardian*, December 3, 2010, www.theguardian.com/world/blog/2010/dec/03/wikileaks-tableau-visualisation-joe-lieberman; and Helen A. Halpin and Peter Harbage, "The Origins and Demise of the Public Option," *Health Affairs* 29, no. 6 (June 2010): 1117–1124.

10. Dana Bash and Ted Barratt, "Sources: Lieberman Likely to Keep Top Democratic Post," *CNN.com*, November 17, 2008, www.cnn.com/2008/POLITICS/11/17/lieberman.senate/.

11. Russell J. Dalton, *The Apartisan American: Dealignment and Changing Electoral Politics* (Washington, DC: CQ Press, 2013).

12. Alan I. Abramowitz and Kyle L. Saunders, "Ideological Realignment in the US Electorate," *Journal of Politics* 60, no. 3 (August 1998): 634–652.

13. Joseph A. Aistrup, *The Southern Strategy Revisited: Republican Top-Down Advancement in the South* (Lexington: University Press of Kentucky, 2015).

14. R. D. Putnam, "Bowling Alone: America's Declining Social Capital," in *Culture and Politics*, ed. L. Crothers and C. Lockhart (New York: Palgrave Macmillan, 2000), 223–234. See also Robert N. Bellah, Richard Madsen, William M. Sullivan, Ann Swidler, and Steven M. Tipton, *Habits of the Heart: Individualism and Commitment in American Life* (New York: Harper & Row, 1985).

15. Scott D. McClurg, "The Electoral Relevance of Political Talk: Examining Disagreement and Expertise Effects in Social Networks on Political Participation," *American Journal of Political Science* 50, no. 3 (July 2006): 737–754.

16. Matthew Levendusky, *The Partisan Sort: How Liberals Became Democrats and Conservatives Became Republicans* (Chicago: University of Chicago Press, 2009).

17. Bill Bishop, *The Big Sort: Why Clustering of Like-Minded America Is Tearing Us Apart* (Boston: Houghton Mifflin, 2008), 302.

18. Samuel J. Abrams and Morris P. Fiorina, "'The Big Sort' that Wasn't: A Skeptical Reexamination," *PS: Political Science and Politics* 45, no. 2 (April 2012): 203–210.

19. Brewer, "The Rise of Partisanship and the Expansion of Partisan Conflict within the American Electorate."

20. Burden, "The Polarizing Effects of Congressional Primaries," 95–115.

21. Jacobson, "Partisan Polarization in Presidential Support."

22. Geoffrey C. Layman and Thomas M. Carsey, "Party Polarization and 'Conflict Extension' in the American Electorate," *American Journal of Political Science* 46, no. 4 (October 2002): 786–802.

23. Edward G. Carmines, Michael J. Ensley, and Michael W. Wagner, "Who Fits the Left-Right Divide? Partisan Polarization in the American Electorate," *American Behavioral Scientist* 56, no. 12 (October 2012): 1631–1653.

24. Elisabeth R. Gerber and Rebecca B. Morton, "Primary Election Systems and Representation," *Journal of Law, Economics, & Organization* 14, no. 2 (October 1998): 304–324.

25. Seth J. Hill, "Institution of Nomination and the Policy Ideology of Primary Electorates," *Quarterly Journal of Political Science* 10, no. 4 (December 2015): 461–487.

26. Karen M. Kaufmann, James G. Gimpel, and Adam H. Hoffman, "A Promise Fulfilled? Open Primaries and Representation," *Journal of Politics*, 65, no. 2 (May 2003): 457–476.

27. John E. Stanga and James F. Sheffield, "The Myth of Zero Partisanship: Attitudes Toward American Political Parties, 1964–84," *American Journal of Political Science* 31, no. 4 (November 1987): 829–855.

28. M. J. Hetherington, "Resurgent Mass Partisanship: The Role of Elite Polarization," *American Political Science Review* 95, no. 3 (September 2001): 619–631.

29. Leonie Huddy and Alexa Bankert, "Political Partisanship as a Social Identity," in *Oxford Research Encyclopedia of Politics*, May 24, 2017, oxfordre.com/politics/view/10.1093/acrefore/9780190228637.001.0001/acrefore-9780190228637-e-250.

30. *American National Election Studies*, "Average Feeling Thermometer Rating Toward Parties 1978–2020," ANES, accessed November 22, 2021, electionstudies.org/resources/anes-guide/top-tables/?id=113.

31. *National Conference of State Legislatures*, "State Primary Election Types," NCSL, accessed November 22, 2021, www.ncsl.org/research/elections-and-campaigns/primary-types.aspx.

32. H. Edward Flentje and Joseph A. Aistrup, *Kansas Politics and Government: The Clash of Political Cultures* (Lincoln: University of Nebraska Press, 2010).

33. Ronald D. Hedlund, Meredith W. Watts, and David M. Hedge, "Voting in an Open Primary," *American Politics Quarterly* 10, no. 2 (April 1982): 197–218.

34. Priscilla L. Southwell, "Open Versus Closed Primaries and Candidate Fortunes, 1972–1984," *American Politics Quarterly* 16, no. 3 (July 1988): 280–295.

35. Kong-Pin Chen and Sheng-Zhang Yang, "Strategic Voting in Open Primaries," *Public Choice* 112, no. 1/2 (July 2002): 1–30.

36. David C. King, "Party Competition and Polarization in American Politics," presentation at the Annual Meeting of the Midwest Political Science Association, Chicago, September 1998.

37. Gerber and Morton, "Primary Election Systems and Representation," 304–324.

38. Kristin Kanthak and Rebecca Morton, "The Effects of Electoral Rules on Congressional Primaries," in *Congressional Primaries and the Politics of Representation*, 116, 126.

39. T. Wayne Parent, Calvin C. Jillson, and Ronald E. Weber, "Voting Outcomes in the 1984 Democratic Party Primaries and Caucuses," *American Political Science Review* 81, no. 1 (March, 1987): 67–84.

40. Douglas J. Ahler, Jack Citrin, and Gabriel S. Lenz, "Do Open Primaries Improve Representation? An Experimental Test of California's 2012 Top-Two Primary," *Legislative Studies Quarterly* 41, no. 2 (May 2016): 237–268.

41. Gray and Caul, "Declining Voter Turnout in Advanced Industrial Democracies, 1950 to 1997."

42. McDonald, "Voter Turnout."

43. Boyd, "The effects of primaries and statewide races on voter turnout."

44. Jack Moran and Mark Fenster, "Voter Turnout in Presidential Primaries: A Diachronic Analysis," *American Politics Quarterly* 10, no. 4 (October 1982): 453–476.

45. David Niven, "The Limits of Mobilization: Turnout Evidence from State House Primaries," *Political Behavior* 23, no. 4 (December 2001): 335–350.

46. Patrick J. Kenney, "Explaining Turnout in Gubernatorial Primaries," *American Politics Quarterly* 11, no. 3 (July 1983): 315–326.

47. David R. Jones, "Party Polarization and Legislative Gridlock," *Political Research Quarterly* 54, no. 1 (March 2001): 125–141.

48. Drew DeSilver, "The Polarized Congress of Today Has Its Roots in the 1970s," *Pew Research Center*, June 20, 2014, www.pewresearch.org/fact-tank/2014/06/12/polarized-politics-in-congress-began-in-the-1970s-and-has-been-getting-worse-ever-since/.

49. Douglas J. Ahler, Jack Citrin, and Gabriel S. Lenz, "Do Open Primaries Help Moderate Candidates? An Experimental Test on the 2012 California Primary," paper presented at the Annual Meeting of the American Political Science Association, 2013.

50. McGhee, Masket, Shor, Rogers, and McCarty, "A Primary Cause of Partisanship?"

51. Michael J. Barber, "Ideological Donors, Contribution Limits, and the Polarization of American Legislatures," *Journal of Politics* 78, no. 1 (January 2016): 296–310.

52. Danielle M. Thomsen, "Ideological Moderates Won't Run: How Party Fit Matters for Partisan Polarization in Congress," *Journal of Politics* 76, no. 3 (July 2014): 786–797.

53. See Geoffrey C. Layman, Thomas M. Carsey, and Juliana Menasce Horowitz, "Party Polarization in American Politics: Characteristics, Causes, and Consequences," *Annual Review of Political Science* 9 (June 2006): 83–110; Seth E. Masket, Jonathan Winburn, and Gerald C. Wright, "The Gerrymanderers Are Coming! Legislative Redistricting Won't Affect Competition or Polarization Much, No Matter Who Does It," *PS: Political Science & Politics* 45, no. 1 (January 2012): 39–43; Michael Barber and Nolan McCarty, "Causes and Consequences of Polarization," in *Political Negotiation: A Handbook*, edited by Jane Mansbridge and Cathie Jo Martin, 37, 39–43 (Washington, DC: Brookings Institution, 2015); John Voorheis, Nolan McCarty, and Boris Shor, "Unequal Incomes, Ideology and Gridlock: How Rising Inequality Increases Political Polarization," *SSRN*, August 21, 2015, ssrn.com/abstract=2649215; Nolan McCarty, Jonathan Rodden, Boris Shor, Chris Tausanovitch, and Christopher Warshaw, "Geography, Uncertainty, and Polarization," *Political Science Research and Methods* 7, no. 4 (March 2018): 775–794.

54. S. Iyengar and J. McGrady, *Media Politics: A Citizen's Guide* (New York: W. W. Norton, 2007).

55. Dan Bernhardt, Stefan Krasa, and Mattias Polborn, "Political Polarization and the Electoral Effects of Media Bias," *Journal of Public Economics* 92, no. 5/6 (June 2008): 1092–1104.

56. Markus Prior, "Media and Political Polarization," *Annual Review of Political Science* 16 (2013): 101–127.

57. Prior, "Media and Political Polarization."

58. Matthew Levendusky and Neil Malhotra, "Does Media Coverage of Partisan Polarization Affect Political Attitudes?" *Political Communication* 33, no. 2 (July 2015): 283–301.

59. Josh Stewart, "Following the Money behind the Nearly $500 Million 2016 Democratic Primary," *Sunlight Foundation*, June 21, 2016, sunlightfoundation.com/2016/06/21/following-the-money-behind-the-nearly-500-million-2016-democratic-primary/.

60. Dan Clark, "Trump Was Outspent by His Closest Primary Opponents," *Politifact*, July 1, 2016, www.politifact.com/new-york/statements/2016/jul/01/michael-caputo/trump-was-outspent-his-closest-primary-opponents/.

61. Bill Allison, Mira Rojanasakul, Brittany Harris, and Cedric Sam, "Tracking the 2016 Presidential Money Race," *Bloomberg*, December 9, 2016, www.bloomberg.com/politics/graphics/2016-presidential-campaign-fundraising/.

62. Christopher Ingraham, "Somebody Just Put a Price Tag on the 2016 Election. It's a Doozy," *Washington Post*, April 14, 2017, www.washingtonpost.com/news/wonk/wp/2017/04/14/somebody-just-put-a-price-tag-on-the-2016-election-its-a-doozy/.

63. Graphiq, "How Much Did Each Presidential Candidate Spend per Vote in the Primaries?" *Mercury News*, August 11, 2016, www.mercurynews.com/2016/07/29/how-much-did-each-presidential-candidate-spend-per-vote-in-the-primaries/.

64. Randall E. Adkins and Andrew J. Dowdle, "The Money Primary: What Influences the Outcome of Pre-Primary Presidential Nomination Fundraising?" *Presidential Studies Quarterly* 32, no. 2 (June 2002): 256–275.

65. For representativeness, especially the suppressive effect primary fundraising demands has on female candidacies for office, see Karin E. Kitchens and Michele L. Swers, "Why Aren't There More Republican Women in Congress? Gender, Partisanship, and Fundraising Support in the 2010 and 2012 Elections," *Politics & Gender* 12, no. 4 (April 2016): 648–676. For effects on incumbency see Jonathan S. Krasno, Donald Philip Green, and Jonathan A. Cowden, "The Dynamics of Campaign Fundraising in House Elections," *Journal of Politics* 56, no. 2 (May 1994): 459–474.

66. Drew Desilver and Patric Van Kessel, "As More Money Flows into Campaigns, Americans Worry about Its Influence," *Pew Research Center*, December 7, 2015, www.pewresearch.org/fact-tank/2015/12/07/as-more-money-flows-into-campaigns-americans-worry-about-its-influence/.

67. J. F., "Why American Elections Cost So Much," *Economist*, February 10, 2014, www.economist.com/the-economist-explains/2014/02/09/why-american-elections-cost-so-much.

68. Sabato, *The Rise of Political Consultants*, xiii.

69. Popkin, *The Reasoning Voter*.

70. Dennis W. Johnson, *Campaigning in the Twenty-first Century: A Whole New Ballgame?* (New York: Routledge, 2011).

71. Schlesinger, *Political Parties and the Winning of Office*, 177–199.

72. Fritz Plasser, "Parties' Diminishing Relevance for Campaign Professionals," *Harvard International Journal of Press/Politics* 6, no. 4 (September 2001): 44–59.

73. In Congressional races, see Paul S. Herrnson, "Campaign Professionalism and Fundraising in Congressional Elections," *Journal of Politics* 54, no. 3 (August 1992): 859–870; and Stephen K. Medvic, *Political Consultants in US Congressional Elections* (Columbus: Ohio State University Press, 2001). For state-level evidence, see Owen G. Abbe and Paul S. Herrnson, "Campaign Professionalism in State Legislative Elections," *State Politics & Policy Quarterly* 3, no. 3 (Fall 2003): 223–245.

74. For a discussion of the deleterious effects professional campaigning has had on the parties, public, and elections, see Mark P. Petracca, "Political Consultants and Democratic Governance," *PS: Political Science & Politics* 22, no. 1 (March 1989): 11–14; David A. Dulio, *For Better or Worse? How Political Consultants Are Changing Elections in the United States* (Albany: State University of New York Press, 2004); Costas Panagopoulos, "Political Consultants, Campaign Professionalization, and Media Attention," *PS: Political Science & Politics* 39, no. 4 (October 2006): 867–869; Dennis W. Johnson, *No Place for Amateurs: How Political Consultants Are Reshaping American Democracy* (New York: Routledge, 2013).

Chapter 9

1. Quoted in Lara M. Brown, "The Presidency and the Nomination Process: Aspirants, Parties and Selections," in *The Presidency and the Political System*, ed. Michael Nelson (Los Angeles: Sage, 2014), 191.
2. Henry Jones Ford, "The Direct Primary," *North American Review* 190, no. 644 (July, 1909): 3.
3. Levitsky and Ziblatt, *How Democracies Die*; see particularly chapters 4–6.
4. Levitsky and Ziblatt, *How Democracies Die*, 231.
5. James Madison, *Notes of Debates in the Federal Convention of 1787* (Athens: Ohio University Press, 2022).
6. Alexis de Tocqueville, *Democracy in America*, vol. 1, trans. Henry Reeve (New York: Vintage, 1990), chapter 15, 255.
7. Jonathan Rauch and Ray La Raja, "Too Much Democracy Is Bad for Democracy," *The Atlantic*, December 2019, 62–68.
8. Nelson W. Polsby, *Consequences of Party Reform* (Oxford: Oxford University Press, 1983), 169–170.
9. Brendan Nyhan, "The Green Lantern Theory of the Presidency," *Brendan Nyhan*, December 14, 2009, www.brendan-nyhan.com/blog/2009/12/the-green-lantern-theory-of-the-presidency.html.
10. Kamarck, "Qualifying for the Debate."
11. Ford, "The Direct Primary."
12. Paul Bond, "Leslie Moonves on Donald Trump: 'It May Not Be Good for America, but It's Damn Good for CBS,'" *Hollywood Reporter*, February 19, 2016, www.hollywoodreporter.com/news/general-news/leslie-moonves-donald-trump-may-871464/.
13. Polsby, *Consequences of Party Reform*, 169.

Bibliography

Abbe, Owen G., and Paul S. Herrnson. "Campaign Professionalism in State Legislative Elections." *State Politics & Policy Quarterly* 3, no. 3 (Fall 2003): 223–245.

Abramowitz, Alan I., and Kyle L. Saunders. "Exploring the Bases of Partisanship in the American Electorate: Social Identity vs. Ideology." *Political Research Quarterly* 59, no. 2 (June 2006): 175–187.

———. "Ideological Realignment in the US Electorate." *Journal of Politics* 60, no. 3 (August 1998): 634–652.

Abrams, Samuel J., and Morris P. Fiorina. "'The Big Sort' that Wasn't: A Skeptical Reexamination." *PS: Political Science & Politics* 45, no. 2 (April 2012): 203–210.

Achen, Christopher, and Larry Bartels. *Democracy for Realists*. Princeton, NJ: Princeton University Press, 2017.

Ackerman, Kenneth D. *Boss Tweed: The Rise and Fall of the Corrupt Pol Who Conceived the Soul of Modern New York*. New York: Carroll & Graf, 2005.

Adams, Sean Patrick, ed. *A Companion to the Era of Andrew Jackson*. Hoboken, NJ: Wiley-Blackwell, 2013.

Addams, Jane. "Ethical Survivals in Municipal Corruption." *International Journal of Ethics* 8, no. 3 (April 1898): 273–291.

Adkins, Randall E. *The Evolution of Political Parties, Campaigns, and Elections: Landmark Documents, 1787–2007*. Washington, DC: CQ Press, 2008.

Adkins, Randall E., and Andrew J. Dowdle. "The Money Primary: What Influences the Outcome of Pre-Primary Presidential Nomination Fundraising?" *Presidential Studies Quarterly* 32, no. 2 (June 2002): 256–275.

Ahler, Douglas J., Jack Citrin, and Gabriel S. Lenz. "Do Open Primaries Help Moderate Candidates? An Experimental Test on the 2012 California Primary." Paper presented at the Annual Meeting of the American Political Science Association, 2013.

———. "Do Open Primaries Improve Representation? An Experimental Test of California's 2012 Top-Two Primary." *Legislative Studies Quarterly* 41, no. 2 (May 2016): 237–268.

Aistrup, Joseph A. *The Southern Strategy Revisited: Republican Top-Down Advancement in the South*. Lexington: University Press of Kentucky, 2015.

Aldrich, John H. *Why Parties? The Origin and Transformation of Political Parties in America*. Chicago: University of Chicago Press, 1995.

Aldrich, John H., and David W. Rohde. *The Logic of Conditional Party Government: Revisiting the Electoral Connection*. Chapel Hill, NC: Political Institutions and Public Choice, 2000.

Aldrich, John H., and James S. Coleman Battista. "Conditional Party Government in the States." *American Journal of Political Science* 46, no. 1 (January 2002): 164–172.

Alexander, Brian. *A Social Theory of Congress: Legislative Norms in the Twenty-First Century*. Lanham, MD: Lexington Books, 2021.

Alilunas, Leo. "The Rise of the 'White Primary' Movement as a Means of Barring the Negro from The Polls." *Journal of Negro History* 25, no. 2 (April 1940): 161–172.

Allison, Bill, Mira Rojanasakul, Brittany Harris, and Cedric Sam. "Tracking the 2016 Presidential Money Race." *Bloomberg*, December 9, 2016. www.bloomberg.com/politics/graphics/2016-presidential-campaign-fundraising/.

Althoff, Phillip, and Samuel C. Patterson. "Political Activism in a Rural County." *Midwest Journal of Political Science* 10, no. 1 (May 1966): 39–51.

American National Election Studies. "Average Feeling Thermometer Rating Toward Parties 1978–2020," ANES, accessed November 22, 2021, electionstudies.org/resources/anes-guide/top-tables/?id=113.

———. "Party Identification 7-Point Scale 1952–2020." *ANES*, accessed November 22, 2021. electionstudies.org/resources/anes-guide/top-tables/?id=21.

Ansolabehere, Stephen, and David M. Konisky. "The Introduction of Voter Registration and Its Effect on Turnout." *Political Analysis* 14, no. 1 (Winter 2006): 83–100.

Ansolabehere, Stephen, John Mark Hansen, Shigeo Hirano, and James M. Snyder Jr. "The Decline of Competition in US Primary Elections, 1908–2004." *The Marketplace of Democracy: Electoral Competition and American Politics* 74 (2006): 82–96.

———. "More Democracy: The Direct Primary and Competition in US Elections." *Studies in American Political Development* 24, no. 2 (August 2010): 190–205.

———. "Primary Elections and Partisan Polarization in the US Congress." *Quarterly Journal of Political Science* 5, no. 2 (2010): 169–191.

Apple, R. W., Jr. "The Democrats Reform Rules on Convention Delegates." *New York Times*, February 20, 1971.

Argersinger, Peter H. "New Perspectives on Election Fraud in the Gilded Age." *Political Science Quarterly* 100, no. 4 (Winter 1985): 669–687.

Aristotle. *The Politics*. Translated by Carnes Lord. Chicago: University of Chicago Press, 1984.

Arthur, Charles. "WikiLeaks Cables Visualization Pulled after Pressure from Joe Lieberman." *Guardian*, December 3, 2010. www.theguardian.com/world/blog/2010/dec/03/wikileaks-tableau-visualisation-joe-lieberman.
Bailyn, Bernard, ed. *The Debate on the Constitution*. New York: Library of America, 1993.
Baker, Kevin. "The Soul of the Machine." *New Republic*, August 17, 2016.
Barber, Benjamin. "The Undemocratic Party System: Citizenship in an Elite/Mass Society." In *A Passion for Democracy*, 119–133. Princeton, NJ: Princeton University Press, 1998.
Barber, Michael, and Nolan McCarty. "Causes and Consequences of Polarization." In *Political Negotiation: A Handbook*, edited by Jane Mansbridge and Cathie Jo Martin, 37–90. Washington, DC: Brookings Institution, 2015.
Barber, Michael J. "Ideological Donors, Contribution Limits, and the Polarization of American Legislatures." *Journal of Politics* 78, no. 1 (January 2016): 296–310.
Barker, David C., Adam B. Lawrence, and Margit Tavits. "Partisanship and the Dynamics of 'Candidate Centered Politics' in American Presidential Nominations." *Electoral Studies* 25, no. 3 (2006): 599–610.
Barry, Ellen. "Lieberman Is Defeated in Primary." *Los Angeles Times*, August 9, 2006.
Bash, Dana, and Ted Barratt. "Sources: Lieberman Likely to Keep Top Democratic Post." *CNN.com*, November 17, 2008. www.cnn.com/2008/POLITICS/11/17/lieberman.senate/.
Baumgartner, Frank R., Bryan D. Jones, and Peter B. Mortensen. "Punctuated Equilibrium Theory: Explaining Stability and Change in Public Policymaking." In *Theories of the Policy Process*, edited by Paul Sabateir and Christopher Weible, 59–103. Boulder, CO: Westview Press, 2014.
Beck, Paul Allen. "The Electoral Cycle and Patterns of American Politics." *British Journal of Political Science* 9, no. 2 (April 1979): 129–156.
Beck, Paul Allen, Lawrence Baum, Aage R. Clausen, and Charles E. Smith Jr. "Patterns and Sources of Ticket Splitting in Subpresidential Voting." *American Political Science Review* 86, no. 4 (December 1992): 916–928.
Becker, Jeffrey. *Ambition in America: Political Power and the Collapse of Citizenship*. Lexington: University Press of Kentucky, 2014.
Bellah, Robert N., Richard Madsen, William M. Sullivan, Ann Swidler, and Steven M. Tipton. *Habits of the Heart: Individualism and Commitment in American Life*. New York: Harper & Row, 1985.
Berg-Anderson, Richard E. "Election Years in which the Direct Primary Has Been Specifically Authorized." *The Green Papers*, May 20, 2021. www.thegreenpapers.com/Hx/DirectPrimaryElectionYears.phtml.
Bernhardt, Dan, Stefan Krasa, and Mattias Polborn. "Political Polarization and the Electoral Effects of Media Bias." *Journal of Public Economics* 92, no. 5/6 (June 2008): 1092–1104.

Berry, Jeffrey M., and Clyde Wilcox. *The Interest Group Society*. New York: Routledge, 2018.

Bianchi, Francesco, Howard Kung, and Roberto Gomez Cram. *Using Social Media to Identify the Effects of Congressional Partisanship on Asset Prices*. No. w28749. National Bureau of Economic Research, 2021.

Bianco, W. T., and I. Sened. "Uncovering Evidence of Conditional Party Government: Reassessing Majority Party Influence in Congress and State Legislatures." *American Political Science Review* 99, no. 3 (September 2005): 361–371.

Bibby, John F. "Party Organizations 1946–1996." In *Partisan Approaches to Postwar American Politics*, edited by Byron E. Shafer, 79–96. New York: Chatham House, 1998.

Bibby, John F., and L. Sandy Maisel. "State Party Organizations: Strengthened and Adapting to Candidate-Centered Politics and Nationalization." In *The Parties Respond: Changes in American Parties and Campaigns*, edited by Mark D. Brewer and L. Sandy Meisel, 19–46. Boulder, CO: Westview Press, 2002.

Binder, Sarah A. *Minority Rights, Majority Rule: Partisanship and the Development of Congress*. Cambridge: Cambridge University Press, 1997.

Birchall, Johnston. *The International Co-operative Movement*. Manchester: Manchester University Press, 1997.

Bishop, Bill. *The Big Sort: Why Clustering of Like-Minded America Is Tearing Us Apart*. Boston: Houghton Mifflin, 2008.

Blau, Joseph Leon, ed. *Social Theories of Jacksonian Democracy: Representative Writings of the Period 1825–1850*. Indianapolis: Hackett, 2003.

Bond, Paul. "Leslie Moonves on Donald Trump: 'It May Not Be Good for America, but It's Damn Good for CBS.'" *Hollywood Reporter*, February 19, 2016. www.hollywoodreporter.com/news/general-news/leslie-moonves-donald-trump-may-871464/.

Born, Richard. "Congressional Incumbency and the Rise of Split-Ticket Voting." *Legislative Studies Quarterly* 25, no. 3 (August 2000): 365–387.

Bowler, Shaun, David J. Lanoue, and Paul Savoie. "Electoral Systems, Party Competition, and Strength of Partisan Attachment: Evidence from Three Countries." *Journal of Politics* 56, no. 4 (November 1994): 991–1007.

Boyd, Richard W. "Decline of US Voter Turnout: Structural Explanations." *American Politics Quarterly* 9, no. 2 (1981): 133–159.

———. "The Effects of Primaries and Statewide Races on Voter Turnout." *Journal of Politics* 51, no. 3 (August 1989): 730–739.

Brady, David W., and Charles S. Bullock III. "Is There a Conservative Coalition in the House?" *Journal of Politics* 42, no. 2 (May 1980): 549–559.

Brady, David W., Hahrie Han, and Jeremy C. Pope. "Primary Elections and Candidate Ideology: Out of Step with the Primary Electorate?" *Legislative Studies Quarterly* 32, no. 1 (January 2011): 79–105.

Brands, H. W. *The Strange Death of American Liberalism.* New Haven, CT: Yale University Press, 2001.

Brent, Peter. "The Australian Ballot: Not the Secret Ballot." *Australian Journal of Political Science* 41, no. 1 (August 2006): 39–50.

Brewer, Mark D. "The Rise of Partisanship and the Expansion of Partisan Conflict within the American Electorate." *Political Research Quarterly* 58, no. 2 (June 2005): 219–229.

Brinkley, Alan. *Liberalism and Its Discontents.* Cambridge, MA: Harvard University Press, 1998.

Brown, Everett S. "The Presidential Election of 1824–1825." *Political Science Quarterly* 40, no. 3 (September 1925): 384–403.

Brown, Lara M. "The Presidency and the Nomination Process: Aspirants, Parties and Selections." In *The Presidency and the Political System*, edited by Michael Nelson, 191–213. Los Angeles: Sage, 2014).

Buffamonti, Jessica. "Identity Politics in America: The Role of Catholicism and Its Implications." Presentation, SUNY Geneseo, 2021. knightscholar.geneseo.edu/cgi/viewcontent.cgi?article=1126&context=great-day-symposium.

Burden, Barry C. "The Polarizing Effects of Congressional Primaries." In *Congressional Primaries and the Politics of Representation*, edited by Peter Gadlerisis, Marni Ezra, and Michael Lyons, 95–115. Lanham, MD: Rowman and Littlefield, 2001.

Burnham, Walter Dean. *Critical Elections and the Mainsprings of American Politics.* New York: Norton, 1970.

Burns, James MacGregor. *The Deadlock of Democracy.* Engel Cliffs, NJ: Prentice Hall, 1963.

Ceaser, James. *Presidential Selection: Theory and Development.* Princeton, NJ: Princeton University Press, 1979.

Calhoon, Robert M. *The Loyalists in Revolutionary America, 1760–1781.* New York: Harcourt, 1973.

California, Joseph. *A Presidential Nation.* New York: Norton, 1975.

Campbell, Angus, Philip E. Converse, Warren E. Miller, and Donald E. Stokes. *The American Voter.* Chicago: University of Chicago Press, 1980.

Campbell, Angus, and Warren E. Miller. "The Motivational Basis of Straight and Split Ticket Voting." *American Political Science Review* 51, no. 2 (June 1957): 293–312.

Campbell, Bruce A., and Richard J. Trilling, eds. *Realignment in American Politics: Toward a Theory.* Austin: University of Texas Press, 2012.

Campbell, Tracy. *Deliver the Vote: A History of Election Fraud, an American Political Tradition, 1742–2004.* New York: Basic Books, 2005.

Canon, David T. "The Institutionalization of Leadership in the US Congress." *Legislative Studies Quarterly* 14, no. 3 (August 1989): 415–443.

Carmines, Edward G., Michael J. Ensley, and Michael W. Wagner. "Who Fits the Left-Right Divide? Partisan Polarization in the American Electorate." *American Behavioral Scientist* 56, no. 12 (October 2012): 1631–1653.

Caro, Robert. *The Years of Lyndon Johnson: The Passage of Power*. New York: Knopf, 2012.

Carson, Jamie L., Michael H. Crespin, Charles J. Finocchiaro, and David W. Rohde. "Redistricting and Party Polarization in the US House of Representatives." *American Politics Research* 35, no. 6 (November 2007): 878–904.

Center for American Women and Politics. "Milestones for Women in American Politics." *CAWP*, 2021, cawp.rutgers.edu/facts/milestones-for-women.

Chance, James. *1912: Wilson, Roosevelt, Taft and Debs—The Election that Changed the Country*. New York: Simon and Schuster, 2004.

Chemerinsky, Erwin. "Challenging Direct Democracy." *Michigan State Law Review* (2007): 293–306.

Chen, Kong-Pin, and Sheng-Zhang Yang. "Strategic Voting in Open Primaries." *Public Choice* 112, no. 1/2 (July 2002): 1–30.

Choma, Russ. "Dave Versus Goliath, by the Numbers." *Open Secrets*, June 11, 2014, opensecrets.org/news/2014/06/dave-versus-goliath-by-the-numbers/.

Clark, Dan. "Trump Was Outspent by His Closest Primary Opponents." *Politifact*, July 1, 2016. www.politifact.com/new-york/statements/2016/jul/01/michael-caputo/trump-was-outspent-his-closest-primary-opponents/.

CNN. "American Votes 2006." *CNN.com*, accessed May 6, 2010. www.cnn.com/ELECTION/2006/.

Coats, R. Morris, and Thomas R. Dalton. "Entry Barriers in Politics and Uncontested Elections." *Journal of Public Economics* 49, no. 1 (October 1992): 75–90.

Cohen, Adam, and Elizabeth Taylor. *American Pharaoh: Mayor Richard J. Daley*. Boston: Little, Brown and Co., 2000.

Cohen, Marty, David Karol, Hans Noel, and John Zaller. *The Party Decides: Presidential Nominations Before and After Reform*. Chicago: University of Chicago Press, 2008.

Cole, Donald B. *Vindicating Andrew Jackson: The 1828 Election and the Rise of the Two-Party System*. Lawrence: University Press of Kansas, 2009.

Conway, M. Margaret. *Political Participation in the United States*. 2nd ed. Washington, DC: CQ Press, 1991.

Cook, Rhodes. *The Presidential Nominating Process: A Place for Us?* Lanham, MD: Rowman and Littlefield, 2004.

Cooper, John Milton, Jr. *Woodrow Wilson: A Biography*. New York: Knopf, 2009.

Corkery, William. "Newt Gingrich and GOPAC: Training the Farm Team that Helped Win the Republican Revolution of 1994." Undergraduate honors thesis, College of William and Mary, 2011.

Cotter, Cornelius P., James L. Gibson, John F. Bibby, and Robert J. Huckshorn. *Party Organizations in American Politics*. Pittsburgh: University of Pittsburgh Press, 1989.

Cotter, Cornelius P., and Bernard C. Hennessy. *Politics without Power: The National Party Committees.* Piscataway, NJ: Transaction, 2009.
Croly, Herbert. "Progressive Democracy." In *American Progressivism: A Reader*, edited by Ronald Pestritto and William Atto, 239–250. Lanham, MD: Lexington Books, 2008.
———. *The Promise of American Life.* Indianapolis: Bobbs-Merrill, 1965.
"The Crump Era." The Benjamin L. Hooks Institute for Social Change, University of Memphis. Accessed February 16, 2022. www.memphis.edu/benhooks/mapping-civil-rights/crump-era.php.
Crunden, Robert M. *Ministers of Reform: The Progressives' Achievement in American Civilization, 1889–1920.* Champaign: University of Illinois Press, 1984.
Cunningham, Noble E. *The Jeffersonian Republicans: The Formation of Party Organization, 1789–1801* (vol. 2). Chapel Hill: University of North Carolina Press, 1957.
Currie, David P. *The Constitution in Congress: The Federalist Period, 1789–1801.* Chicago: University of Chicago Press, 1997.
Dahl, Robert. *Democracy and Its Critics.* New Haven, CT: Yale University Press, 1989.
———. *How Democratic Is the American Constitution?* New Haven, CT: Yale University Press, 1989.
Dallek, Robert. *Flawed Giant: Lyndon Johnson and His Times, 1961–1973.* Oxford: Oxford University Press, 1998.
Dalton, Russell J. *The Apartisan American: Dealignment and Changing Electoral Politics.* Washington, DC: CQ Press, 2013.
Dalton, Russell J., Ian McAllister, and Martin P. Wattenberg. "The Consequences of Partisan Dealignment." In *Parties without Partisans: Political Change in Advanced Industrial Democracies*, edited by Russell J. Dalton and Martin P. Wattenberg, 37–63. Oxford: Oxford University Press, 2002.
Dalton, Russell J., David M. Farrell, and Ian McAllister. *Political Parties and Democratic Linkage: How Parties Organize Democracy.* Oxford: Oxford University Press, 2011.
Dark, Taylor E. "Organized Labor and Party Reform: A Reassessment." *Polity* 28, no. 4 (Summer 1996): 497–520.
Davis, James W. *US Presidential Primaries and the Caucus-Convention System: A Sourcebook.* Westport, CT: Greenwood, 1997.
DeSilver, Drew. "The Polarized Congress of Today Has Its Roots in the 1970s." *Pew Research Center*, June 20, 2014. www.pewresearch.org/fact-tank/2014/06/12/polarized-politics-in-congress-began-in-the-1970s-and-has-been-getting-worse-ever-since/.
———. "Turnout Was High in the 2016 Primary Season, but Just Short of 2008 Record." *Pew Research Center*, June 10, 2016. www.pewresearch.org/fact-tank/2016/06/10/turnout-was-high-in-the-2016-primary-season-but-just-short-of-2008-record/.
Desilver, Drew, and Patric Van Kessel. "As More Money Flows into Campaigns, Americans Worry about Its Influence." *Pew Research Center*, December 7,

2015. www.pewresearch.org/fact-tank/2015/12/07/as-more-money-flows-into-campaigns-americans-worry-about-its-influence/.

DiGaetano, A. "The Rise and Development of Urban Political Machines: An Alternative to Merton's Functional Analysis." *Urban Affairs Quarterly* 24, no. 2 (December 1988): 242–267.

Dinkin, Robert J. *Campaigning in America: A History of Election Practices.* Westport, CT: Praeger, 1989.

Dorsett, Lyle W. *The Pendergast Machine.* New York: Oxford University Press, 1968.

Dowling, Conor M., and Michael G. Miller. *Super PAC!: Money, Elections, and Voters after Citizens United.* New York: Routledge, 2014.

Downs, Anthony. *An Economic Theory of Democracy.* New York: HarperCollins, 1957.

Dulio, David A. *For Better or Worse? How Political Consultants Are Changing Elections in the United States.* Albany: State University of New York Press, 2004.

Duverger, Maurice. "Duverger's Law: Forty Years Later." In *Electoral Laws and Their Political Consequences*, edited by Bernard Grofman and Arend Lijphart, 69–84. New York: Agathon Press, 2003.

———. *Political Parties.* New York: John Wiley and Sons, 1962.

Ecelbarger, Gary. *The Great Comeback: How Abraham Lincoln Beat the Odds to Win the 1860 Republican Nomination.* New York: Macmillan, 2008.

The Economist. "The Perils of Extreme Democracy." *Economist*, April 23, 2011. www.economist.com/leaders/2011/04/20/the-perils-of-extreme-democracy.

Ellis, Joseph. *American Sphinx: The Character of Thomas Jefferson.* New York: Knopf, 1997.

Ellwood, John W., and Robert J. Spitzer. "The Democratic National Telethons: Their Successes and Failures." *Journal of Politics* 41, no. 3 (August 1979): 828–864.

Enten, Harry. "Why Donald Trump Isn't a Real Candidate, in One Chart." *FiveThirtyEight*, June 16, 2015. fivethirtyeight.com/features/why-donald-trump-isnt-a-real-candidate-in-one-chart/.

Epstein, Leon D. *Political Parties in Western Democracies.* Piscataway, NJ: Transaction, 1980.

Ethington, Philip. "The Metropolis and Multicultural Ethics." In *Progressivism and the New Democracy*, ed. Sidney Milkis and Jerome Mileur, 192–225. Amherst: University of Massachusetts Press, 1999.

Ewing, Cortez A. M. *Primary Elections in the South: A Study in Uniparty Politics.* Norman: University of Oklahoma Press, 1953.

Farrell, David M., and Paul Webb. "Political Parties as Campaign Organizations." In *Parties without Partisans: Political Change in Advanced Industrial Democracies*, edited by Russell J. Dalton and Martin P. Wattenberg, 102–128. Oxford: Oxford University Press, 2002.

Ferling, John E. *The Ascent of George Washington: The Hidden Political Genius of an American Icon.* New York: Bloomsbury, 2010.

Filene, Peter G. "An Obituary for the Progressive Movement." *American Quarterly* 22, no. 1 (Spring 1970): 20–34.
Fiorina, Morris P., Samuel J. Abrams, and Jeremy C. Pope. *Culture War? The Myth of a Polarized America*. New York: Pearson Longman, 2005.
Fiorina, Morris P., and Matthew S. Levendusky. "Disconnected: The Political Class versus the People." *Red and Blue Nation* 1 (2006): 49–71.
Fiorina, Morris P., and David W. Rohde. *Home Style and Washington Work: Studies of Congressional Politics*. Ann Arbor: University of Michigan Press, 1991.
Flanagan, Scott C., and Russell J. Dalton. "Parties under Stress: Realignment and Dealignment in Advanced Industrial Societies." *West European Politics* 7, no. 1 (December 2007): 7–23.
Flentje, H. Edward, and Joseph A. Aistrup. *Kansas Politics and Government: The Clash of Political Cultures*. Lincoln: University of Nebraska Press, 2010.
Ford, Henry Jones. "The Direct Primary." *North American Review* 190, no. 644 June 1909, 1–14.
———. *The Rise and Growth of American Politics: A Sketch of Constitutional Development*. New York: The Macmillan Company, 1898.
Formisano, Ronald P. "Federalists and Republicans: Parties, Yes—System, No." In *The Evolution of American Electoral Systems*, edited by Paul Kleppener, 33–76. Westport, CT: Greenwood Press, 1981.
Fry, Brian, and Jos C. N. Raddschelders. *Mastering Public Administration from Max Weber to Dwight Waldo*. Washington: CQ Press, 2008.
Galderisi, Peter F., and Marni Ezra. "Congressional Primaries in Historical and Theoretical Context." In *Congressional Primaries and the Politics of Representation*, edited by Peter F. Galderisi, Marni Ezra, and Michael Lyons, 11–28. Lanham, MD: Rowman and Littlefield, 2001.
Gans-Morse, Jordan, Sebastián Mazzuca, and Simeon Nichter. "Varieties of Clientelism: Machine Politics During Elections." *American Journal of Political Science* 58, no. 2 (April 2014): 415–432.
Gerber, Elisabeth R., and Rebecca B. Morton. "Primary Election Systems and Representation." *Journal of Law, Economics, & Organization* 14, no. 4 (December 2015): 304–324.
Giulia, Sandri, Antonella Seddone, and Fulvio Venturino, eds. *Party Primaries in Comparative Perspective*. Farnham, UK: Ashgate, 2015.
Glass, Andrew, and Jonathan Cottin. "Democratic Reform Drive Falters as Spotlight Shifts to Presidential Race." *National Journal*, June 19, 1971.
Glazer, Nathan, and Daniel P. Moynihan. *Beyond the Melting Pot: The Negroes, Puerto Ricans, Jews, Italians, and Irish of New York City*. Cambridge, MA: MIT Press, 1970.
Goodman, J. David. "Crowley's Loss Heralds an 'End of an Era.'" *New York Times*, June 28, 2018.

Goodnow, Frank Johnson. "The American Conception of Liberty." In *American Progressivism: A Reader*, edited by Ronald Pestritto and William Atto, 55–64. Lanham, MD: Lexington Books, 2008.

Gould, Lewis. *Four Hats in the Ring: The 1912 Election and the Birth of Modern American Politics*. Lawrence: University Press of Kansas, 2008.

———. *Grand Old Party: A History of the Republican Party*. New York: Random House, 2003.

Gould, Lewis T. *America in the Progressive Era, 1890–1914*. New York: Routledge, 2014.

Graphiq. "How Much Did Each Presidential Candidate Spend per Vote in the Primaries?" *Mercury News*, August 11, 2016. www.mercurynews.com/2016/07/29/how-much-did-each-presidential-candidate-spend-per-vote-in-the-primaries/.

Gray, Mark, and Miki Caul. "Declining Voter Turnout in Advanced Industrial Democracies, 1950 to 1997: The Effects of Declining Group Mobilization." *Comparative Political Studies* 33, no. 9 (November 2000): 1091–1122.

Greene, John. *I Like Ike: The Presidential Election of 1952*. Lawrence: University Press of Kansas, 2017.

Hale, Dennis. "The Natural History of Citizenship." In *Friends and Citizens: Essays in Honor of Wilson Carey McWilliams*, edited by Peter Dennis Bathory and Nancy L. Schwartz, 159–170. Lanham, MD: Rowman and Littlefield, 2001.

Halpin, Helen A., and Peter Harbage. "The Origins and Demise of the Public Option." *Health Affairs* 29, no. 6 (June 2010): 1117–1124.

Hamilton, Elizabeth. "Lieberman Reflects on Candidacy." *Hartford Courant*, April 15, 2004.

Hartz, Louis. *The Liberal Tradition in America: An Interpretation of American Political Thought Since the Revolution*. New York: Houghton Mifflin Harcourt, 1955.

Hayden, Tom. *The Port Huron Statement: The Visionary Call of the 1960s Revolution*. New York: Thunder's Mouth Press, 2005.

Hedlund, Ronald D., Meredith W. Watts, and David M. Hedge. "Voting in an Open Primary." *American Politics Quarterly* 10, no. 2 (April 1982): 197–218.

Hein, Clarence J. "The Adoption of Minnesota's Direct Primary Law." *Minnesota History* 35, no. 8 (December 1957): 341–351.

Held, David. *Models of Democracy*. Stanford, CA: Stanford University Press, 1996.

Herrnson, Paul S. "Campaign Professionalism and Fundraising in Congressional Elections." *Journal of Politics* 54, no. 3 (August 1992): 859–870.

Hershey, Marjorie Randon. *Party Politics in America*. New York: Routledge, 2017.

Hetherington, M. J. "Resurgent Mass Partisanship: The Role of Elite Polarization." *American Political Science Review* 95, no. 3 (September 2001): 619–631.

Hibbard, Caroline M. *Charles I and the Popish Plot*. Chapel Hill: University of North Carolina Press, 2017.

Hill, Seth J. "Institution of Nomination and the Policy Ideology of Primary Electorates." *Quarterly Journal of Political Science* 10, no. 4 (December 2015): 461–487.

Hine, Darlene Clark, Steven F. Lawson, and Merline Pitre. *Black Victory: The Rise and Fall of the White Primary in Texas.* Columbia: University of Missouri Press, 2003.

Hirano, Shigeo, Gabriel S. Lenz, Maksim Pinkovskiy, and James M. Snyder Jr. "Voter Learning in State Primary Elections." *American Journal of Political Science* 59, no. 1 (March 2015): 91–108.

Hirano, Shigeo, and James M. Snyder Jr. *Primary Elections in the United States.* Cambridge: Cambridge University Press, 1957.

Hofstadter, Richard. *The Age of Reform: From Bryan to FDR.* New York: Vintage, 1955.

Hoogenboom, Ari. "The Pendleton Act and the Civil Service." *American Historical Review* 64, no. 2 (January 1959): 301–318.

Hopkins, James F. "Election of 1824." In *History of American Presidential Elections, 1789–1968,* edited by Arthur M. Schlesinger, 4. London: Chelsea House, 1971.

Huddy, Leonie, and Alexa Bankert. "Political Partisanship as a Social Identity." In *Oxford Research Encyclopedia of Politics,* May 24, 2017. oxfordre.com/politics/view/10.1093/acrefore/9780190228637.001.0001/acrefore-9780190228637-e-250.

Hume, David. *Essays: Moral, Political and Literary.* Indianapolis: Liberty Classics, 1987.

Ingraham, Christopher. "Somebody Just Put a Price Tag on the 2016 Election. It's a Doozy." *Washington Post,* April 14, 2017.

Iyengar, S., and J. McGrady. *Media Politics: A Citizen's Guide.* New York: W. W. Norton, 2007.

Jackson, Andrew. "First Annual Message." *The American Presidency Project,* ed. Gerhard Peters and John T. Woolley. Accessed November 30, 2021. www.presidency.ucsb.edu/ws/index.php?pid=29471.

Jackson, John S. "The Era of Party Reform." In *The American Political Party System: Continuity and Change Over Ten Presidential Elections,* 47–61. Washington, DC: Brookings Institution, 2015.

Jackson, John S. III, and William Crotty. *The Politics of Presidential Selection.* New York: HarperCollins, 1996.

Jacobson, G. C. "Partisan Polarization in Presidential Support: The Electoral Connection." *Congress & the Presidency: A Journal of Capital Studies* 30, no. 1 (March 2003): 1–36.

James, Marquis. *Andrew Jackson: Portrait of a President.* New York: Grosset & Dunlap, 1937.

Jefferson, Thomas. "Letter from Thomas Jefferson to Francis Hopkinson, 13 March 1789." *Founders Online.* Accessed April 12, 2022. founders.archives.gov/documents/Jefferson/01-14-02-0402.

Jeffries, John. *A Third Term for FDR: The Election of 1940.* Lawrence: University Press of Kansas, 2017.

J. F. "Why American Elections Cost So Much." *Economist,* February 10, 2014. www.economist.com/the-economist-explains/2014/02/09/why-american-elections-cost-so-much.

John, R. R. "Affairs of Office: The Executive Departments, the Election of 1828, and the Making of the Democratic Party." In *The Democratic Experiment: New Directions in American Political History*, edited by Meg Jacobs, William Novack, and Julian Zeilizer, 50–84. Princeton: Princeton University Press, 2003.

Johnson, Dennis W. *Campaigning in the Twenty-first Century: A Whole New Ballgame?* New York: Routledge, 2011.

———. *No Place for Amateurs: How Political Consultants Are Reshaping American Democracy.* New York: Routledge, 2013.

Johnston, Robert D. "Re-Democratizing the Progressive Era: The Politics of Progressive Era Political Historiography." *Journal of the Gilded Age and Progressive Era* 1, no. 1 (January 2002): 68–92.

Jones, David R. "Party Polarization and Legislative Gridlock." *Political Research Quarterly* 54, no. 1 (March 2001): 125–141.

Jordan, David M. *FDR, Dewey, and the Election of 1944.* Bloomington: Indiana University Press, 2011.

Jouvenel, Betrand de. "The Chairman's Problem." *American Political Science Review* 55, no. 2 (June 1961): 368–372.

Kamarck, Elaine. *Primary Politics: Everything You Need to Know about How America Nominates Its Presidential Candidates.* Washington, DC: Brookings Institution Press, 2015.

———. "Qualifying for the Debate: The Lost Role of Peer Review." *Brookings Institution*, September 11, 2019. www.brookings.edu/blog/fixgov/2019/09/11/qualifying-for-the-debate-the-lost-role-of-peer-review/.

———. "Why Is the Presidential Nominating System Such a Mess?" *Center for Effective Public Management at Brookings*, January 2016. www.brookings.edu/wp-content/uploads/2016/07/primaries.pdf.

Kammen, Michael. *A Machine That Would Go of Itself.* New York: St. Martin's Press, 1986.

Kanthak, Kristin, and Rebecca Morton. "The Effects of Electoral Rules on Congressional Primaries." In *Congressional Primaries and the Politics of Representation*, edited by Peter Gadlerisi, Marni Ezra, and Michael Lyons, 218–244. Lanham, MD: Rowman and Littlefield, 2001.

Katz, Richard S., and Robin Kolodny. "Party Organization as an Empty Vessel: Parties in American Politics." In *How Parties Organize: Change and Adaptation in Party Organizations in Western Democracies*, ed. Richard S. Katz and Peter Mair, 59–76. Thousand Oaks, CA: Sage, 1995.

Kaufmann, Karen M., James G. Gimpel, and Adam H. Hoffman. "A Promise Fulfilled? Open Primaries and Representation." *Journal of Politics* 65, no. 2 (May 2003): 457–476.

Keith, Bruce E., David B. Magleby, Candice J. Nelson, Elizabeth A. Orr, Mark C. Westlye, and Raymond E. Wolfinger. *The Myth of the Independent Voter.* Berkeley: University of California Press, 1992.

Keller, Morton. *America's Three Regimes: A New Political History.* Oxford: Oxford University Press, 2007.
Kenney, Patrick J. "Explaining Primary Turnout: The Senatorial Case." *Legislative Studies Quarterly* 11, no. 1 (February 1986): 65–73.
———. "Explaining Turnout in Gubernatorial Primaries." *American Politics Quarterly* 11, no. 3 (February 1986): 315–326.
Kent, Frank R. *The Democratic Party: A History.* Whitefish, MT: Kessinger Publishing, 2005.
Key, V. O., Jr. *Politics, Parties, and Pressure Groups.* New York: Crowell, 1955.
———. *The Responsible Electorate: Rationality in Presidential Voting, 1936–1960.* New York: Vintage Books, 1966.
———. *Southern Politics in State and Nation: A New Edition.* Knoxville: The University of Tennessee Press, 1994.
———. "A Theory of Critical Elections." *Journal of Politics* 17, no. 1 (February, 1955): 3–15.
Keyssar, Alexander. *The Right to Vote.* New York: Basic Books, 2000.
Kitschelt, Herbert, and Steven I. Wilkinson. "Citizen-Politician Linkages: An Introduction." In *Patrons, Clients, and Policies: Patterns of Democratic Accountability and Political Competition,* edited by Herbert Kitschelt and Steven I. Wilkinson, 1–49. Cambridge: Cambridge University Press, 2007.
King, David C. "Party Competition and Polarization in American Politics." Presentation at the Annual Meeting of the Midwest Political Science Association, Chicago, September, 1988.
Kirschner, Don S. "The Ambiguous Legacy: Social Justice and Social Control in the Progressive Era." *Historical Reflections/Réflexions Historiques* 2, no. 1 (Summer 1975): 69–88.
Kitchens, Karin E., and Michele L. Swers. "Why Aren't There More Republican Women in Congress? Gender, Partisanship, and Fundraising Support in the 2010 and 2012 Elections." *Politics & Gender* 12, no. 4 (April 2016): 648–676.
Klinkner, Philip. *The Losing Parties: Out Party National Committees, 1956–1993.* New Haven, CT: Yale University Press, 1994.
Kloppenberg, James T. *Toward Democracy.* Oxford: Oxford University Press, 2016.
Knuckey, Jonathan. "Classification of Presidential Elections: An Update." *Polity* 31, no. 4 (Summer 1999): 639–653.
Kolodny, Robin. *Pursuing Majorities: Congressional Campaign Committees in American Politics.* Norman: University of Oklahoma Press, 1998.
Kramnick, Isaac, and Theodore Lowi. *American Political Thought: A Norton Anthology.* New York: Norton, 2009.
Krasno, Jonathan S., Donald Philip Green, and Jonathan A. Cowden. "The Dynamics of Campaign Fundraising in House Elections." *Journal of Politics* 56, no. 2 (May 1994): 459–474.

Krehbiel, Keith, Kenneth A. Shepsle, and Barry R. Weingast. "Why Are Congressional Committees Powerful?" *American Political Science Review* 81, no. 3 (September 1987): 929–945.

Kuriwaki, Shiro. "The Swing Voter Paradox: Electoral Politics in a Nationalized Era." PhD diss., Harvard University, 2021.

Kurlansky, Mark. *1968: The Year that Rocked the World*. New York: Random House, 2004.

Ladd, Everett. *Transformation of the American Political System*. New York: Norton, 1975.

La Follette, Robert. "The Danger Threatening Representative Government" (1897). *U.S. History Primary Source Reader | HIS 20 BCC CUNY*, bcc-cuny.digication.com/ushistoryreader/Robert_La_Follette_The_Threat_to_Representative_Go.

———. *La Follette's Autobiography: A Personal Narrative of Political Experiences*. Madison, WI: Robert M. La Follette Co., 1913.

———. "Peril in the Machine." *Chicago Times-Herald*, February 23, 1897. Reproduced at *Wisconsin Historical Society*, www.wisconsinhistory.org/Records/Newspaper/BA1995.

La Raja, Raymond J., and Brian F. Schaffner. *Campaign Finance and Political Polarization: When Purists Prevail*. Ann Arbor: University of Michigan Press, 2015.

Lawler, Peter Augustine, and Robert Martin Schaefer, eds. *American political rhetoric: A reader* Lanham, MD: Rowman and Littlefield, 2005.

Layman, Geoffrey C., and Thomas M. Carsey. "Party Polarization and 'Conflict Extension' in the American Electorate." *American Journal of Political Science* 46, no. 4 (October 2002): 786–802.

Layman, Geoffrey C., Thomas M. Carsey, and Juliana Menasce Horowitz. "Party Polarization in American Politics: Characteristics, Causes, and Consequences." *Annual Review of Political Science* 9 (June 2006): 83–110.

Levendusky, Matthew. *The Partisan Sort: How Liberals Became Democrats and Conservatives Became Republicans*. Chicago: University of Chicago Press, 2009.

Levendusky, Matthew, and Neil Malhotra. "Does Media Coverage of Partisan Polarization Affect Political Attitudes?" *Political Communication* 33, no. 2 (July 2015): 283–301.

Levitsky, Steven, and Daniel Ziblatt. *How Democracies Die*. New York: Broadway Books, 2018.

Lovejoy, Allen. *La Follette and the Establishment of the Direct Primary in Wisconsin, 1890–1904*. New Haven, CT: Yale University Press, 1941.

Luttbeg, Norman, and Michael Gant. *American Electoral Behavior, 1952–1992*. Itasca, IL: F. E. Peacock Publishers, 1995.

Madison, James. *Federalist* no. 10. In *The Debate on the Constitution*, edited by Bernard Bailyn, 404–412. New York: Library of America, 1993.

———. *Notes of Debates in the Federal Convention of 1787*. Athens: Ohio University Press, 2022.

Magleby, David B., Candice J. Nelson, and Mark C. Westlye. "The Myth of the Independent Voter Revisited." In *Facing the Challenge of Democracy: Explorations in the Analysis of Public Opinion and Political Participation*, edited by Paul M. Sniderman and Benjamin Highton, 238–263. Princeton, NJ: Princeton University Press, 2012.

Mailer, Norman. "The Siege of Chicago." In *Reporting Vietnam, Part One: American Journalism 1959–1969*, compiled by Milton J. Bates, Lawrence Lichty, Paul Miles, Ronald H. Spector, and Marilyn Young, 628–642. New York: The Library of America, 1998.

Mair, Peter. "Party Organizations: From Civil Society to the State." In *How Parties Organize: Change and Adaptation in Party Organizations in Western Democracies*, edited by Richard S. Katz and Peter Mair, 1–20. Thousand Oaks, CA: Sage, 1995.

Malbin, Michael J., ed. *The Election after Reform: Money, Politics, and the Bipartisan Campaign Reform Act*. Lanham, MD: Rowman and Littlefield, 2006.

Marshall, Bryan W., and Patrick J. Haney. "The Impact of Party Conflict on Executive Ascendancy and Congressional Abdication in US Foreign Policy." *International Politics*, July 13, 2021. doi.org/10.1057/s41311-021-00326-z.

Martin, Douglas. "Anne Wexler, an Influential Political Operative and Lobbyist, Is Dead at 79." *New York Times*, August 8, 2009.

Martínez, Christopher A., Mariana Llanos, and Raymond Tatalovich. "Impeaching the President: Mapping the Political Landscape in the House of Representatives." *Congress & the Presidency*, July 8, 2021. doi.org/10.1080/07343469.2021.1934186.

Masket, Seth E., Jonathan Winburn, and Gerald C. Wright. "The Gerrymanderers Are Coming! Legislative Redistricting Won't Affect Competition or Polarization Much, No Matter Who Does It." *PS: Political Science & Politics* 45, no. 1 (January 2012): 39–43.

Mattei, Franco, and John S. Howes. "Competing Explanations of Split-Ticket Voting in American National Elections." *American Politics Quarterly* 28, no. 3 (2000): 379–407.

Mattson, Kevin. *Creating a Democratic Public: The Struggle for Urban Participatory Democracy during the Progressive Era*. University Park: Penn State Press, 2010.

May, Clifford D. "Buckleys Are Backing a Democrat?" *New York Times*, August 16, 1988.

Mayer, William G. "Changes in Elections and the Party System: 1992 in Historical Perspective." In *The New American Politics*, 19–50. New York: Routledge, 2018.

———. *The Divided Democrats: Ideology Unity, Party Reform and Presidential Elections*. Boulder, CO: Westview Press, 1996.

Mayer, William G., and Andrew E. Busch. *The Front-Loading Problem in Presidential Nominations*. Washington, DC: Brookings Institution, 2003.

Mayhew, David. *Electoral Realignments: A Critique of an American Genre.* New Haven, CT: Yale University Press, 2002.

McAllister, Ian, and Robert Darcy. "Sources of Split-Ticket Voting in the 1988 American Elections." *Political Studies* 40, no. 4 (December 1992): 695–712.

McCarty, Nolan, Jonathan Rodden, Boris Shor, Chris Tausanovitch, and Christopher Warshaw. "Geography, Uncertainty, and Polarization." *Political Science Research and Methods* 7, no. 4 (March 2018): 775–794.

McClory, Toni. *Understanding the Arizona Constitution.* Tucson: University of Arizona Press, 2010.

McClurg, Scott D. "The Electoral Relevance of Political Talk: Examining Disagreement and Expertise Effects in Social Networks on Political Participation." *American Journal of Political Science* 50, no. 3 (July 2006): 737–754.

McCormick, Richard Levis. "The Discovery that Business Corrupts Politics: A Reappraisal of the Origins of Progressivism." In *The Party Period and Public Policy*, 311–356. Oxford: Oxford University Press, 1986.

McCormick, Richard P. *The Presidential Game.* Oxford: Oxford University Press, 1982.

McCright, Aaron M., Chenyang Xiao, and Riley E. Dunlap. "Political Polarization on Support for Government Spending on Environmental Protection in the USA, 1974–2012." *Social Science Research* 48 (July 2014): 251–260.

McDonald, Forrest. *The Presidency of George Washington.* Lawrence: University Press of Kansas, 1974.

McGerr, Michael. *A Fierce Discontent: The Rise and Fall of the Progressive Movement in America, 1870–1920.* New York: Free Press, 2003.

McDonald, Michael P. "National General Election VEP Turnout Rates, 1789–Present." *United States Elections Project*, 2018. www.electproject.org/national-1789-present.

———. "Voter Turnout." *United States Elections Project*, 2020. www.electproject.org/home/voter-turnout/voter-turnout-data.

McGhee, Eric, Seth Masket, Boris Shor, Steven Rogers, and Nolan McCarty. "A Primary Cause of Partisanship? Nomination Systems and Legislator Ideology." *American Journal of Political Science* 58, no. 2 (April 2014): 337–351.

McSweeney, Dean, and John E. Owens, eds. *The Republican Takeover of Congress.* Cham, Switzerland: Palgrave Macmillan, 1998.

McWilliams, Wilson Carey. "Standing at Armageddon." In *Progressivism and the New Democracy*, edited by Sidney Milkis and Jerome Mileur, 117–129. Amherst: University of Massachusetts Press, 1999.

Meacham, Jon. *American Lion: Andrew Jackson in the White House.* New York: Random House, 2009.

Medina, Jennifer, and Patrick Healy. "As Outsider, Lieberman Walks a Tricky Path." *New York Times*, September 9, 2006.

Medvic, Stephen K. *Political Consultants in US Congressional Elections.* Columbus: Ohio State University Press, 2001.

Memoli, Michael A. "Eric Cantor Upset: How Dave Brat Pulled Off a Historic Political Coup." *Los Angeles Times*, June 11, 2014.

Michels, Robert. *Political Parties.* New York: Free Press, 1958.
Milkis, Sidney. *Theodore Roosevelt, the Progressive Party, and the Transformation of American Democracy.* Lawrence: University Press of Kansas, 2009.
Miller, James. *Democracy Is in the Streets: From Port Huron to the Siege of Chicago.* Cambridge, MA: Harvard University Press, 1994.
Miller, Warren E., and J. Merrill Shanks. *The New American Voter.* Cambridge, MA: Harvard University Press, 1996.
Moran, Jack, and Mark Fenster. "Voter Turnout in Presidential Primaries: A Diachronic Analysis." *American Politics Quarterly* 10, no. 4 (October 1982): 453–476.
Morone, James. *The Democratic Wish.* New York: Basic Books, 1990.
Murphy, Kevin P. *Political Manhood: Red Bloods, Mollycoddles, and the Politics of Progressive Era Reform.* New York: Columbia University Press, 2008.
Murray, Robert Keith. *The 103rd Ballot: The Legendary 1924 Democratic Convention that Forever Changed Politics.* New York: HarperCollins, 2016.
Mushkat, Jerome. *Tammany: The Evolution of a Political Machine, 1789–1865.* Syracuse, NY: Syracuse University Press, 1971.
Nagourney, Adam. "A Referendum on Iraq Policy." *New York Times,* August 9, 2006.
National Conference of State Legislatures. "State Primary Election Types." *NCSL,* accessed November 22, 2021. www.ncsl.org/research/elections-and-campaigns/primary-types.aspx.
National Conference on Practical Reform of Primary Elections. New York: W. C. Hollister & Bro., 1898. Accessed on Google Books.
Nelson, Candice J. *Grant Park: The Democratization of Presidential Elections, 1968–2008.* Washington, DC: Brookings Institution, 2011.
Nelson, Michael. *Resilient America: Electing Nixon in 1968, Channeling Dissent, and Dividing Government.* Lawrence: University Press of Kansas, 2014.
Neuhaus, Richard J. *The Naked Public Square: Religion and Democracy in America.* Grand Rapids, MI: Wm. B. Eerdmans Publishing, 1986.
Newman, Andy, and Tyler Pager. "How a Political Machine Works: Candidates Running for 21 Seats, All Unaware." *New York Times,* August 24, 2018.
Niven, David. "The Limits of Mobilization: Turnout Evidence from State House Primaries." *Political Behavior* 23, no. 4 (December 2001): 335–350.
Noble, David W. *The Paradox of Progressive Thought.* Minneapolis: University of Minnesota Press, 1958.
North, J. A. "Democratic Politics in Republican Rome." *Past & Present,* no. 126 (February 1990): 3–21.
Nugent, Walter. *Progressivism: A Very Short Introduction.* Oxford: Oxford University Press, 2010.
Nyhan, Brendan. "The Green Lantern Theory of the Presidency." *Brendan Nyhan,* December 14, 2009. www.brendan-nyhan.com/blog/2009/12/the-green-lantern-theory-of-the-presidency.html.
Ogg, David. *England in the Reign of Charles II.* Westport, CT: Greenwood Press, 1979.
Overacker, Louise. *Presidential Primary.* New York: Arno Press, 1974.

Painter, Nell Irvin. *Standing at Armageddon: A Grassroots History of the Progressive Era*. New York: Norton, 2008.

Panagopoulos, Costas. "Political Consultants, Campaign Professionalization, and Media Attention." *PS: Political Science & Politics* 39, no. 4 (October 2006): 867–869.

Parent, T. Wayne, Calvin C. Jillson, and Ronald E. Weber. "Voting Outcomes in the 1984 Democratic Party Primaries and Caucuses." *American Political Science Review* 81, no. 1 (March, 1987): 67–84.

Parsons, Lynn Hudson. *The Birth of Modern Politics: Andrew Jackson, John Quincy Adams, and the Election of 1828*. Oxford: Oxford University Press, 2009.

Pasley, Jeffrey L., Andrew W. Robertson, and David Waldstreicher, eds. *Beyond the Founders: New Approaches to the Political History of the Early American Republic*. Chapel Hill: University of North Carolina Press, 2009.

Pateman, Carol. *Participation and Democratic Theory*. Cambridge: Cambridge University Press, 1990.

Patterson, James T. "A Conservative Coalition Forms in Congress, 1933–1939." *Journal of American History* 52, no. 4 (March 1966): 757–772.

Patterson, Samuel C. "Party Opposition in the Legislature: The Ecology of Legislative Institutionalization." *Polity* 4, no. 3 (Spring 1972): 344–366.

Patterson, Samuel C., and Gregory A. Caldeira. "Party Voting in the United States Congress." *British Journal of Political Science* 18, no. 1 (January 1988): 111–131.

Perlstein, Rick. *Nixonland: The Rise of a President and the Fracturing of America*. New York: Scribner, 2008.

Persily, Nathaniel A. "The Peculiar Geography of Direct Democracy: Why the Initiative, Referendum and Recall Developed in the American West." *Michigan Law and Policy Review* 2 (January 1997): 11–41.

Peters, Charles. *Five Days in Philadelphia*. New York: Public Affairs, 2005.

Peters, Gerhard, and John T. Woolley, eds. *The American Presidency Project*. www.presidency.ucsb.edu.

Petracca, Mark P. "Political Consultants and Democratic Governance." *PS: Political Science & Politics* 22, no. 1 (March 1989): 11–14.

Pietrusza, David. *1920: The Year of the Six Presidents*. New York: Basic Books, 2007.

———. *1948: Harry Truman's Improbable Victory and the Year that Transformed America*. New York: Union Square Press, 2011.

Plasser, Fritz. "Parties' Diminishing Relevance for Campaign Professionals." *Harvard International Journal of Press/Politics* 6, no. 4 (September 2001): 44–59.

Polsby, Nelson W. *Consequences of Party Reform*. Oxford: Oxford University Press, 1983.

———. "The Institutionalization of the US House of Representatives." *American Political Science Review* 62, no. 1 (March 1968): 144–168.

———. "The Reform of Presidential Selection and Democratic Theory." *PS: Political Science & Politics* 16, no. 4 (Autumn 1983): 695–698.
Polsby, Nelson, Aaron Wildavsky, Steen Schier, and David Hopkins. *Presidential Elections: Strategies and Structures of American Politics.* Lanham, MD: Rowman and Littlefield, 2012.
Polsky, Andrew J. "Partisan Regimes in American Politics." *Polity* 44, no. 1 (January 2012): 51–80.
Pomper, Gerald. *Nominating the President: The Politics of Convention Choice.* New York: Norton, 1996.
Poole, Keith T., and Howard Rosenthal. "Analysis of Congressional Coalition Patterns: A Unidimensional Spatial Model." *Legislative Studies Quarterly* 12, no. 1 (February 1987): 55–75.
Popkin, Samuel L. *The Reasoning Voter: Communication and Persuasion in Presidential Campaigns.* Chicago: University of Chicago Press, 1994.
"People's Party Platform." *Omaha Morning World-Herald*, July 5, 1892. Available at wwnorton.com/college/history/eamerica/media/ch22/resources/documents/populist.htm.
Preimesberger, John. *Presidential Elections: 1789–1992.* Washington, DC: CQ Press, 1995.
Prior, Markus. "Media and Political Polarization." *Annual Review of Political Science* 16 (2013): 101–127.
Progressive Party. "Minor/Third Party Platforms: Progressive Party Platform of 1912." *The American Presidency Project*, ed. Gerhard Peters and John T. Woolley. Accessed January 10, 2019. www.presidency.ucsb.edu/documents/progressive-party-platform-1912.
Putnam, R. D. "Bowling Alone: America's Declining Social Capital." In *Culture and Politics*, edited by L. Crothers and C. Lockhard, 223–234. New York: Palgrave Macmillan, 2000.
Raab, Selwyn. *Five Families: The Rise, Decline, and Resurgence of America's Most Powerful Mafia Empires.* New York: Thomas Dunne Books, 2005.
Rackaway, Chapman. "Weak Parties and Strong Partisans." *In American Political Parties Under Pressure*, edited by Chapman Rackaway and Laurie L. Rice, 169–187. Cham, Switzerland: Palgrave Macmillan, 2017.
Radosh, Ronald. *Divided They Fell: The Demise of the Democratic Party, 1964–1996.* New York: Free Press, 1996.
Ranney, Austin. *Curing the Mischiefs of Faction: Party Reform in America.* Berkeley: University of California Press, 1975.
———. "Turnout and Representation in Presidential Primary Elections." *American Political Science Review* 66, no. 1 (March 1972): 21–37.
Rauch, Jonathan, and Ray La Raja. "Too Much Democracy Is Bad for Democracy." *The Atlantic*, December 2019, 62–68.

Redlawsk, David P. "What Voters Do: Information Search During Election Campaigns." *Political Psychology* 25, no. 4 (August 2004): 595–610.
Reeves, Thomas C. "Chester A. Arthur and Campaign Assessments in the Election of 1880." *Historian* 31, no. 4 (December, 1969): 573–582.
Reichley, James. *The Life of the Parties: A History of American Political Parties*. Lanham, MD: Rowman and Littlefield, 2000.
Remini, Robert V. *Henry Clay: Statesman for the Union*. New York: Norton, 1991.
———. *The Life of Andrew Jackson*. New York: Harper & Row, 1988.
Reston, James. "Humphrey Staff Sure of Nomination." *New York Times*, June 25, 1968.
Riordan, William L. *Plunkitt of Tammany Hall: A Series of Very Plain Talks on Very Practical Politics*. New York: Penguin, 1995.
Ritchie, Donald. *Electing FDR: The New Deal Campaign of 1932*. Lawrence: University Press of Kansas, 2007.
Rodgers, Daniel T. *Atlantic Crossings: Social Politics in a Progressive Age*. Cambridge, MA: Harvard University Press, 1998.
Rogers, Josh. "McCain Wins Lieberman Endorsement." *Reuters*, December 16, 2007. www.reuters.com/article/us-usa-politics-lieberman/mccain-wins-lieberman-endorsement-idUSN1634401920071217.
Rohde, David W. *Parties and Leaders in the Postreform House*. Chicago: University of Chicago Press, 2010.
———. "Studying Congressional Norms: Concepts and Evidence." *Congress & the Presidency: A Journal of Capital Studies* 15, no. 2 (September 1988): 139–145.
Roosevelt, Theodore. *An Autobiography*. New York: Library of America, 2004.
———. "The New Nationalism." In *Theodore Roosevelt: Letters and Speeches*. New York: Library of America, 2005.
———. "Who Is a Progressive?" In *American Progressivism: A Reader*. Lanham, MD: Lexington Books, 2008.
Royko, Mike. *Boss: Richard J. Daley of Chicago*. New York: Penguin, 1988.
Rusk, J. G. "The Effect of the Australian Ballot Reform on Split Ticket Voting: 1876–1908." *American Political Science Review* 64, no. 4 (December 1970): 1220–1238.
Sabato, L. *The Rise of Political Consultants: New Ways of Winning Elections*. New York: Basic Books, 1981.
Saiz, Martin, and Hans Geser, eds. *Local Parties in Political and Organizational Perspective*. Boulder, CO: Westview, 1999.
Sanchez, Jáime, Jr. "Revisiting McGovern-Fraser: Party Nationalization and the Rhetoric of Reform." *Journal of Political History* 32, no. 1 (January 2020): 1–24.
Sandri, Giulia, Antonella Seddone, and Fulvio Venturino, eds. *Party Primaries in Comparative Perspective*. Farnham, UK: Ashgate, 2015.
Scarrow, S. E. "The Nineteenth-Century Origins of Modern Political Parties: The Unwanted Emergence of Party-Based Politics." In *Handbook of Party Politics*, edited by Richard Katz and William Crotty, 6–24. Thousand Oaks, CA: Sage, 2006.

Schattschneider, E. E. *Party Government.* New York: Holt, Rinehart, and Winston, 1942.

Schlesinger, J. A. *Political Parties and the Winning of Office.* Ann Arbor: University of Michigan Press, 1994.

Schneider, Helmut. "Branding in Politics—Manifestations, Relevance and Identity-Oriented Management." *Journal of Political Marketing* 3, no. 3 (December 2002): 41–67.

Schudson, Michael. *The Good Citizen: A History of American Civil Life.* New York: The Free Press, 1998.

Schultz, David A., and Robert Maranto. *The Politics of Civil Service Reform.* New York: Peter Lang, 1998.

Scott, James C. "Corruption, Machine Politics, and Political Change." *American Political Science Review* 63, no. 4 (December 1969): 1142–1158.

Shafer, Byron E. *Quiet Revolution: The Struggle for the Democratic Party and the Shaping of Post-Reform Politics.* New York: Russell Sage Foundation, 1983.

Shafritz, Jay, E. W. Russell, and Christopher Borick. *Introduction to Public Administration.* 8th ed. New York: Pearson, 2013.

Shea, Daniel M. *Transforming Democracy: Legislative Campaign Committees and Political Parties.* Albany: State University of New York Press, 1995.

Shefter, Martin. *Political Parties and the State: The American Historical Experience.* Princeton, NJ: Princeton University Press, 1993.

———. "Regional Receptivity to Reform: The Legacy of the Progressive Era." *Political Science Quarterly* 98, no. 3 (Autumn 1983): 459–483.

Shepsle, Kenneth A., and Barry R. Weingast. "The Institutional Foundations of Committee Power." *American Political Science Review* 81, no. 1 (March 1987): 85–104.

Silbey, Joel H. *The American Political Nation, 1838–1893.* Stanford, CA: Stanford University Press, 1991.

Silbey, Joel H., and Allan G. Bogue, eds. *The History of American Electoral Behavior.* Princeton, NJ: Princeton University Press, 2015.

Simkhovitch, Mary. "Friendship and Politics." *Political Science Quarterly* 17, no. 2 (June 1902): 189–205.

Sinclair, Barbara. "Senate Styles and Senate Decision Making, 1955–1980." *Journal of Politics* 48, no. 4 (November 1986): 877–908.

Smith, Jean Edward. *FDR.* New York: Random House, 2007.

Smith, Kevin B., and Alan Greenblatt. *Governing States and Localities.* 6th ed. Los Angeles: Sage, 2018.

Smith, Steven S., and Melanie J. Springer. "Choosing Presidential Candidates." In *Reforming the Presidential Nomination Process,* edited by Steven S. Smith and Melanie J. Springer, 1–22. Washington, DC: Brookings Institution, 2009.

Sorauf, Frank J. "State Patronage in a Rural County." *American Political Science Review* 50, no. 4 (December 1956): 1046–1056.

Southwell, Priscilla L. "Open Versus Closed Primaries and Candidate Fortunes, 1972–1984." *American Politics Quarterly* 16, no. 3 (July 1988): 280–295.

Squire, Peverill. "Competition and Uncontested Seats in US House Elections." *Legislative Studies Quarterly* 14, no. 2 (May 1989): 281–295.

———. "Uncontested Seats in State Legislative Elections." *Legislative Studies Quarterly* 25, no. 1 (February, 2000): 131–146.

Staloff, Darren. *Hamilton, Adams, Jefferson: The Politics of Enlightenment and the American Founding*. New York: Macmillan, 2005.

Stanga, John E., and James F. Sheffield. "The Myth of Zero Partisanship: Attitudes toward American Political Parties, 1964–84." *American Journal of Political Science* 31, no. 4 (November 1987): 829–855.

Starr, Paul. *The Creation of the Media: Political Origins of Mass Communications*. Princeton: Princeton University Press, 2004.

Steel, Ronald. *In Love with Night: The American Romance with Robert Kennedy*. New York: Simon and Schuster, 2000.

Stern, Sol. "The Battle of Chicago, 1968." *Tablet Magazine*, August 26, 2018. www.tabletmag.com/sections/news/articles/the-battle-of-chicago-1968.

Stettner, Edward. *Shaping Modern Liberalism: Herbert Croly and Progressive Thought*. Lawrence: University Press of Kansas, 1993.

Stewart, Josh. "Following the Money behind the Nearly $500 Million 2016 Democratic Primary." *Sunlight Foundation*, June 21, 2016, sunlightfoundation.com/2016/06/21/following-the-money-behind-the-nearly-500-million-2016-democratic-primary/.

Stid, Daniel D. *The President as Statesman: Woodrow Wilson and the Constitution*. Lawrence: University Press of Kansas, 1998.

Storing, Herbert J. "Introduction." In *The Complete Anti-Federalist*, edited by Herbert J. Storing, vol. 1, 3–6. Chicago: University of Chicago Press, 1981.

Sundquist, James L. *Dynamics of the Party System: Alignment and Realignment of Political Parties in the United States*. Washington, DC: Brookings Institution, 1983.

Talisee, Robert. *Overdoing Democracy: Why We Must Put Politics in its Place*. Oxford: Oxford University Press, 2019.

Theriault, Sean M. "Party Polarization in the US Congress: Member Replacement and Member Adaptation." *Party Politics* 12, no. 4 (2006): 483–503.

Thompson, Dennis. "The Primary Purpose of Presidential Primaries." *Political Science Quarterly* 125, no. 2 (Summer 2010): 205–232.

Thomsen, Danielle M. "Ideological Moderates Won't Run: How Party Fit Matters for Partisan Polarization in Congress." *Journal of Politics* 76, no. 3 (July 2014): 786–797.

Tocqueville, Alexis de. *Democracy in America*, vol. 1. Translated by Henry Reeve. New York: Vintage, 1990.

Tolles, Frederick B. "The American Revolution Considered as a Social Movement: A Re-evaluation." *American Historical Review* 60, no. 1 (October 1954): 1–12.

Trounstine, Jessica. "Representation and Accountability in Cities." *Annual Review of Political Science* 13 (February 2010): 407–423.

Tucker, David. "Edward Hull 'Boss' Crump." *Tennessee Encyclopedia*, March 1, 2018. tennesseeencyclopedia.net/entries/edward-hull-and-crump/.
Turner, Julius. "Primary Elections as the Alternative to Party Competition in 'Safe' Districts." *Journal of Politics* 15, no. 2 (May 1953): 197–210.
Uslaner, Eric M. "Partisanship and Coalition Formation in Congress." *Political Methodology* 2 (Fall 1975): 381–414.
Van Buren, Martin. *Inquiry into the Origin and Course of Political Parties in the United States*. New York: Augustus M. Kelly, 1967.
Van Deusen, Glyndon G. *The Jacksonian Era, 1828–1848*. New York: Harper & Row, 1969.
Vann, Burrel. "Persuasive Action and Ideological Polarization in Congress." *Social Problems* 68, no. 4 (November 2021): 809–830.
Voorheis, John, Nolan McCarty, and Boris Shor. "Unequal Incomes, Ideology and Gridlock: How Rising Inequality Increases Political Polarization." *SSRN*, August 21, 2015, dx.doi.org/10.2139/ssrn.2649215.
Walker, Daniel. *What Hath God Wrought: The Transformation of America 1815–1848*. Oxford: Oxford University Press, 2007.
Ware, Alan. *The American Direct Primary: Party Institutionalization and Transformation in the North*. Cambridge: Cambridge University Press, 2002.
———. "Anti-partism and Party Control of Political Reform in the United States: The Case of the Australian Ballot." *British Journal of Political Science* 30, no. 1 (January, 2000): 1–29.
Washington, George. *George Washington's Farewell Address*. Krill Press via PublishDrive, 2015.
Wattenberg, Martin P. *The Decline of American Political Parties, 1952–1996*. Cambridge: Harvard University Press, 2009.
Weingast, Barry R. "Floor Behavior in the US Congress: Committee Power under the Open Rule." *American Political Science Review* 83, no. 3 (September 1989): 795–815.
Weinstein, James. *The Corporate Ideal in the Liberal State: 1900–1918*. Westport, CT: Praeger, 1969.
White, Richard. *The Republic for which It Stands*. Oxford: Oxford University Press, 2017.
White, Theodore. *The Making of the President, 1960*. New York: Atheneum, 1961.
———. *The Making of the President, 1964*. New York: Harper Perennial, 1965.
Wiebe, Robert. *The Search for Order, 1877–1920*. New York: Hill and Wang, 1983.
Wieck, Paul R. "Defying the Bosses in Illinois and Texas." *New Republic*, March 1, 1971.
Wilentz, S. *Chants Democratic: New York City and the Rise of the American Working Class, 1788–1850*. Oxford: Oxford University Press, 2004.
Williams, Joyce E., and Vicky M. MacLean. "In Search of the Kingdom: The Social Gospel, Settlement Sociology, and the Science of Reform in America's

Progressive Era." *Journal of the History of the Behavioral Sciences* 48, no. 4 (August 2012): 339–362.

Willman, Robert. "The Origins of 'Whig' and 'Tory' in English Political Language." *Historical Journal* 17, no. 2 (June 1974): 247–264.

Wills, Garry. *Nixon Agonistes: The Crisis of the Self-Made Man.* New York: Penguin Books, 1979.

Wilson, James. *Collected Works of James Wilson.* 2 vols. Edited by Kermit L. Hall and Mark David Hall. Indianapolis: Liberty Fund, 2007.

Wilson, James Lindley. *Democratic Equality.* Princeton. NJ: Princeton University Press, 2019.

Wilson, James Q. *The Amateur Democrat: Club Politics in Three Cities.* Chicago: University of Chicago Press, 1966.

———. *Political Organizations.* Princeton, NJ: Princeton University Press, 1995.

Wilson, Woodrow. "First Annual Message." December 2, 1913. *The American Presidency Project*, ed. Gerhard Peters and John T. Woolley. Accessed January 10, 2019. www.presidency.ucsb.edu/documents/first-annual-message-18.

———. *The New Freedom.* New York: Doubleday, Page and Company, 1913.

———. "The Study of Administration." *Political Science Quarterly* 2, no. 2 (June 1887): 197–222.

Wing, Ian Sue, and Joan L. Walker. "The Geographic Dimensions of Electoral Polarizations in the 2004 US Presidential Vote." In *Progress in Spatial Analysis*, edited by Antonia Páez, Julie Gallo, Ron Buliung, and Sandy Dall'erba, 253–285. New York: Springer, 2010.

Witcover, Jules. *Party of the People: A History of the Democrats.* New York: Random House, 2003.

Wolfinger, Raymond E., and Joan Heifetz. "Safe Seats, Seniority, and Power in Congress." *American Political Science Review* 59, no. 2 (June 1965): 337–349.

Wolin, Sheldon. *Democracy Incorporated: Managed Democracy and the Specter of Inverted Totalitarianism.* Princeton, NJ: Princeton University Press, 2008.

Young, Nancy Beck. *Two Suns of the Southwest: Lyndon Johnson, Barry Goldwater and the 1964 Battle between Liberalism and Conservatism.* Lawrence: University Press of Kansas, 2019.

Zimmer, Kerstin. "The Comparative Failure of Machine Politics, Administrative Resources and Fraud." *Canadian Slavonic Papers* 47, no. 3/4 (September–December 2005): 361–384.

Index

A Fierce Discontent, 38, 55
Achen, Christopher, 6, 117
Adams, John Quincy, 23, 24, 25, 138
Adams, Sherman, 98
Adelson, Sheldon, 181
American National Election Study, 144, 146, 156
American Political Science Association, 58
Anti-federalist, 17, 18, 20, 57
Apple, R. W., 123
Aristotle, 4, 59, 84
Arizona, 66, 67, 72
Arthur, Chester, 32
Articles of Confederation, 17
Australian Ballot, 62, 64, 65, 76

Barr, Joseph, 120
Bartels, Larry, 6
Bayh, Birch, 121
Bennet, Michael, 176
Bentivolio, Kerry, 14
Biden, Joseph, 187, 188
Bill of Rights, 17
Bipartisan Campaign Reform Act, 142
Bishop, William, 155
Bloomberg, Michael, 176
Bode, Ken, 115
Booker, Corey, 176, 184
Boston, 21, 29, 44

Boston Globe, 91
Brat, David, 3
Buchanan, Patrick, 100, 176
Buckley, William F., 151
Bullock, Steve, 176
Burnham, Walter Dean, 133
Burns, James Macgregor, 108
Bush, George Walker, 176
Bush, John E. "Jeb," 126
Buttigieg, Pete, 176

Calhoun, John C., 138
California, 66, 67, 72, 91, 98, 100, 110, 128, 163, 173
California, Joseph, 123
Campbell, John, 50, 81
Cannon, Joseph, 135
Cantor, Eric, 3
Carter, James Earl "Jimmy," 180
Catholic (Church), 15, 27, 28, 37, 104
caucus, 20–24, 35, 65, 76, 81, 84, 86–87, 118, 121, 137–139, 153, 163
Cheney, Richard, 153
Chicago, 29–30, 32, 40, 42, 63, 65, 98, 103, 109–110, 111, 113–115, 132
Christie, Chris, 170
Citizens United v. FEC, 142–143

Index

Civil War, 38, 40, 46, 74, 113
Clark, Champ, 91
Clay, Henry, 23, 138
Cleveland, Grover, 177
Clinton, Hillary Rodham, 92, 158, 170, 177
Committee on Party Structure and Delegate Selection, 114
Commons, John R., 65
Congress, United States, 1, 12, 17, 25, 27, 43, 90, 109, 125, 134–136, 139, 142, 147, 152, 154, 156, 166, 189
Connecticut, 72, 113, 150, 151, 153
Conscience of a Conservative, 100
Conservative Coalition, 135, 147
Constitution and parties, 9–10, 12–13, 14
Constitution, United States, 7, 9, 10, 12–14, 17, 18, 22, 50, 64, 66, 67, 71, 74, 75, 80, 127–128
Conway, Margaret, 81
Coolidge, Calvin, 177
Cousins v Wigoda, 118
Crafword, William, 137–139
Croly, Herbert, 8, 38, 57–58, 62
Cronkite, Walter, 112
Crowley, Joseph, 125
Crump, E. H., 31
Cuomo, Mario, 176
Curley, James, 29, 44

Dahl, Robert, 6-May
Daley, Richard, 29–31, 44, 110–111, 114
Davis, John W., 63
de Jouvenel, Bertrand, 80–81
Dealignment, 133
Debs, Eugene, 40
Democracy, ancient Greece, 4-Mar
Democracy for Realists, 6
Democrat, 41, 97, 106, 109, 146, 151–153, 188

Democratic Choice, 113
Democratic Equality, 4
Democratic National Committee, 65, 114–115, 121–122, 140
Democratic National Convention, 24, 103–123
Democratic-Republican Party, 138–139
DeSapio, Carmine, 45
deTocqueville, Alexis, 181
Dewey, John, 53, 107
Dewey, Thomas, 95, 97–98
direct democracy, 3–4, 6, 8–9, 11, 35, 40, 48–49, 57, 60, 65, 66, 68, 77, 86, 106, 127–130, 178, 183
Direct Legislation League, 66
direct primary, 66, 68–69, 71, 72, 74, 77–78, 80, 86–89, 92–94, 102, 125–136, 140–141, 143–145, 147, 148, 150, 152–154, 157, 164–167, 170–171, 190
Downs, Anthony, 51
Dukakis, Michael, 176
DuPont, Pierre, 136

Eisenhower, Dwight David, 96, 98–100
Election, general, 2–3, 31, 2, 52, 63, 68, 75, 77–78, 85, 93, 146, 150–153, 157–158, 160–166, 170, 175, 179–181
Election, primary, 1, 3, 8–9, 11, 32, 35, 52, 61, 66, 68–69, 72, 81, 127, 132, 154, 159, 163
Electoral College, 20, 23–24, 100, 138–139, 188

Faction, 13, 16, 18–19, 31, 47, 69, 88–89, 97, 99, 115, 122, 131, 137–138, 144, 175
Federal Election Commission, 142
Federalist, 12
Federalist #10, 13–14, 18, 19, 47, 147

Federalist #6, 128
Fiorina, Carly, 170
Ford, Henry Jones, 177, 182–183
Franklin, Benjamin, 59
Fraser, Donald, 114

Garfield, James, 32
Gettysburg Address, 6
Gilkeson, B. F., 65
Gingrich, Newton, 181
Goldwater, Barry, 96, 99–101, 104, 155, 180
Goodnow, Frank Johnson, 58
GOPAC, 136
Gould, Lewis, 93
Great Depression, 97
Green Party, 187
Guiliani, Rudolf, 152

Hamilton, Alexander, 18, 128
Hanna, Mark, 91
Harding, Warren, 92, 94, 177
Harris, Fred, 114, 122
Harris, Kamala, 176
Harrison, Carter, 42
Harrison, Benjamin, 177
Hart, Gary, 176
Hayden, Thomas, 106–108, 120
Haymarket Riot, 38
Hickenlooper, John, 176
Hofstadter, Richard, 60, 62
Homestead Steel Strike, 38
Hoover, Herbert, 104
House of Representatives, United States, 109, 119, 125, 135–136, 138–139, 147, 153, 158
How Democracies Die, 3, 177
Hughes Commission, 113
Hughes, Charles Evans, 94
Hughes, Harold, 113, 121
Humphrey, Hubert, 96, 103, 105, 110–113, 115

Huntington, Samuel, 107

Initiative, 7, 9, 64–66, 67, 68, 127–129, 132, 168
Inslee, Jay, 176
Iowa Caucus, 99, 181

Jackson, Andrew, 21–27, 40, 63, 82–83, 137–139
James, Duke of York, 15
Jefferson, Thomas, 1, 8
Jim Crow, 75, 90
Johnson, Hiram, 66
Johnson, Lyndon Baines, 96, 99–101, 104–106, 109–110, 116, 180
Joseph, Geraldine, 115, 121

Kamarck, Elaine, 55, 113, 182
Kansas, 46, 72, 74, 160–161
Kansas City, 29, 31
Kefauver, Estes, 96
Kemp, Jack, 152
Kennedy, John Fitzgerald, 96, 104–105, 116
Kennedy, Robert, 109–110
Key, V. O., 108, 137
"King Caucus," 23, 63, 81, 139
King Charles II, 15
King, Martin Luther, 108

Lafollette, Robert, 86, 87
Lamont, Ned, 151–152
Levin, Mark, 2
Levitsky, Steven, 3, 177
Libertarian Party, 187
Lieberman, Joseph, 151–153
Lincoln, Abraham, 63, 177
Linkage institution, 9–11, 19–21, 31, 36, 87, 127, 129, 141–142, 150, 164, 168, 172–173
Lippman, Walter, 46
Lodge, Henry Cabot, 98, 104

Long, Huey, 29, 177

"Machine," 26, 28, 29, 30, 31, 32, 33, 40, 41, 42, 43, 44, 45, 48, 63, 69, 76, 86, 87, 111, 114, 125, 129, 131, 132, 133, 134, 135, 140, 143, 145, 147, 193
Madison, James, 6, 12–14, 18–20, 29, 50, 179
Mailer, Norman, 110
Majority Leader (U.S. House), 1–2, 105
Massachusetts, 17, 23, 49, 65, 67, 69, 72, 104, 106, 184
McAdoo, William, 92
McCain, John, 152, 173
McCarthy, Eugene, 103, 109–110, 112–113, 115
McCotter, Thaddeus, 14
McGerr, Michael, 55
McGovern, George, 180
McGovern-Fraser Commission, 65, 103, 112–114, 119, 122–123, 146
McGovern-Fraser reforms, 101, 122, 159–160, 164
McKinley, William, 91
Memphis, 31
Milkis, Sydney, 50
Minnesota, 68–69, 72, 98, 114, 122
Monroe, James, 25
Moonves, Leslie, 183
Mugwumps, 32, 61

National Republican Party, 24, 137, 139
National Conference on Practical Reform of Primary Elections, 65
Negative partisanship, 158–159
New Deal, 97, 99
New Hampshire, 69, 73, 100, 146, 164, 181
New York (State), 73, 99, 100, 104, 176

New York City, 21, 28–32, 42, 45, 83, 89, 125, 152, 176
New York Times, 105, 123
Nixon, Richard, 100, 104, 155, 156, 180
Noel, Hans, 149
Nominating Convention, 49, 63, 68, 82, 90, 139–140, 184
Nordhoff, Charles, 43
Norris, George, 87
Nyhan, Brendan, 182

Obama, Barack, 152, 170, 179
Ocasio-Cortez, Alexandria, 125–126, 187–188
Organized interest group, 12, 19, 143, 167, 170, 172, 174
Osawatomie, KS, 46
Overacker, Denise, 89, 92, 94

Pacific Gas and Electric, 173
Parliament (British), 15–16, 20
participatory democracy, 6, 11, 24, 40, 48, 86, 107, 115, 117–120, 123, 128–129, 178
Party "boss," 31, 41, 43, 45, 83, 110, 111
Party organization, 21, 137, 140–141, 143
Party registration, 49, 157
Pendergast, Thomas, 29, 31
Pendleton Act, 64
Peoples' Party, 35, 38, 74
Pericles, 183
Perlstein, Rick, 113
Perot, H. Ross, 189
Plunkitt of Tammany Hall, 28
Plunkitt, George Washington, 28, 42, 50
Polarization, electoral, 155, 156, 157, 163, 166
Polarization, legislative, 166–167
Polsby, Nelson, 182–183

Pomper, Gerald, 101, 115
Populism, 74
Port Huron Statement, 106–108, 118, 120
primary, closed, 160, 162
primary, defined, 3
primary, open, 126, 161–162, 167
Progressive (movement), 8, 11, 37, 38, 56, 58, 62, 88, 187
Progressive Era, 8, 23, 57, 61, 68, 70, 75, 130–131
Progressive Reforn, 42, 46, 62, 65, 132, 145
Putnam, Robert, 155

Quiet Revolution, 119

Ranked Choice Voting, 186
Ranney, Austin, 62, 84, 87
Reagan, Ronald, 101, 154, 179
Reed, Thomas, 135
Referenda, 6–7, 48, 62, 64–66, 67, 69, 127–129
Reichley, James, 83
Representative democracy, 3, 5–6, 9, 36, 48, 57, 159, 178, 183
Republican National Committee, 126
Reston, James, 105
Riordan, William, 42
Rockefeller, Nelson, 99–100, 104
Rockwell, Norman, 181
Roosevelt, Franklin Delano, 75, 94, 96–97, 104, 116
Roosevelt, Theodore, 7, 41, 43–44, 46–48, 50, 55, 90–91, 93, 130
Rothstein, Arnold, 45
Rousseau, Jean-Jacques, 88
Rubio, Marco, 126
Rush, G. Fred, 65

Sanchez Jr., Jamie, 121
Sanders, Bernard, 153, 170, 188

Schattschneider, E. E., 18–19, 115
Schlesinger, Alan, 151–152
Schlesinger, Arthur, 141
Seward, William, 83
Shafer, Byron, 118–119
Shays' Rebellion, 17
Simkhovitch, Mary, 42, 44–45
Socialist Party, 40, 47, 178
"spoils" system, 25, 26, 27, 29, 32, 40, 43, 61, 132
Southern Strategy, 155
Speaker of the House, 1, 91, 135
SpeechNOW v. FEC, 142, 143
split ticket voting, 145
Spoils system, 27–29, 32
Stalwarts, 32, 69
Stassen, Harold, 95–96, 98
Stevenson, Adlai, 96
Steyer, Thomas, 176
Stokes, Carl, 112–113
Students for a Democratic Society, 106
Sullivan, "Big" Tim, 45
SuperPAC, 143

Taft, Robert, 97–99, 101
Taft, William Howard, 90–91, 93, 96, 177
Talisse, Robert, 7
Tammany Hall, 28, 40, 41, 42, 45, 50, 61
TEA Party, 2
The Port Huron Statement, 106–108, 118, 120
Top-two primary, 160, 163–164
Tory, 16
Town hall, 5, 57–60, 66, 78
Truman, Harry, 79, 96, 98, 116, 177
Trump, Donald, 126, 158, 164, 170, 175, 177, 179, 183–184, 188
Turnout, 24, 27, 40, 53, 77–78, 82, 94, 128, 131, 145–145, 150, 162, 164–166, 181, 186–187, 189

Tweed Ring, 30, 41–42
Tweed, William "Boss," 43, 125, 175

U'Ren, William S., 66

Van Buren, Martin, 26, 131, 137
Vietnam Conflict, 99, 108–109, 115

Wallace, George, 115, 188
War for Independence, 13, 16–18
Ware, Alan, 62, 85–86, 89
Warren, Earl, 98
Washington, George, 18, 158
Weaver, James, 38
Wexler, Anne, 113
Whig, 16

White, Theodore, 105, 113
Wiecker, Lowell, 151
Williams, William Carey, 36
Willkie, Wendell, 96
Wilson, James Lindley, 4, 5
Wilson, Woodrow, 43, 48, 50, 56, 62, 91
Wisconsin, 48, 55–56, 68, 73, 95, 105, 161
Wood, Leonard, 93
Woodruff, Clinton, 65

Yang, Andrew, 176, 186

Ziblatt, Daniel, 3, 177